Christianity *and* Other Religions

Selected Readings

Concepts of God: Images of the Divine in Five Religious Traditions, Keith Ward,
   ISBN 1–85168–064–0

Ethics in the World Religions, edited by Joseph Runzo and Nancy M. Martin,
   ISBN 1–85168–247–3

The Ethics of Uncertainty: A New Christian Approach to Moral Decision-Making,
   ISBN 1–85168–217–1

The Fifth Dimension: An Exploration of the Spiritual Realm, John Hick,
   ISBN 1–85168–191–4 (pb); ISBN 1–85168–190–6 (hb)

God and the Universe of Faiths, John Hick, ISBN 1–85168–071–3

God, Chance and Necessity, Keith Ward, ISBN 1–85168–116–7

God, Faith and the New Millennium: Christian Belief in an Age of Science, Keith Ward,
   ISBN 1–85168–155–8

Great Thinkers on Great Questions, Roy Abraham Varghese, ISBN 1–85168–144–2

Interfaith Theology: A Reader, Dan Cohn-Sherbok, ISBN 1–85168–276–7

Inter-religious Dialogue: A Short Introduction, Martin Forward, ISBN 1–85168–275–9

Love, Sex and Gender in the World Religions, edited by Joseph Runzo and Nancy M.
   Martin, ISBN 1–85168–223–6

The Meaning of Life in the World Religions, edited by Joseph Runzo and Nancy M.
   Martin, ISBN 1–85168–200–7

Paths from Science Towards God: The End of all our Exploring, Arthur Peacocke,
   ISBN 1–85168–245–7

The Phenomenon of Religion, Moojan Momen, ISBN 1–85168–161–2

What Christians Believe, David Craig, ISBN 1–85168–218–X

Wilfred Cantwell Smith: A Reader, edited by Kenneth Cracknell,
   ISBN 1–85168–249–X

Christianity
and
Other
Religions

Selected Readings

Revised Edition, edited by
John Hick and Brian Hebblethwaite

ONEWORLD

OXFORD

CHRISTIANITY AND OTHER RELIGIONS

Oneworld Publications
185 Banbury Road
Oxford OX2 7AR
England
www.oneworld-publications.com

A selection of essays entitled 'Christianity and other
Religions: Selected Readings' was published in 1980
by Collins, Fount Paperbacks, and by Fortress Press in
1981. This book has been fully revised and updated to
include seven new chapters.
© John Hick and Brian Hebblethwaite 2001

ISBN 1–85168–279–1

Cover design by Design Deluxe
Typeset by Saxon Graphics Ltd, Derby
Printed and bound in Britain by Bell & Bain Ltd, Glasgow

Contents

Introduction

Already in 1980, when John Hick and I prepared our first selection of readings, the relation between Christianity and the other religions of the world had become one of the most pressing themes for Christian self-understanding. It was already quite impossible for Christians to ignore the existence of other flourishing world faiths, providing spiritual homes for hundreds of millions of people. The collapse of Western colonialism and the loss of Western self-confidence had already reinforced the need for a drastic reappraisal of the missionary task. The mainstream Christian churches had been forced to reckon with their relative failure to make much headway in Asia and the Middle East. The small indigenous churches in the non-Christian lands were also having to re-think their attitudes to the majority faiths around them.

These problems have become even more pressing over the last two decades, with the rapid growth of global intercommunication and the increasingly multifaith nature of many large cities in Europe and North America. On the one hand, there is a greatly increased awareness, in schools and universities, as well as through the media, of the histories and spiritual riches of the world religions. (Our greatly enlarged bibliography is but one indication of this.) Also there are far more personal contacts between Christians and people of other faiths, as well as between their leaders and representatives. On the other hand, the growth of militant sections of Islam and of Jewish Zionist nationalism, and the revivals of Christian Serbian nationalism and of Hindu nationalism in India – to mention but four recent developments – have made people aware of the dangers of inter-religious conflict and of the need for peace and co-operation between the religions. The World Parliament of Religions, at its centenary meeting in Chicago in 1993, reaffirmed this pressing need, and, at the same time, urged the promulgation of a global ethic for international politics and economics.

This new selection of readings – only four of the eleven presented here appeared in our first edition – illustrates the continuing attempt by Christian thinkers, both Protestant and Catholic, to come to terms with the fact of many flourishing world faiths, each with a long history behind it, and each manifestly capable of renewal and development in face of the challenges of the modern world. For the most part our authors are theologians, reflecting on the implications of the fact of religious plurality. But, increasingly, we find that even the theologians are caught up in the practicalities of interfaith relations and the pressures of global politics. Readers will find that our new selection is considerably more 'engaged' than its predecessor.

We have retained the extracts from the Second Vatican Council's declaration on the relationship of the Church to non-Christian religions, since this was such a watershed document in the history of the Roman Catholic Church; but the relative openness to other faiths which that declaration made possible has proved much easier to sustain and develop in the world of theology than in that of the Vatican itself. The present Pope's address and the extracts from the Congregation for the Doctrine of the Faith's recent declaration, with which our selection ends, show how a more traditional, conservative interpretation of Vatican II is tending to prevail, at least officially, and how hard it is for Christianity to modify its claims for the uniqueness and finality of Christ.

Once again we present our selected readings in chronological order; but the fact that we begin and end with more traditional views is an indication of the lack of any linear development towards the radical end of the spectrum. But, all the same, the pressures making for more radical views are reflected, in different ways, in at least seven out of our eleven contributions.

The spectrum of positions illustrated here ranges from the 'exclusivism' of Karl Barth, who presents an uncompromising view of God's self-revelation in Jesus Christ over against all human religious experience and aspiration (including those of the Christians) to the 'pluralism' of John Hick, who urges us to see our own 'salvific' religious experience, nurtured in whichever religious tradition, as one among many transformative paths from ego-centredness to a new orientation centred on the transcendent divine reality.

These two positions are illustrated further by Lesslie Newbigin, Paul Knitter, and Wilfred Cantwell Smith. Newbigin's version of exclusivism is more nuanced and informed by long experience of interfaith encounter than was Barth's. Knitter's pluralism is particularly interesting in coming from a Roman Catholic theologian. It is a version of pluralism firmly rooted in the shared soteriological pressure for liberation. It is this that, for Knitter, makes Christian Christocentrism but one way of responding to that pressure. Cantwell Smith's virtual pluralism is much more individualistic; he plays down doctrinal exclusivism in favour of personal authenticity nurtured in whatever tradition one finds oneself. Yet one may well think that his moral universalism still has specifically Christian doctrinal implications.

The remaining selections fall more or less explicitly between these two extremes. Most obviously 'inclusivist' – to continue to use the, by now, customary terminology – is the classic statement by Karl Rahner that faithful members of non-Christian religions may be thought of and welcomed by Christians as 'anonymous Christians'.

Hans Küng insists that pragmatic solutions to the question of religious truth are not enough. After surveying the options and rejecting atheism, exclusivism and pluralism, Küng finds himself questioning inclusivism for its inevitable arrogance. Christians have no monopoly of truth, and are themselves open to moral and religious criticism. All religions must be judged by both humane and religious criteria, and each religion has its own internal criterion by which to judge itself and others. By Christianity's own internal criterion – Jesus Christ – the fellowship of solidarity with others is required. Peace among religions is essential for peace among nations. If this sounds like a pragmatic solution after all, we have to note Küng's final insistence on the future consummation, where all particularities will be transcended in the end when God is all in all.

Aloysius Pieris insists that any theology must grow out of its own cultural situation. A third world Christian theology has to emerge from the revolutionary potential of the non-Christian religions which have shaped the vast majority of third world people. This too looks like a form of pragmatism. We, like Küng, would no doubt wish to press Pieris on the question of religious truth.

Jürgen Moltmann's frank and penetrating survey of the state of interfaith dialogue today leads him to present a fresh understanding of mission as an invitation to life. Freed from aggressive imperialism, Christianity, like all religions, should see its task as a matter of inviting all human beings to the affirmation and protection of life. Once again, the question still remains whether the proclamation of Christ as saviour is necessary, not only for Christians, but for everyone else as well.

As with our first selection of readings twenty years ago, we are left with the teasing – and very practical – question of whether the Christianity of the future can or should retain its traditional Christocentrism in however all-embracing a form, or whether it can or should embrace the thoroughgoing religious pluralism of John Hick and others.

Brian Hebblethwaite
Cambridge, November 2000

1

KARL BARTH: The Revelation of God as the Abolition of Religion

Karl Barth (1886–1968), the Swiss Protestant theologian, was described by Pope Pius XII as the greatest theologian since Thomas Aquinas. His unfinished Church Dogmatics *represents the most thorough and uncompromising statement of Christian theology based solely on God's self-revelation in Jesus Christ. In the extract printed here he argues that religion is unbelief; the only true religion is faithful witness to God's Word in Christ. Later in the* Church Dogmatics *he softens this line a little in allowing that there are 'other lights' in ethics and religion worldwide, but they can only be recognized as such in the light of Jesus Christ, who is the light of the world.*

RELIGION AS UNBELIEF

A theological evaluation of religion and religions must be characterized primarily by the great cautiousness and charity of its assessment and judgements. It will observe and understand and take man in all seriousness as the subject of religion. But it will not be man apart from God, in a human *per se*. It will be man for whom (whether he knows it or not) Jesus Christ was born, died, and rose again. It will be man who (whether he has already heard it or not) is intended in the Word of God. It will be man who (whether he is aware of it or not) has in Christ his Lord. It will always understand religion as a vital utterance and activity of this man. It will not ascribe to this life-utterance and activity of his a unique 'nature', the so-called 'nature of religion', which it can then use as a gauge to weigh and balance one human thing against another, distinguishing the 'higher' religion from the 'lower', the 'living' from the 'decomposed', the 'ponderable' from the 'imponderable'. It will not omit to do this from carelessness or indifference towards the manifoldness with which we have to do in this human sphere, nor because a prior definition of the 'nature' of the phenomena in this sphere is either impossible or in itself irrelevant, but because what we have to know of the nature of religion from the standpoint of God's revelation does not allow us to make any but the most incidental use of an immanent definition of the nature of religion. It is not, then, that this 'revealed' nature of religion is not fitted in either form or content to differentiate between the good and the bad, the true and the false in the religious world. Revelation singles out the Church as the *locus* of true religion. But this does not mean that the Christian religion as such is the fulfiled nature of human religion. It does not mean that the Christian religion is the true religion, fundamentally superior to all other religions. We can never stress too much the connection between the truth of the Christian religion and the grace of revelation. We have to give particular emphasis to the fact that through grace the Church lives by grace, and to that extent it is the *locus* of true religion. And if this is so, the Church will as little boast of its 'nature', i.e. the perfection in which it fulfils the 'nature' of religion, as it can attribute that nature to other religions. We cannot differentiate and separate the Church from other religions on the basis of a general concept of the nature of religion ...

A truly theological treatment of religion and religions, as it is demanded and possible in the Church as the *locus* of the Christian religion, will need to be distinguished from all other forms of treatment by the exercise of a very marked tolerance towards its object. Now this tolerance must not be confused with the moderation of those who actually have their own religion or religiosity, and are secretly zealous for it, but who can exercise self-control, because they have told themselves or have been told that theirs is not the only faith, that fanaticism is a bad thing, that love must always have the first and the last word. It must not be confused with the clever aloofness of the rationalistic Know-All – the typical Hegelian belongs to the same category – who thinks that he can deal comfortably and in the end successfully with all religions in the light of a concept of a perfect religion which is gradually evolving in history. But it also must not be confused with the relativism and impartiality of a historical scepticism, which does not ask about truth and untruth in the field of religious phenomena, because it thinks that truth can be known only in the form of its own doubt about all truth. That the so-called 'tolerance' of this kind is unattainable is revealed by the fact that the object, religion and religions, and therefore man, are not taken seriously, but are at bottom patronized. Tolerance in the sense of moderation, or superior knowledge, or scepticism is actually the worst form of intolerance. But the religion and religions must be treated with a tolerance which is informed by the forbearance of Christ, which derives therefore from the knowledge that by grace God has reconciled to himself godless man and his religion. It will see man carried, like an obstinate child in the arms of its mother, by what God has determined and done for his salvation in spite of his own opposition. In detail, it will neither praise nor reproach him. It will understand his situation – understand it even in the dark and terrifying perplexity of it – not because it can see any meaning in the situation as such, but because it acquires a meaning from outside, from Jesus Christ. But confronted by this object it will not display the weak or superior or weary smile of a quite inappropriate indulgence. It will see that man is caught in a way of acting that cannot be recognized as right and holy, unless it is first and at the same time recognized as thoroughly wrong and unholy. Self-evidently, this kind of tolerance, and therefore a theological consideration of religion, is possible only for those who are ready to abase themselves and their religion together with man, with every individual man, knowing that they first, and their religion, have need of tolerance, a strong forbearing tolerance.

We begin by stating that religion is unbelief. It is a concern, indeed, we must say that it is the one great concern, of godless man ...

In the light of what we have already said, this proposition is not in any sense a negative value-judgement. It is not a judgement of religious science or philosophy based upon some prior negative judgement concerned with the nature of religion. It does not affect only other men with their religion. Above all, it affects ourselves also as adherents of the Christian religion. It formulates the judgement of divine revelation upon all religion. It can be explained and expounded, but it cannot be derived from any higher principle than revelation, nor can it be proved by any phenomenology or history of religion. Since it aims only to repeat the judgement of God, it does not involve any human renunciation of human values, and contesting of the true and the good and the beautiful which a closer inspection will reveal in almost all religions, and which we naturally expect to find in abundant measure in our own religion, if we hold to it with any conviction. What happens is simply that man is taken by God and judged and condemned by God. That means, of course, that we are struck to the very roots, to the heart. Our whole existence is called in question. But where that is the case there can be no place for sad and pitiful laments at the non-recognition of relative human greatness ...

To realize that religion is really unbelief, we have to consider it from the standpoint of the revelation attested in Holy Scripture. There are two elements in that revelation which make it unmistakably clear.

1. Revelation is God's self-offering and self-manifestation. Revelation encounters man on the presupposition and in confirmation of the fact that man's attempts to know God from his own standpoint are wholly and entirely futile; not because of any necessity in principle, but because of a practical necessity of fact. In revelation God tells man that he is God, and that as such he is his Lord. In telling him this, revelation tells him something utterly new, something which apart from revelation he does not know and cannot tell either himself or others. It is true that he could do this, for revelation simply states the truth. If it is true that God is God and that as such he is the Lord of man, then it is also true that man is so placed towards him, that he could know him. But this is the very truth which is not available to man, before it is told him in revelation. If he really can know God this capacity rests upon the fact that he really does know him, because God has offered and manifested himself to him. The capacity, then, does not rest upon the fact, which is true enough, that man could know him. Between 'he could' and 'he can' there lies the absolute decisive 'he cannot', which can be removed and turned into its opposite only by revelation. The truth that God is God and our Lord, and the further truth that we could know him as God and Lord, can only come to us through the truth itself. This 'coming to us' of the truth is revelation. It does not reach us in a neutral condition, but in an action which stands to it, as the coming of truth, in a very definite, indeed a determinate relationship. That is to say, it reaches us as religious men; i.e. it reaches us in the attempt to know God from our standpoint. It does not reach us, therefore, in the activity which corresponds to it. The activity which corresponds to revelation would have to be faith; the recognition of the self-offering and self-manifestation of God. We need to see that in view of God all our activity is in vain even in the best life; i.e. that of ourselves we are not in a position to apprehend the truth, to let God be God and our Lord. We need to renounce all attempts even to try to apprehend this truth. We

need to be ready and resolved simply to let the truth be told us, and therefore to be apprehended by it. But that is the very thing for which we are not resolved and ready. The man to whom the truth has really come will concede that he was not at all ready and resolved to let it speak to him. The genuine believer will not say that he came to faith from faith, but – from unbelief, even though the attitude and activity with which he met revelation, and still meets it, is religion. For in faith, man's religion as such is shown by revelation to be resistance to it. From the standpoint of revelation religion is clearly seen to be a human attempt to anticipate what God in his revelation wills to do and does do. It is the attempted replacement of the divine work by a human manufacture. The divine reality offered and manifested to us in revelation is replaced by a concept of God arbitrarily and wilfully evolved by man ...

'Arbitrarily and wilfully' means here by his own means, by his own human insight and constructiveness and energy. Many different images of God can be formed once we have engaged in this undertaking, but their significance is always the same ...

The image of God is always that reality of perception or thought in which man assumes and asserts something unique and ultimate and decisive either beyond or within his own existence, by which he believes himself to be posited or at least determined and conditioned. From the standpoint of revelation, man's religion is simply an assumption and assertion of this kind, and as such it is an activity which contradicts revelation – contradicts it, because it is only through truth that truth can come to man. If a man tries to grasp at truth of himself he tries to grasp at it *a priori*. But in that case he does not do what he has to do when the truth comes to him. He does not believe. If he did, he would listen; but in religion he talks. If he did, he would accept a gift; but in religion he takes something for himself. If he did, he would let God himself intercede for God: but in religion he ventures to grasp at God. Because it is a grasping, religion is the contradiction of revelation, the concentrated expression of human unbelief, i.e. an attitude and activity which is directly opposed to faith. It is a feeble but defiant, an arrogant but hopeless, attempt to create something which man could do, but now cannot do, or can do only because and if God himself creates it for him: the knowledge of the truth, the knowledge of God. We cannot therefore interpret the attempt as a harmonious co-operating of man with the revelation of God, as though religion were a kind of outstretched hand which is filled by God in his revelation.

Again, we cannot say of the evident religious capacity of man that it is, so to speak, the general form of human knowledge, which acquires its true and proper content in the shape of revelation. On the contrary, we have here an exclusive contradiction. In religion man bolts and bars himself against revelation by providing a substitute, by taking away in advance the very thing which has to be given by God ...

He has, of course, the power to do this. But what he achieves and acquires in virtue of this power is never the knowledge of God as Lord and God. It is never the truth. It is a complete fiction, which has not only little but no relation to God. It is an anti-God who has first to be known as such and discarded when the truth comes to him. But it can be known as such, as a fiction, only as the truth does come to him ...

Revelation does not link up with a human religion which is already present and practised. It contradicts it, just as religion previously contradicted revelation. It displaces it, just as religion previously displaced revelation; just as faith cannot link up with a mistaken faith, but must contradict and displace it as unbelief, as an act of contradiction ...

2. As the self-offering and self-manifestation of God, revelation is the act by which in grace he reconciles man to himself by grace. As a radical teaching about God, it is also the radical assistance of God which comes to us as those who are unrighteous and unholy, and as such damned and lost. In this respect, too, the affirmation which revelation makes and presupposes of man is that he is unable to help himself either in whole or even in part. But again, he ought not to have been so helpless. It is not inherent in the nature and concept of man that he should be unrighteous and unholy and therefore damned and lost. He was created to be the image of God, i.e. to obedience towards God and not to sin, to salvation and not to destruction. But he is not summoned to this as to a state in which he might still somehow find himself, but as one in which he no longer finds himself, from which he has fallen by his own fault. But this, too, is a truth which he cannot maintain: it is not present to him unless it comes to him in revelation, i.e. in Jesus Christ, to be declared to him in a new way – the oldest truth of all in a way which is quite new. He cannot in any sense declare to himself that he is righteous and holy, and therefore saved, for in his own mouth as his own judgement of himself it would be a lie. It is truth as the revealed knowledge of God. It is truth in Jesus Christ. Jesus Christ does not fill out and improve all the different attempts of man to think of God and to represent him according to his own standard. But as the self-

offering and self-manifestation of God he replaces and completely outbids those attempts, putting them in the shadows to which they belong. Similarly, in so far as God reconciles the world to himself in him, he replaces all the different attempts of man to reconcile God to the world, all our human efforts at justification and sanctification, at conversion and salvation. The revelation of God in Jesus Christ maintains that our justification and sanctification, our conversion and salvation, have been brought about and achieved once and for all in Jesus Christ. And our faith in Jesus Christ consists in our recognizing and admitting and affirming and accepting the fact that everything has actually been done for us once and for all in Jesus Christ. He is the assistance that comes to us. He alone is the Word of God that is spoken to us. There is an exchange of status between him and us: his righteousness and holiness are ours, our sin is his; he is lost for us, and we for his sake are saved. By this exchange (καταλλαγή, 2 Corinthians 5:19) revelation stands or falls. It would not be the active, redemptive self-offering and self-manifestation of God, if it were not centrally and decisively the *satisfactio* and *intercessio Jesu Christi*.

And now we can see a second way in which revelation contradicts religion, and conversely religion necessarily opposes revelation. For what is the purpose of the universal attempt of religions to anticipate God, to foist a human product into the place of his Word, to make our own images of the one who is known only where he gives himself to be known, images which are first spiritual, and then religious, and then actually visible? What does the religious man want when he thinks and believes and maintains that there is a unique and ultimate and decisive being, that there is a divine being (θείου), a godhead, that there are gods and a single supreme God, and when he thinks that he himself is posited, determined, conditioned, and overruled by this being? Is the postulate of God or gods, and the need to objectify the Ultimate spiritually or physically, conditioned by man's experience of the actual superiority and lordship of certain natural and supernatural, historical and eternal necessities, potencies, and ordinances? Is this experience (or the postulate and need which correspond to it) followed by the feeling of man's impotence and failure in face of this higher world, by the urge to put himself on peaceful and friendly terms with it, to interest it on his behalf, to assure himself of its support, or better still, to enable himself to exercise an influence on it, to participate in its power and dignity and to co-operate in its work? Does man's attempt to justify and sanctify himself, follow the attempt to think of God and represent him? Or is the relationship the direct opposite? Is the primary thing man's obscure urge to justify and sanctify himself, i.e. to confirm and strengthen himself in the awareness and exercise of his skill and strength to master life, to come to terms with the world, to make the world serviceable to him? Is religion with its dogmatics and worship and precepts the most primitive, or better perhaps, the most intimate and intensive part of the technique, by which we try to come to terms with life? Is it that the experience of that higher world, or the need to objectify it in the thought of God and the representation of God, must be regarded only as an exponent of this attempt, that is, as the ideal construction inevitable within the framework of this technique? Are the gods only reflected images and guarantees of the needs and capacities of man, who in reality is lonely and driven back upon himself and his own willing and ordering and creating? Are sacrifice and prayer and asceticism and morality more basic than God and the gods? Who is to say? In face of the two possibilities we are in a circle which we can consider from any point of view with exactly the same result. What is certain is that in respect of the practical content of religion it is still a matter of an attitude and activity which does not correspond to God's revelation, but contradicts it. At this point, too, weakness and defiance, helplessness and arrogance, folly and imagination are so close to one another that we can scarcely distinguish the one from the other. Where we want what is wanted in religion, i.e. justification and sanctification as our own work, we do not find ourselves – and it does not matter whether the thought and representation of God has a primary or only a secondary importance – on the direct way to God, who can then bring us to our goal at some higher stage on the way. On the contrary, we lock the door against God, we alienate ourselves from him, we come into direct opposition to him. God in his revelation will not allow man to try to come to terms with life, to justify and sanctify himself. God in his revelation, God in Jesus Christ, is the one who takes on himself the sin of the world, who wills that all our care should be cast upon him, because he careth for us ...

It is the characteristically pious element in the pious effort to reconcile him to us which must be an abomination to God, whether idolatry is regarded as its presupposition or its result, or perhaps as both. Not by any continuing along this way, but only by radically breaking away from it, can we come, not to our own goal but to God's goal, which is the direct opposite of our goal ...

TRUE RELIGION

The preceding expositions have established the fact that we can speak of 'true religion' only in the sense in which we speak of a 'justified sinner'.

Religion is never true in itself and as such. The revelation of God denies that any religion is true, i.e. that it is in truth the knowledge and worship of God and the reconciliation of man with God. For as the self-offering and self-manifestation of God, as the work of peace which God himself has concluded between himself and man, revelation is the truth beside which there is no other truth, over against which there is only lying and wrong. If by the concept of a 'true religion' we mean truth which belongs to religion in itself and as such, it is just as unattainable as a 'good man', if by goodness we mean something which man can achieve on his own initiative. No religion is true. It can only become true, i.e. according to that which it purports to be and for which it is upheld. And it can become true only in the way in which man is justified, from without; i.e. not of its own nature and being but only in virtue of a reckoning and adopting and separating which are foreign to its own nature and being, which are quite inconceivable from its own standpoint, which come to it quite apart from any qualifications or merits. Like justified man, true religion is a creature of grace. But grace is the revelation of God. No religion can stand before it as true religion. No man is righteous in its presence. It subjects us all to the judgement of death. But it can also call dead men to life and sinners to repentance. And similarly in the wider sphere where it shows all religion to be false, it can also create true religion. The abolishing of religion by revelation need not mean only its negation: the judgement that religion is unbelief. Religion can just as well be exalted in revelation, even though the judgement still stands. It can be upheld by it and concealed in it. It can be justified by it, and – we must at once add – sanctified. Revelation can adopt religion and mark it off as true religion. And it not only can. How do we come to assert that it can, if it has not already done so? There is a true religion: just as there are justified sinners. If we abide strictly by that analogy – and we are dealing not merely with an analogy, but in a comprehensive sense with the thing itself – we need have no hesitation in saying that the Christian religion is the true religion.

In our discussion of 'religion as unbelief' we did not consider the distinction between Christian and non-Christian religion. Our intention was that whatever we said about the other religions affected the Christian similarly. In the framework of that discussion we could not speak in any special way about Christianity. We could not give it any special or assured place in face of that judgement. Therefore the discussion cannot be understood as a preliminary polemic against the non-Christian religions, with a view to the ultimate assertion that the Christian religion is the true religion. If this were the case our task now would be to prove that, as distinct from the non-Christian religions, the Christian is not guilty of idolatry and self-righteousness, that it is not therefore unbelief but faith, and therefore true religion; or, which comes to the same thing, that it is no religion at all, but as against all religions, including their mystical and atheistical self-criticism, it is in itself the true and holy and as such the unspotted and incontestable form of fellowship between God and man. To enter on this path would be to deny the very thing we have to affirm. If the statement is to have any content we can dare to state that the Christian religion is the true one only as we listen to the divine revelation. But a statement which we dare to make as we listen to the divine revelation can only be a statement of faith. And a statement of faith is necessarily a statement which is thought and expressed in faith and from faith, i.e. in recognition and respect of what we are told by revelation. Its explicit and implicit content is unreservedly conditioned by what we are told. But that is certainly not the case if we try to reach the statement that the Christian religion is the true religion by a road which begins by leaving behind the judgement of revelation, that religion is unbelief, as a matter which does not apply to us Christians but only to others, the non-Christians, thus enabling us to separate and differentiate ourselves from them with the help of this judgement. On the contrary, it is our business as Christians to apply this judgement first and most acutely to ourselves: and to others, the non-Christians, only in so far as we recognize ourselves in them, i.e. only as we see in them the truth of this judgement of revelation which concerns us, in the solidarity, therefore, in which, anticipating them in both repentance and hope, we accept this judgement to participate in the promise of revelation. At the end of the road we have to tread there is, of course, the promise to those who accept God's judgement, who let themselves be led beyond their unbelief. There is faith in this promise, and, in this faith, the presence and reality of the grace of God, which, of course, differentiates our religion, the Christian, from all others as the true religion. This exalted goal cannot be reached except by this humble road. And it would not be a truly humble road if we tried to tread it except in the consciousness that any 'attaining' here can consist only in the utterly humble and thankful adoption of something which we would not attain if it were not already attained in God's revelation before we set out on the road.

We must insist, therefore, that at the beginning of a knowledge of truth of the Christian religion there stands the recognition that this religion, too, stands under the judgement that religion is unbelief, and that it is not acquitted by any inward worthiness, but only by the grace of God, proclaimed and effectual in his revelation. But concretely this judgement affects the whole practice of our faith: our Christian conceptions of God and the things of God, our Christian theology, our Christian worship, our forms of Christian fellowship and order, our Christian morals, poetry, and art, our attempts to give individual and social form to the Christian life, our Christian strategy and tactics in the interest of our Christian cause, in short our Christianity, to the extent that it is *our* Christianity, the human work which we undertake and adjust to all kinds of near and remote aims and which as such is seen to be on the same level as the human work in other religions. This judgement means that all this Christianity of ours, and all the details of it, are not as such what they ought to be and pretend to be, a work of faith, and therefore of obedience to the divine revelation. What we have here is in its own way – a different way from that of other religions, but no less seriously – unbelief, i.e. opposition to the divine revelation, and therefore active idolatry and self-righteousness. It is the same helplessness and arbitrariness. It is the same self-exaltation of man which means his most profound abasement. But this time it is in place of and in opposition to the self-manifestation and self-offering of God, the reconciliation which God himself has accomplished, it is in disregard of the divine consolations and admonitions that great and small Babylonian towers are erected, which cannot as such be pleasing to God, since they are definitely not set up to his glory ...

We are here concerned with an order which can be forgotten or infringed only to the detriment of a real knowledge of the truth of the Christian religion. Again, to ascribe the demonstrative power for this truth to the religious self-consciousness as such is to the dishonouring of God and the eternal destruction of souls. Even outwardly, in its debate with non-Christian religions, the Church can never do more harm than when it thinks that it must abandon the apostolic injunction, that grace is sufficient for us. The place to which we prefer to look is only mist, and the reed upon which we have to lean will slip through our fingers. By trying to resist and conquer other religions, we put ourselves on the same level. They, too, appeal to this or that immanent truth in them. They, too, can triumph in the power of the religious self-consciousness, and sometimes they have been astonishingly successful over wide areas. Christianity can take part in this fight. There is no doubt that it does not lack the necessary equipment, and can give a good account of itself alongside the other religions. But do not forget that if it does this it has renounced its birthright. It has renounced the unique power which it has as the religion of revelation. This power dwells only in weakness. And it does not really operate, nor does the power with which Christianity hopes to work, the power of religious self-consciousness which is the gift of grace in the midst of weakness, unless Christianity has first humbled instead of exalting itself. By its neglect of this order, Christianity has created great difficulties for itself in its debate with other religions ...

We must not allow ourselves to be confused by the fact that a history of Christianity can be written only as a story of the distress which it makes for itself. It is a story which lies completely behind the story of that which took place between Yahweh and his people, between Jesus and his apostles. It is a story whose source and meaning and goal, the fact that the Christian is strong only in his weakness, that he is really satisfied by grace, can in the strict sense nowhere be perceived directly. Not even in the history of the Reformation! What can be perceived in history is the attempt which the Christian makes, in continually changing forms, to consider and vindicate his religion as a work which is in itself upright and holy. But he continually feels himself thwarted and hampered and restrained by Holy Scripture, which does not allow this, which even seems to want to criticize this Christian religion of his. He obviously cannot shut out the recollection that it is in respect of this very work of his religion that he cannot dispense with the grace of God and therefore stands under the judgement of God. At this point we are particularly reminded of the history of the Reformation. But in the very light of that history we see that the recollection has always been there, even in the pre- and post-Reformation periods. Yet the history of Christianity as a whole reveals a tendency which is quite contrary to this recollection. It would be arbitrary not to recognize this, and to claim that the history of Christianity, as distinct from that of other religions, is the story of that part of humanity, which, as distinct from others, has existed only as the part which of grace lives by grace. In the strict sense there is no evidence of this throughout the whole range of Christianity. What is evident is in the first instance a part of humanity which no less contradicts the grace and revelation of God because it claims them as its own peculiar and most sacred treasures, and its religion is to that extent a religion of revelation. Contradiction is contradiction. That it exists at this point, in respect of the religion of revelation, can be denied even less than at other points. Elsewhere we might claim in extenuation that it simply exists in fact, but not in direct contrast with revelation. But in the history of Christianity, just because it is the religion of revelation, the sin is, as it were, committed with a high hand. Yes, sin! For contradiction against grace is unbelief, and unbelief is sin, indeed it is *the* sin. It is therefore a fact that we can speak of the truth of the Christian religion only within the doctrine of the *iustificatio impii.* The statement that even Christianity is unbelief gives rise to a whole mass of naïve and rationalizing contradictions. Church history itself is a history of this contradiction. But it is this very fact which best shows us how true and right the statement is. We can as little avoid the contradiction as jump over our own shadow.

We cannot expect that at a fourth or fifth or sixth stage the history of Christianity will be anything but a history of the distress which Christianity creates for itself. May it not lack in future reformation, i.e. expressions of warning and promise deriving from Holy Scripture! But before the end of all things we cannot expect that the Christian will not always show himself an enemy of grace, in spite of all intervening restraints.

Notwithstanding the contradiction and therefore our own existence, we can and must perceive that for our part we and our contradiction against grace stand under the even more powerful contradiction of grace itself. We can and must – in faith. To believe means, in the knowledge of our sin to rely upon the righteousness of God which makes an infinite satisfaction for our sin. Concretely, it means, in the knowledge of our contradiction against grace to cleave to the grace of God which infinitely contradicts this contradiction. In this knowledge of grace, in the knowledge that it is the justification of the ungodly, that it is grace for the enemies of grace, the Christian faith attains to its knowledge of the truth of the Christian religion. There can be no more question of any immanent rightness or holiness of this particular religion as the ground and content of the truth of it than there can be of any other religion claiming to be the true religion in virtue of its inherent advantages. The Christian cannot avoid abandoning any such claim. He cannot avoid confessing that he is a sinner even in his best actions as a Christian. And that is not, of course, the ground, but the symptom of the truth of the Christian religion. The abandoning and confessing means that the Christian Church is the place where, confronted with the revelation and grace of God, by grace men live by grace ...

There is, of course, one fact which powerfully and decisively confirms the assertion, depriving it of its arbitrary character and giving to it a necessity which is absolute. But to discern this fact, our first task – and again and again we shall have to return to this 'first' – must be to ignore the whole realm of 'facts' which we and other human observers as such can discern and assess. For the fact about which we are speaking stands in the same relationship to this realm as does the sun to the earth. That the sun lights up this part of the earth and not that means for the earth no less than this, that day rules in the one part and night in the other. Yet the earth is the same in both places. In neither place is there anything in the earth itself to dispose it for the day. Apart from the sun, it would everywhere be enwrapped in eternal night. The fact that it is partly in the day does not derive in any sense from the nature of the particular part as such. Now it is in exactly the same way that the light of the righteousness and judgement of God falls upon the world of man's religion, upon one part of that world, upon the Christian religion, so that that religion is not in the night but in the day, it is not perverted but straight, it is not false religion but true. Taken by itself, it is still human religion and therefore unbelief, like all other religions. Neither in the root nor in the crown of this particular tree, neither at the source nor at the outflow of this particular stream, neither on the surface nor in the depth of this particular part of humanity can we point to anything that makes it suitable for the day of divine righteousness and judgement. If the Christian religion is the right and true religion the reason for it does not reside in facts which might point to itself or its own adherents, but in the fact which as the righteousness and the judgement of God confronts it as it does all other religions, characterizing and differentiating it and not one of the others as the right and true religion ...

2

KARL RAHNER: Christianity and the Non-Christian Religions

Karl Rahner (1904–1984) was a member of the Society of Jesus and Professor of Dogmatics in the universities of Innsbruck, Munich and Münster. One of the leading theologians of the Roman Catholic Church, he was a theological consultant at the Second Vatican Council. Many of his essays have been published in the volumes of Theological Investigations *(London and New York, 1961–1992). His* Foundations of Christian Faith *appeared in 1976 (English trans., London and New York, 1978). The following expositions are the notes of a lecture given on 28 April 1961 in Eichstatt (Bavaria) at a meeting of the Abendländische Akademie. They expound Rahner's much discussed notion of people of other religions as 'anonymous Christians'.*

'Open Catholicism' involves two things. It signifies the fact that the Catholic Church is opposed by historical forces which she herself cannot disregard as if they were purely 'worldly' forces and a matter of indifference to her but which, on the contrary, although they do not stand in a positive relationship of peace and mutual recognition to the Church, do have a significance for her. 'Open Catholicism' means also the task of becoming related to these forces in order to understand their existence (since this cannot be simply acknowledged), in order to bear with and overcome the annoyance of their opposition and in order to form the Church in such a way that she will be able to overcome as much of this pluralism as should not exist, by understanding herself as the higher unity of this opposition. 'Open Catholicism' means therefore a certain attitude towards the present-day pluralism of powers with different outlooks on the world. We do not, of course, refer to pluralism merely as a fact which one simply acknowledges without explaining it. Pluralism is meant here as a fact which ought to be thought about and one which, without denying that – in part at least – it should not exist at all, should be incorporated once more from a more elevated viewpoint into the totality and unity of the Christian understanding of human existence. For Christianity, one of the gravest elements of this pluralism in which we live and with which we must come to terms, and indeed the element most difficult to incorporate, is the pluralism of religions. We do not refer by this to the pluralism of Christian denominations. This pluralism too is a fact, and a challenge and task for Christians. But we are not concerned with it here.

Our subject is the more serious problem, at least in its ultimate and basic form, of the different religions which still exist even in Christian times, and this after a history and mission of Christianity which has already lasted two thousand years. It is true, certainly, that all these religions together, including Christianity, are faced today with an enemy which did not exist for them in the past. We refer to the decided lack of religion and the denial of religion in general. This denial, in a sense, takes the stage with the ardour of a religion and of an absolute and sacred system which is the basis and the yard-stick of all further thought. This denial, organized on the basis of a State, represents itself as *the* religion of the future – as the decided, absolute secularization of human existence excluding all mystery. No matter how paradoxical this may sound, it does remain true that precisely this state of siege in which religion in general finds itself, finds one of its most important weapons and opportunities for success in the fact that humanity is so torn in its religious adherence. But quite apart from this, this pluralism is a greater threat and a reason for greater unrest for Christianity than for any other religion. For no other religion – not even Islam – maintains so absolutely that it is *the* religion, the one and only valid revelation of the one living God, as does the Christian religion.

The fact of the pluralism of religions, which endures and still from time to time becomes virulent anew even after a history of two thousand years, must therefore be the greatest scandal and the greatest vexation for Christianity. And the threat of this vexation is also greater for the individual Christian today than ever before. For in the past, the other religion was in practice the religion of a completely different cultural environment. It belonged to a history with which the individual only communicated very much on the periphery of his own history; it was the religion of those who were even in every other respect alien to oneself. It is not surprising, therefore, that people did not wonder at the fact that these 'others' and 'strangers' had also a different religion. No wonder that in general people could not seriously consider these other religions as a challenge posed to themselves or even as a possibility for themselves. Today things have changed. The West is no longer shut up in itself; it can no longer regard itself simply as the centre of the history of this world and as the centre of culture, with a religion which even from this point of view (i.e. from a point of view which has really nothing to do with a decision of faith but which simply carries the weight of something quite self-evident) could appear as the obvious and indeed sole way of honouring God to be thought of for a European. Today everybody is the next-door neighbour and spiritual neighbour of everyone else in the world. And so everybody today is determined by the inter-communication of all those situations of life which affect the whole world. Every religion which exists in the world is – just like all cultural possibilities and actualities of other people – a question posed, and a possibility offered, to every person. And just as one experiences someone else's culture in practice as something relative to one's own and as something existentially demanding, so it is also involuntarily with alien religions. They have become part of one's own existential situation – no longer merely theoretically but in the concrete – and we experience them therefore as something which puts the absolute claim of our own Christian faith into question. Hence, the question about the understanding of and the continuing existence of religious pluralism as a factor of our immediate Christian existence is an urgent one and part of the question as to how we are to deal with today's pluralism.

This problem could be tackled from different angles. In the present context we simply wish to try to describe a few of those basic traits of a Catholic dogmatic interpretation of the non-Christian religions which may help us to come closer to a solution of the question about the Christian position in regard to the religious pluralism in the world of today. Since it cannot be said, unfortunately, that Catholic theology – as practised in more recent times – has really paid sufficient attention to the questions to be posed here, it will also be impossible to maintain that what we will have to say here can be taken as the common thought of Catholic theology. What we have to say carries, therefore, only as much weight as the reasons we can adduce, which reasons can again only be briefly indicated. Whenever the propositions to be mentioned carry a greater weight than this in theology, anyone trained in theology will realize it quite clearly from what is said. When we say that it is a question here of a *Catholic* dogmatic interpretation of the non-Christian religions, this is not meant to indicate that it is necessarily a question also of theories controverted among Christians themselves. It simply means that we will not be able to enter explicitly into the question as to whether the theses to be stated here can also hope to prove acceptable to Protestant theology. We say too that we are going to give a dogmatic interpretation, since we will pose our question not as empirical historians of religion but out of the self-understanding of Christianity itself, i.e. as dogmatic theologians.

1st Thesis: We must begin with the thesis which follows, because it certainly represents the basis in the Christian faith of the theological understanding of other religions. This thesis states that Christianity understands itself as the absolute religion, intended for all men, which cannot recognize any other religion beside itself as of equal right. This proposition is self-evident and basic for Christianity's understanding of itself. There is no need here to prove it or to develop its meaning. After all, Christianity does not take valid and lawful religion to mean primarily that relationship of man to God which man himself institutes on his own authority. Valid and lawful religion does not mean man's own interpretation of human existence. It is not the reflection and objectification of the experience which man has of himself and by himself.

Valid and lawful religion for Christianity is rather God's action on men, God's free self-revelation by communicating himself to man. It is God's relationship to men, freely instituted by God himself and revealed by God in this institution. *This* relationship of God to man is basically the same for all men, because it rests on the Incarnation, death and resurrection of the one Word of God become flesh. Christianity is God's own interpretation in his Word of this relationship of God to man founded in Christ by God himself. And so Christianity can recognize itself as the true and lawful religion for all men only where and when it enters with existential power and demanding force into the realm of another religion and – judging it by itself – puts it in question. Since the time of Christ's coming – ever since he came in the flesh as the Word of God in absoluteness and reconciled, i.e. united the world with

God by his death and resurrection, not merely theoretically but really – Christ and his continuing historical presence in the world (which we call 'Church') is *the* religion which binds man to God.

Already we must, however, make one point clear as regards this first thesis (which cannot be further developed and proved here). It is true that the Christian religion itself has its own pre-history which traces this religion back to the beginning of the history of humanity – even though it does this by many basic steps. It is also true that this fact of having a pre-history is of much greater importance, according to the evidence of the New Testament, for the theoretical and practical proof of the claim to absolute truth made by the Christian religion than our current fundamental theology is aware of. Nevertheless, the Christian religion as such has a beginning in history; it did not always exist but began at some point in time. It has not always and every-where been *the* way of salvation for men – at least not in its historically tangible ecclesio-sociological constitution and in the reflex fruition of God's saving activity in, and in view of, Christ. As a historical quantity Christianity has, therefore, a temporal and spatial starting point in Jesus of Nazareth and in the saving event of the unique Cross and the empty tomb in Jerusalem. It follows from this, however, that this absolute religion – even when it begins to be this for practically all men – must come in a historical way to men, facing them as the only legitimate and demanding religion for them. It is therefore a question of whether this moment, when the existentially real demand is made by the absolute religion in its historically tangible form, takes place really at the same chronological moment for all people, or whether the occurrence of this moment has itself a history and thus is not chronologically simultaneous for all people, cultures and spaces of history. (This is a question which up until now Catholic theology has not thought through with suffi-cient clarity and reflection by really confronting it with the length and intricacy of real human time and history.) Normally the beginning of the objective obligation of the Christian message for all men – in other words, the abolition of the validity of the Mosaic religion *and* of all other religions which (as we will see later) may also have a period of validity and of being-willed-by-God – is thought to occur in the apostolic age. Normally, therefore, one regards the time between this beginning and the actual acceptance of the personally guilty refusal of Christianity in a non-Jewish world and history as the span between the already given promulgation of the law and the moment when the one to whom the law refers takes cognizance of it.

It is not just an idle academic question to ask whether such a conception is correct or whether, as we maintain, there could be a different opinion in this matter, i.e. whether one could hold that the beginning of Christianity for actual periods of history, for cultures and religions, could be postponed to those moments in time when Christianity became a real historical factor in an individual history and culture – a real historical moment in a particular culture. For instance, one concludes from the first, usual answer that *everywhere* in the world, since the first Pentecost, baptism of children dying before reaching the use of reason is necessary for their supernatural salvation, although this was not necessary before that time. For other questions, too, a correct and considered solution of the present question could be of great importance, as for instance for the avoidance of immature conversions, for the justification and importance of 'indirect' missionary work, etc. One will have to ask oneself whether one can still agree today with the first opinion mentioned above, in view of the history of the missions which has already lasted two thousand years and yet is still to a great extent in its beginnings – for even Suarez himself, for instance, had already seen (at least with regard to the *Jews*) that the *promulgatio* and *obligatio* of the Christian religion, and not merely the *divulgatio* and *notitia promulgationis*, take place in historical sequence. We cannot really answer this question here, but it may at least be pointed out as an open question; in practice, the correctness of the second theory may be presupposed since it alone corresponds to the real historicity of Christianity and salvation-history.

From this there follows a delicately differentiated understanding of our first thesis: we maintain positively only that, as regards destination, Christianity is the absolute and hence the only religion for all men. We leave it, however, an open question (at least in principle) at what exact point in time the absolute obligation of the Christian religion has in fact come into effect for every man and culture, even in the sense of the *objective* obligation of such a demand. Nevertheless – and this leaves the thesis formulated still sufficiently exciting – wherever in practice Christianity reaches man in the real urgency and rigour of his actual existence, Christianity – once understood – presents itself as the only still valid religion for this man, a necessary means for his salvation and not merely an obligation with the necessity of a precept. It should be noted that this is a question of the necessity of a *social* form for salvation. Even though this is Christianity and not some other religion, it may surely still be said without hesitation that this thesis contains

t of the individual. For, as far as the Gospel is concerned, we have no
ly conclusive reason for thinking so pessimistically of men. On the other
d, and contrary to every merely human experience, we do have every
on for thinking optimistically of God and his salvific will which is more
erful than the extremely limited stupidity and evil-mindedness of men.
vever little we can say with certitude about the final lot of an individual
e or outside the officially constituted Christian religion, we have every
on to think optimistically – i.e. truly hopefully and confidently in a
stian sense – of God who has certainly the last word and who has
led to us that he has spoken his powerful word of reconciliation and
veness into the world. If it is true that the eternal Word of God has
me flesh and has died the death of sin for the sake of our salvation and in
of our guilt, then the Christian has no right to suppose that the fate of
orld – having regard to the whole of the world – takes the same course
count of man's refusal as it would have taken if Christ had not come.
t and his salvation are not simply one of two possibilities offering them-
to man's free choice; they are the need of God which bursts open and
ms the false choice of man by overtaking it. In Christ God not only gives
sibility of salvation, which in that case would still have to be effected by
imself, but the actual salvation itself, however much this includes also
ht decision of human freedom which is itself a gift from God. Where
ady existed, grace came in superabundance. And hence we have every
o suppose that grace has not only been offered even outside the
an Church (to deny this would be the error of Jansenism) but also that,
at many cases at least, grace gains the victory in man's free acceptance
is being again the result of grace.
urse, we would have to show more explicitly than the shortness of time
that the empirical picture of human beings, their life, their religion
r individual and universal history does not disprove this optimism of a
ich knows the whole world to be subjected to the salvation won by
But we must remember that the theoretical and ritualistic factors in
d evil are only a very inadequate expression of what man actually
ishes in practice. We must remember that the same transcendence of
en the transcendence elevated and liberated by God's grace) can be
in many different ways and under the most varied labels. We must
consideration that whenever the religious person acts really reli-
he makes use of, or omits unthinkingly, the manifold forms of

implicitly another thesis which states that in concrete human existence as
such, the nature of religion itself must include a social constitution – which
means that religion can exist only in a social form. This means, therefore,
that man, who is commanded to have a religion, is also commanded to seek
and accept a social form of religion. It will soon become clear what this
reflection implies for the estimation of non-Christian religions.

Finally, we may mention one further point in this connection. What is
vital in the *notion* of *paganism* and hence also of the non-Christian pagan religions (taking 'pagan' here as a theological concept without any disparaging
intent) is not the actual refusal to accept the Christian religion but the
absence of any sufficient historical encounter with Christianity which would
have enough historical power to render the Christian religion really present
in this pagan society and in the history of the people concerned. If this is so,
then paganism ceases to exist in this sense by reason of what is happening
today. For the Western world is opening out into a universal world history in
which every people and every cultural sector becomes an inner factor of
every other people and every other cultural sector. Or rather, paganism is
slowly entering a new phase: there is *one* history of the world, and in this *one*
history both the Christians and the non-Christians (i.e. the old and new
pagans together) live in one and the same situation and face each other in
dialogue, and thus the question of the theological meaning of the other religions arises once more and with even greater urgency.

2nd Thesis: Until the moment when the Gospel really enters into the
historical situation of an individual, a non-Christian religion (even outside
the Mosaic religion) does not merely contain elements of a natural
knowledge of God, elements, moreover, mixed up with human depravity
which is the result of original sin and later aberrations. It contains also supernatural elements arising out of the grace which is given to men as a gratuitous
gift on account of Christ. For this reason a non-Christian religion can be
recognized as a *lawful* religion (although only in different degrees) without
thereby denying the error and depravity contained in it. This thesis requires
a more extensive explanation.

We must first of all note the point up to which this evaluation of the non-
Christian religions is valid. This is the point in time when the Christian
religion becomes a historically real factor for those who are of this religion.
Whether this point is the same, theologically speaking, as the first Pentecost,

or whether it is different in chronological time for individual peoples and religions, is something which even at this point will have to be left to a certain extent an open question. We have, however, chosen our formulation in such a way that it points more in the direction of the opinion which seems to us the more correct one in the matter although the *criteria* for a more exact determination of this moment in time must again be left an open question.

The thesis itself is divided into two parts. It means first of all that it is *a priori* quite possible to suppose that there are supernatural, grace-filled elements in non-Christian religions. Let us first of all deal with this statement. It does not mean, of course, that all the elements of a polytheistic conception of the divine, and all the other religious, ethical and metaphysical aberrations contained in the non-Christian religions, are to be or may be treated as harmless either in theory or in practice. There have been constant protests against such elements throughout the history of Christianity and throughout the history of the Christian interpretation of the non-Christian religions, starting with the Epistle to the Romans and following on the Old Testament polemics against the religion of the 'heathens'. Every one of these protests is still valid in what was really meant and expressed by them. Every such protest remains a part of the message which Christianity and the Church has to give to the peoples who profess such religions. Furthermore, we are not concerned here with an *a posteriori* history of religions. Consequently, we also cannot describe empirically what should not exist and what is opposed to God's will in these non-Christian religions, nor can we represent these things in their many forms and degrees. We are here concerned with dogmatic theology and so can merely repeat the universal and unqualified verdict as to the unlawfulness of the non-Christian religions right from the moment when they came into real and historically powerful contact with Christianity (and at first only thus!). It is clear, however, that this condemnation does not mean to deny the very basic differences within the non-Christian religions especially since the pious, God-pleasing pagan was already a theme of the Old Testament, and especially since this God-pleasing pagan cannot simply be thought of as living absolutely outside the concrete socially constituted religion and constructing his own religion on his native foundations – just as St Paul in his speech on the Areopagus did not simply exclude a positive and basic view of the pagan religion.

The decisive reason for the first part of our thesis is basically a theological consideration. This consideration (prescinding from certain more precise

qualifications) rests ultimately on the fact that, if we wish to must profess belief in the universal and serious salvific towards all men which is true even within the post-par salvation dominated by original sin. We know, to be sure sition of faith does not say anything certain about the *indi* man understood as something which has in fact been desires the salvation of everyone. And this salvation wil salvation won by Christ, the salvation of supernatural gra man, the salvation of the beatific vision. It is a salvation re those millions upon millions of people who lived perh before Christ – and also for those who have lived after cultures and epochs of a very wide range which were still from the viewpoint of those living in the light of the Ne the one hand, we conceive salvation as something spe there is no salvation apart from Christ, if according to C supernatural divinization of mankind can never be repl will on the part of man but is necessary as somethin earthly life; and if, on the other hand, God has reall intended this salvation for all men – then these two asp ciled in any other way than by stating that every hum truly exposed to the influence of divine, supernatural interior union with God and by means of which God whether the individual takes up an attitude of ac towards this grace. It is senseless to suppose cruelly – a acceptance by the man of today, in view of the enorm Christian history of salvation and damnation – tha outside the official and public Christianity are so ev offer of supernatural grace ought not even to be ma since these individuals have already rendered them an offer by previous, subjectively grave offences a law.

If one gives more exact theological thought to thi regard nature and grace as two phases in the life follow each other in time. It is furthermore imposs of supernatural, divinizing grace made to all men salvific purpose of God, should in general (presc few exceptions) remain ineffective in most cases religious institutions by making a consciously critical choice among and between them. We must consider the immeasurable difference – which it seems right to suppose to exist even in the Christian sphere – between what is objectively wrong in moral life and the extent to which this is really realized with subjectively grave guilt. Once we take all this into consideration, we will not hold it to be impossible that grace is at work, and is even being accepted, in the spiritual, personal life of the individual, no matter how primitive, unenlightened, apathetic and earth-bound such a life may at first sight appear to be. We can say quite simply that, wherever, and in so far as, the individual makes a moral decision in his life (and where could this be declared to be in any way absolutely impossible – except in precisely 'pathological' cases?), this moral decision can also be thought to measure up to the character of a supernaturally elevated, believing and thus saving act, and hence to be more in actual fact than merely 'natural morality'. Hence, if one believes seriously in the universal salvific purpose of God towards all men in Christ, it need not and cannot really be doubted that gratuitous influences of properly Christian supernatural grace are conceivable in the life of all men (provided they are first of all regarded as individuals) and that these influences can be presumed to be accepted in spite of the sinful state of men and in spite of their apparent estrangement from God.

Our second thesis goes even further than this, however, and states in its second part that, from what has been said, the actual religions of 'pre-Christian' humanity too must not be regarded as simply illegitimate from the very start, but must be seen as quite capable of having a positive significance. This statement must naturally be taken in a very different sense which we cannot examine here for the various particular religions. This means that the different religions will be able to lay claim to being lawful religions only in very different senses and to very different degrees. But precisely this variability is not at all excluded by the notion of a 'lawful religion', as we will have to show in a moment. A lawful religion means here an institutional religion whose 'use' by man at a certain period can be regarded on the whole as a positive means of gaining the right relationship to God and thus for the attaining of salvation, a means which is therefore positively included in God's plan of salvation.

That such a notion and the reality to which it refers can exist even where such a religion shows many theoretical and practical errors in its concrete form becomes clear in a theological analysis of the structure of the Old

Covenant. We must first of all remember in this connection that only in the New Testament – in the Church of Christ understood as something which is eschatologically final and *hence* (and only for this reason) 'indefectible' and infallible – is there realized the notion of a Church which, because it is instituted by God in some way or other, already contains the permanent norm of differentiation between what is right (i.e. willed by God) and what is wrong in the religious sphere, and contains it both as a permanent institution and as an intrinsic element of this religion. There was nothing like this in the Old Testament, although it must undoubtedly be recognized as a lawful religion. The Old Covenant – understood as a concrete, historical and religious manifestation – contained what is right, willed by God, *and* what is false, erroneous, wrongly developed and depraved. But there was no permanent, continuing and institutional court of appeal in the Old Covenant which could have differentiated authoritatively, always and with certainty for the conscience of the individual between what was willed by God and what was due to human corruption in the actual religion. Of course, there were the prophets. They were not a permanent institution, however, but a conscience which had always to assert itself anew on behalf of the people in order to protest against the corruption of the religion as it existed at the time, thus – incidentally – confirming the existence of this corruption. The official, institutional forms known as the 'kingdom' and the priesthood were so little proof against this God-offending corruption that they could bring about the ruin of the Israelitic religion itself. And since there were also pseudo-prophets, and no infallible 'institutional' court of appeal for distinguishing genuine and false prophecy, it was – in the last analysis – left to the conscience of the individual Israelite himself to differentiate between what in the concrete appearance of the Israelitic religion was the true covenant with God and what was a humanly free, and so in certain cases falsifying, interpretation and corruption of this God-instituted religion. There might have been objective criteria for such a distinction of spirits, but their application could not simply be left to an 'ecclesiastical' court – not even in the most decisive questions – since official judgements could be wrong even about these questions and in fact were completely wrong about them.

This and nothing more – complete with its distinction between what was willed by God and what was human, all too human, a distinction which was ultimately left to be decided by the individual – was the concrete Israelitic religion. The Holy Scriptures do indeed give us the official and valid deposit to help us differentiate among the spirits which moved the history of the Old Testament religion. But since the infallible delimitation of the canon of the Old Testament is again to be found only in the New Testament, the exact and final differentiation between the lawful and the unlawful in the Old Testament religion is again possible only by making use of the New Testament as something eschatologically final. The unity of the concrete religion of the Old Testament, which (ultimately) could be distinguished only gropingly and at one's own risk, was however the unity willed by God, providential for the Israelites in the order of salvation and indeed the lawful religion for them. In this connection it must furthermore be taken into consideration that it was meant to be this only for the Israelites and for no one else; the institution of those belonging to the Jewish religion without being of the Jewish race (i.e. of the proselytes), was a very much later phenomenon. Hence it cannot be a part of the notion of a lawful religion in the above sense that it should be free from corruption, error and objective moral wrong in the concrete form of its appearance, or that it should contain a clear objective and permanent final court of appeal for the conscience of the individual to enable the individual to differentiate clearly and with certainty between the elements willed and instituted by God and those which are merely human and corrupt.

We must therefore rid ourselves of the prejudice that we can face a non-Christian religion with the dilemma that it must either come from God in everything it contains and thus correspond to God's will and positive providence, or be simply a purely human construction. If man is under God's grace even in these religions – and to deny this is certainly absolutely wrong – then the possession of this supernatural grace cannot but show itself, and cannot but become a formative factor of life in the concrete, even where (though not only where) this life turns the relationship to the absolute into an explicit theme, viz. in religion. It would perhaps be possible to say in theory that where a certain religion is not only accompanied in its concrete appearance by something false and humanly corrupted but also makes this an explicitly and consciously adopted element – an explicitly declared condition of its *nature* – this religion is wrong in its deepest and most specific being and hence can no longer be regarded as a lawful religion – not even in the widest sense of the word. This may be quite correct in theory. But we must surely go on to ask whether there is any religion apart from the Christian religion (meaning here even only the Catholic religion) with an authority which could elevate falsehood into one of its really essential parts and which could thus face man with an alternative of either accepting this falsehood as the most real and decisive factor of the religion or leaving this religion. Even if one could perhaps say something like this of Islam as such, it would have to be denied of the majority of religions. It would have to be asked in every case to what extent the followers of such religions would actually agree with such an interpretation of their particular religion. If one considers furthermore how easily a concrete, originally religious act can be always directed in its intention towards one and the same absolute, even when it manifests itself in the most varied forms, then it will not even be possible to say that theoretical polytheism, however deplorable and objectionable it may be objectively, must always and everywhere be an absolute obstacle to the performance in such a religion of genuinely religious acts directed to the one true God. This is particularly true since it cannot be proved that the practical religious life of the ancient Israelites, in so far as it manifested itself in popular theory, was always more than mere henotheism.

Furthermore, it must be borne in mind that the individual ought to and must have the possibility in his life of partaking in a genuine saving relationship to God, and this at all times and in all situations of the history of the human race. Otherwise there could be no question of a serious and also actually effective salvific design of God for all men, in all ages and places. In view of the social nature of man and the previously even more radical social solidarity of men, however, it is quite unthinkable that man, being what he is, could actually achieve this relationship to God – which he must have and which if he is to be saved, is and must be made possible for him by God – in an absolutely private interior reality and this outside of the actual religious bodies which offer themselves to him in the environment in which he lives. If man had to be and could always and everywhere be a *homo religiosus* in order to be able to save himself as such, then he was this *homo religiosus* in the concrete religion in which 'people' lived and had to live at that time. He could not escape this religion, however much he may have and did take up a critical and selective attitude towards this religion on individual matters, and however much he may have and did put different stresses in practice on certain things which were at variance with the official theory of this religion. If, however, man can always have a positive, saving relationship to God, and if he always had to have it, then he has always had it within *that* religion which in practice was at his disposal by being a factor in his sphere of existence. As already stated above, the inherence of the individual exercise of religion in a social religious order is one of the essential traits of true religion as it exists in practice. Hence, if one were to expect from someone who lives outside the Christian religion that he should have exercised his genuine, saving relationship to God absolutely outside the religion which society offered him, then such a conception would turn religion into something intangibly interior, into something which is always and everywhere performed only indirectly, a merely transcendental religion without anything which could become tangible in categories. Such a conception would annul the above-mentioned principle regarding the necessarily social nature of all religion in the concrete, so that even the Christian Church would then no longer have the necessary pre-supposition of general human and natural law as proof of her necessity. And since it does not at all belong to the notion of a lawful religion intended by God for man as something positively salvific that it should be pure and positively willed by God in all its elements, such a religion can be called an absolutely legitimate religion for the person concerned. That which God has intended as salvation for him reached him, in accordance with God's will and by his permission (no longer adequately separable in practice), in the *concrete* religion of his actual realm of existence and historical condition, but this fact did not deprive him of the right and the limited possibility to criticize and to heed impulses of religious reform which by God's providence kept on recurring within such a religion. For a still better and simpler understanding of this, one has only to think of the natural and socially constituted morality of a people and culture. Such a morality is never pure but is always also corrupted, as Jesus confirmed even in the case of the Old Testament. It can always be disputed and corrected, therefore, by the individual in accordance with his conscience. Yet, taken in its totality, it is *the* way in which the individual encounters the natural divine law according to God's will, and the way in which the natural law is given real, actual power in the life of the individual who cannot reconstruct these tablets of the divine law anew on his own responsibility and as a private metaphysician.

The morality of a people and of an age, taken in its totality, is therefore the legitimate and concrete form of the divine law (even though, of course, it can and may have to be corrected), so that it was not until the New Testament that the institution guaranteeing the purity of this form became (with the necessary reservations) an element of this form itself. Hence, if there existed a divine moral law and religion in the life of man *before* this moment, then its absolute purity (i.e. its constitution by divinely willed elements alone) must not be made the condition of the lawfulness of its existence. In fact, if every man who comes into the world is pursued by God's grace – and if one of the effects of this grace, even in its supernatural and salvifically elevating form, is to cause changes in consciousness (as is maintained by the better theory in Catholic theology) even though it cannot be simply *as* such a direct object of certain reflection – then it cannot be true that the actually existing religions do not bear any trace of the fact that all men are in some way affected by grace. These traces may be difficult to distinguish even to the enlightened eye of the Christian. But they must be there. And perhaps we may only have looked too superficially and with too little love at the non-Christian religions and so have not really seen them. In any case it is certainly not right to regard them as new conglomerates of natural theistic metaphysics and as a humanly incorrect interpretation and institutionalization of this 'natural religion'. The religions existing in the concrete must contain supernatural, gratuitous elements, and in using *these* elements the pre-Christian was able to attain God's grace: presumably, too, the pre-Christian exists even to this day, even though the possibility is gradually disappearing *today*. If we say that there were lawful religions in pre-Christian ages even outside the realm of the Old Testament, this does not mean that these religions were lawful in *all* their elements – to maintain this would be absurd. Nor does it mean that *every* religion was lawful; for in certain cases several forms, systems and institutions of a religious kind offered themselves within the historically concrete situation of the particular member of a certain people, culture, period of history, etc., so that the person concerned had to decide as to *which* of them was here and now, and on the whole, the more correct way (and hence for him *in concreto* the only correct way) of finding God.

This thesis is not meant to imply that the lawfulness of the Old Testament religion was of exactly the same kind as that which we are prepared to grant in a certain measure to the extra-Christian religions. For in the Old Testament the prophets saw to it (even though not by way of a permanent institution) that there existed a possibility of distinguishing in public salvation-history between what was lawful and what was unlawful in the history of the religion of the Israelites. This cannot be held to be true to the same extent outside this history, although this again does not mean that outside the Old Testament there could be no question of any kind of divinely guided salvation-history in the realm of public history and institutions.

The main difference between such a salvation-history and that of the Old Testament will presumably lie in the fact that the historical, factual nature of the New Testament has *its* immediate pre-history in the *Old Testament* (which pre-history, in parenthesis, is insignificantly brief in comparison with the general salvation-history which counts perhaps a million years – for the former can be known with any certainty only from the time of Abraham or of Moses). Hence, the New Testament unveils *this* short span of salvation-history distinguishing its divinely willed elements and those which are contrary to God's will. It does this by a distinction which we cannot make in the same way in the history of any other religion. The second part of this second thesis, however, states two things positively. It states that even religions other than the Christian and the Old Testament religions contain quite certainly elements of a supernatural influence by grace which must make itself felt even in these objectifications. And it also states that by the fact that in practice man as he really is can live his proffered relationship to God only in society, man must have had the right and indeed the duty to live this his relationship to God within the religious and social realities offered to him in his particular historical situation.

3rd Thesis: If the second thesis is correct, then Christianity does not simply confront the member of an extra-Christian religion as a mere non-Christian but as someone who can and must already be regarded in this or that respect as an anonymous Christian. It would be wrong to regard the pagan as someone who has not yet been touched in any way by God's grace and truth. If, however, he has experienced the grace of God – if, in certain circumstances, he has already accepted this grace as the ultimate, unfathomable entelechy of his existence by accepting the immeasurableness of his dying existence as opening out into infinity – then he has already been given revelation in a true sense even before he has been affected by missionary preaching from without. For this grace, understood as the *a priori* horizon of all his spiritual acts, accompanies his consciousness subjectively, even though it is not known objectively. And the revelation which comes to him from without is not in such a case the proclamation of something as yet absolutely unknown, in the sense in which one tells a child here in Bavaria, for the first time in school, that there is a continent called Australia. Such a revelation is then the expression in objective concepts of something which this person has already attained or could already have attained in the depth of his rational existence. It is not possible here to prove more exactly that this *fides implicita* is something which dogmatically speaking can occur in a so-called pagan. We can do no more here than to state our thesis and to indicate the direction in which the proof of this thesis might be found. But if it is true that a person who becomes the object of the Church's missionary efforts is or may be already someone on the way towards his salvation, and someone who in certain circumstances finds it, without being reached by the proclamation of the Church's message – and if it is at the same time true that this salvation which reaches him in this way is Christ's salvation, since there is no other salvation – then it must be possible to be not only an anonymous theist but also an anonymous Christian. And then it is quite true that in the last analysis, the proclamation of the Gospel does not simply turn someone absolutely abandoned by God and Christ into a Christian, but turns an anonymous Christian into someone who now also knows about his Christian belief in the depths of his grace-endowed being by objective reflection and in the profession of faith which is given a social form in the Church.

It is not thereby denied, but on the contrary implied, that this explicit self-realization of his previously anonymous Christianity is itself part of the development of this Christianity itself – a higher stage of development of this Christianity demanded by his being – and that it is therefore intended by God in the same way as everything else about salvation. Hence, it will not be possible in any way to draw the conclusion from this conception that, since man is already an anonymous Christian even without it, this explicit preaching of Christianity is superfluous. Such a conclusion would be just as false (and for the same reasons) as to conclude that the sacraments of baptism and penance could be dispensed with because a person can be justified by his subjective acts of faith and contrition even before the reception of these sacraments.

The reflex self-realization of a previously anonymous Christianity is demanded (1) by the incarnational and social structure of grace and of Christianity, and (2) because the individual who grasps Christianity in a clearer, purer and more reflective way has, other things being equal, a still greater chance of salvation than someone who is merely an anonymous Christian. If, however, the message of the Church is directed to someone who is a 'non-Christian' only in the sense of living by an anonymous Christianity not as yet fully conscious of itself, then her missionary work must take this fact into account and must draw the necessary conclusions when deciding on its missionary strategy and tactics. We may say at a guess that this is still not the case in sufficient measure. The exact meaning of all this, however, cannot be developed further here.

4th Thesis: It is possibly too much to hope, on the one hand, that the religious pluralism which exists in the concrete situation of Christians will disappear in the foreseeable future. On the other hand, it is nevertheless absolutely permissible for the Christian himself to interpret this non-Christianity as Christianity of an anonymous kind which he does always still go out to meet as a missionary, seeing it as a world which is to be brought to the explicit consciousness of what already belongs to it as a divine offer or already pertains to it also over and above this as a divine gift of grace accepted unreflectedly and implicitly. If both these statements are true, then the Church will not so much regard herself today as the exclusive community of those who have a claim to salvation but rather as the historically tangible vanguard and the historically and socially constituted explicit expression of what the Christian hopes is present as a hidden reality even outside the visible Church.

To begin with, however much we must always work, suffer and pray anew and indefatigably for the unification of the whole human race, in the one Church of Christ, we must nevertheless expect, for theological reasons and not merely by reason of a profane historical analysis, that the religious pluralism existing in the world and in our own historical sphere of existence will not disappear in the foreseeable future. We know from the gospel that the opposition to Christ and to the Church will not disappear until the end of time. If anything, we must even be prepared for a heightening of this antagonism to Christian existence. If, however, this opposition to the Church cannot confine itself merely to the purely private sphere of the individual but must also be of a public, historical character, and if this opposition is said to be present in a history which today, in contrast to previous ages, possesses a worldwide unity, then the continuing opposition to the Church can no longer exist merely locally and outside a certain limited sector of history such as that of the West. It must be found in our vicinity and everywhere else. And this is part of what the Christian must expect and must learn to endure. The Church, which is at the same time the homogenous characterization of an in itself homogeneous culture (i.e. the medieval Church), will no longer exist if history can no longer find any way to escape from or go back on the period of its planetary unity. In a unified world history in which everything enters into the life of everyone, the 'necessary' public opposition to Christianity is a factor in the existential sphere of all Christianity. If this Christianity, thus always faced with opposition and unable to expect seriously that this will ever cease, nevertheless believes in God's universal salvific will – in other words, believes that God can be victorious by his secret grace even where the Church does not win the victory but is contradicted – then this Church cannot feel herself to be just *one* dialectic moment in the whole of history but has already overcome this opposition by her faith, hope and charity. In other words, the others who oppose her are merely those who have not yet recognized what they nevertheless really already are (or can be) even when, on the surface of existence, they are in opposition; they are already anonymous Christians, and the Church is not the communion of those who possess God's grace as opposed to those who lack it, but is the communion of those who can explicitly confess what they *and* the others hope to be. Non-Christians may think it presumption for the Christian to judge everything which is sound or restored (by being sanctified) to be the fruit in every man of the grace of his Christ, and to interpret it as anonymous Christianity; they may think it presumption for the Christian to regard the non-Christian as a Christian who has not yet come to himself reflectively. But the Christian cannot renounce this 'presumption' which is really the source of the greatest humility both for himself and for the Church. For it is a profound admission of the fact that God is greater than man and the Church. The Church will go out to meet the non-Christian of tomorrow with the attitude expressed by St Paul when he said: What therefore you do not know and yet worship [and yet *worship*!] that I proclaim to you (Acts 17:23). On such a basis one can be tolerant, humble and yet firm towards all non-Christian religions.

3

VATICAN II: Declaration on the Relation of the Church to Non-Christian Religions

The Second Vatican Council, summoned by Pope John XXIII, met in four sessions from 1962 to 1964. It marked a turning point in the history of the Roman Catholic Church in the twentieth century. It initiated major changes in the Church's liturgy, and opened up new and much more positive attitudes to other Christians, to other religions and to the secular world.

INTRODUCTION

In this age when the human race is daily becoming more closely united and ties between different peoples are becoming stronger, the Church considers more closely her own relation to non-Christian religions. Since it is her task to foster unity and love among men, and indeed among nations, she first considers in this declaration what men have in common and what draws them into fellowship together.

For, since God made all races of men and gave them the whole earth to inhabit (cf. Acts 17:26), all nations form a single community with a common origin; they also have a single final end which is God. God's providence and his evident goodness and his plan of salvation extend to all men (cf. Wisdom 8:1; Acts 14:17; Romans 2:6–7; 1 Timothy 2:4), until the time when all the elect are made one in the holy city, where all nations will walk in the brightness of God's glory which will be its light (cf. Apocalypse 21:23 ff.).

From his different religions, man seeks the answer to the riddles and problems of human existence; these exercise him no less deeply today than in the past: What is man? What is the meaning and purpose of life? What are goodness and sin? What is the origin and purpose of suffering? Which is the way to attain true happiness? What is death, judgement and reward after death? What, lastly, is that ultimate and indescribable mystery, embracing the whole of our existence, which is both our origin and our end?

VARIOUS NON-CHRISTIAN RELIGIONS

From ancient times down to the present day there is found in various peoples a certain recognition of that hidden power which is present in history and human affairs, and in fact sometimes an acknowledgement of a supreme Godhead, or even of a Father. This recognition and acknowledgement give those people's lives a deep and pervading religious sense. With the advance of the civilizations with which they are connected, these religions endeavour to use more refined concepts and more developed language to answer these questions. Thus in Hinduism, men probe the mystery of God and express it with a rich fund of myths and a penetrating philosophy. They seek liberation from the constrictions of this world by various forms of asceticism, deep meditation or loving and trustful recourse to God. In the various forms of Buddhism the basic inadequacy of this changing world is recognized and men are taught how with confident application they can achieve a state of complete liberation, or reach the highest level of illumination, either through their own efforts or with help from above. There are other religions too, all over the world, which try to alleviate in various ways the anxieties of man's heart. To this end they put forward various 'ways' – doctrines and moral teaching as well as sacred rites.

The Catholic Church rejects nothing which is true and holy in these religions. She has a sincere respect for those ways of acting and living, those moral and doctrinal teachings which may differ in many respects from what she holds and teaches, but which none the less often reflect the brightness of that Truth which is the light of all men. But she proclaims, and is bound to proclaim unceasingly, Christ, who is 'the way, the truth, and the life' (John 14:6). In him men find the fullness of their religious life and in him God has reconciled all things to himself (cf. 2 Corinthians 5:18–19).

She therefore urges her sons, using prudence and charity, to join members of other religions in discussions and collaboration. While bearing witness to their own Christian faith and life, they must acknowledge those good spiritual and moral elements and social and cultural values found in other religions, and preserve and encourage them.

ISLAM

The Church also regards with esteem the Muslims who worship the one, subsistent, merciful and almighty God, the Creator of heaven and earth, who has spoken to man. Islam willingly traces its descent back to Abraham, and just as he submitted himself to God, the Muslims endeavour to submit themselves to his mysterious decrees. They venerate Jesus as a prophet, without, however, recognizing him as God, and they pay honour to his virgin mother Mary and sometimes also invoke her with devotion. Further, they expect a day of judgement when God will raise all men from the dead and reward them. For this reason they attach importance to the moral life and worship God, mainly by prayer, alms-giving and fasting.

If in the course of the centuries there has arisen not infrequent dissension and hostility between Christian and Muslim, this sacred Council now urges everyone to forget the past, to make sincere efforts at mutual understanding and to work together in protecting and promoting for the benefit of all men, social justice, good morals as well as peace and freedom.

THE JEWISH RELIGION

Probing the mystery of the Church, this sacred Council remembers the bond by which the people of the New Testament are spiritually linked to the line of Abraham.

The Church of Christ recognizes that in God's plan of salvation, the beginning of her own election and faith are to be found in the Patriarchs, Moses and the Prophets. She fully acknowledges that all believers in Christ, who are Abraham's sons in faith (cf. Galatians 3:7), are included in Abraham's calling and that the salvation of the Church is mystically prefigured in the exodus of the chosen people from the land of their bondage. The Church cannot, therefore, forget that it was through that people, with whom God in his ineffable mercy saw fit to establish the Old Covenant, that she herself has received the revelation of the Old Testament. She takes her nourishment from the root of the cultivated olive tree on to which the wild-olive branches of the Gentiles have been grafted (cf. Romans 11:17–24). The

Church believes that Christ, who is our Peace, has reconciled Jews and Gentiles through the Cross and has made us both one in himself (cf. Ephesians 2:14–16).

The Church also always keeps before her eyes the words of the Apostle Paul concerning his kinsmen 'to whom belongeth the adoption as of children, and the glory, and the testament, and the giving of the law and the service of God and the promises: whose are the fathers, and of whom is Christ, according to the flesh' (Romans 9:4–5), the son of the Virgin Mary. She recalls too that the apostles, the foundations and pillars of the Church and very many of those first disciples who proclaimed the Gospel of Christ to the world, were born of the Jewish people.

Holy Scripture is witness that Jerusalem has not known the time of her visitation (cf. Luke 19:44). The Jews have not, for the most part, accepted the gospel; some indeed have opposed its diffusion (cf. Romans 11:28). Even so, according to the Apostle Paul, the Jews still remain very dear to God, for the sake of their fathers, since he does not repent of the gifts he makes or the calls he issues (cf. Romans 11:28–9). In company with the Prophets and the same Apostle, the Church looks forward to that day, known to God alone, when all peoples will call on the Lord with one voice and 'serve him with one accord' (Soph. 3:9; cf. Isaiah 66:23; Psalm 65:4; Romans 11:11–32).

Given this great spiritual heritage common to Christians and Jews, it is the wish of this sacred Council to foster and recommend a mutual knowledge and esteem, which will come from biblical and theological studies, and brotherly discussions.

Even if the Jewish authorities, together with their followers, urged the death of Christ (cf. John 19:6), what was done to him in his passion cannot be blamed on all Jews living at that time indiscriminately, or on the Jews of today. Although the Church is the new People of God, the Jews should not be presented as rejected by God or accursed, as though this followed from Scripture. Therefore all must take care that in instruction and in preaching the Word of God, they do not teach anything which is not in complete agreement with the truth of the Gospel and the spirit of Christ.

Further, the Church condemns all persecutions of any men; she remembers her common heritage with the Jews and, acting not from any political motives, but rather from a spiritual and evangelical love, deplores all hatred, persecutions and other manifestations of antisemitism, whatever the period and whoever was responsible.

But Christ, the Church holds and always has held, in his infinite love, underwent his passion and death voluntarily for the sins of all men in order that all might achieve salvation. It is the task of the Church in its preaching to proclaim the cross of Christ as a sign of God's universal love and as the source of all grace.

ANY SORT OF DISCRIMINATION EXCLUDES UNIVERSAL BROTHERHOOD

We cannot call on God, the Father of all men, if there are any men whom we refuse to treat as brothers, since all men are created in God's image. Man's relation to God the Father is connected with his relation to his fellow men in such a way that Scripture says 'He that loveth not, knoweth not God' (1 John 4:8).

There remain, then, no grounds for any theory or practice which leads to discrimination between men or races in matters concerning the dignity of man, and the rights which stem from it.

Therefore the Church condemns all discrimination between men and all conflict of race, colour, class or creed, as being contrary to the mind of Christ. Accordingly, following in the footsteps of the Apostles Peter and Paul, this sacred Council earnestly appeals to believers in Christ to 'conduct themselves well among the Gentiles' (1 Peter 2:12) if possible, and do their best to be at peace with all men (cf. Romans 12:18), so that they may be true sons of the Father who is in heaven (cf. Matthew 5:45).

4

WILFRED CANTWELL SMITH:
The Christian in a Religiously Plural
World

Wilfred Cantwell Smith (1916–2000) was Professor of the Comparative History of Religions at Harvard University. Having specialized, in early writings, in Islamic studies, he turned to the wider problem of world religion in a series of influential books, The Meaning and End of Religion *(1962, reprinted New York and London, 1978),* Questions of Religious Truth *(London, 1967),* Belief and History *(Charlottesville, 1977),* Faith and Belief *(Princeton, 1979),* Towards a World Theology *(London, 1980). Cantwell Smith insisted throughout his writings on the primacy of 'personal truth' over the truth of doctrines.*

We live, if I may coin a phrase, in a time of transition. The observation is a platitude; but the transitions themselves through which we are moving, the radical transformations in which we find ourselves involved, are far from hackneyed. Rather, there is excitement and at times almost terror in the newness to which all our cherished past is giving way. In area after area we are becoming conscious of being participants in a process, where we thought we were carriers of a pattern.

I wish to attempt to discern and to delineate something at least of the momentous current that, if I mistake not, has begun to flow around and through the Christian Church. It is a current which, although we are only beginning to be aware of it, is about to become a flood that could sweep us quite away unless we can through greatly increased consciousness of its force and direction learn to swim in its special and mighty surge.

I refer to the movement that, had the word 'ecumenical' not been appropriated lately to designate rather an internal development within the ongoing Church, might well have been called by that name, in its literal
meaning of a worldwide humanity. I mean the emergence of a true
cosmopolitanism, or according to the wording of my title, the Christian
Church in a religiously plural world, which of course is the only world there
is. Like the other, *the* 'ecumenical' movement, this transformation, too, begins
at the frontier, on the mission field, the active confrontation of the Church
with mankind's other faiths, other religious traditions. We shall begin there,
too, but shall presently see that the issues raised cannot be left out there in the
distance. They penetrate back into the scholar's study, and pursue us into
what we were brought up to think of as the most intimate and most sanctified
recesses of our theological traditions.

Regarding the missionary movement itself, I shall begin by stating quite
bluntly and quite vigorously: the missionary enterprise is in profound and
fundamental crisis. There has been some temptation to recognize this more
on the practical than on the theoretical level. There has been some temptation, perhaps, even not to recognize it at all! – or at least, not to recognize
how serious, and how far-reaching, it is: that the whole Church is involved,
and not merely 'those interested in missions'.

At the practical level the situation is acute enough. It is not only in China
that the traditional missionary venture has come or is coming to an end. Take
the problem of recruitment: more have remarked on the fact that volunteers
today are either scarce or curious, than that today no mission board can in
fact offer any young person a life vocation on the mission field. Since some
persons in the Church at home seem not to realize the kind of feeling on these
matters to be found in the non-Western world, I shall quote from the report
of a Christian Missionary Activities Enquiry Committee appointed in 1954
by the state government of Madhya Pradesh in India. Among its recommen-
dations were the following:

> Those missionaries whose primary object is proselytization should be asked
> to withdraw. The large influx of foreign missionaries is undesirable and
> should be checked ...
> The use of medical or other professional service as a direct means of
> making conversions should be prohibited by law ...
> Any attempt by force or fraud, or threats of illicit means or grants of
> financial or other aid, or by fraudulent means or promises, or by moral and

material assistance, or by taking advantage of any person's inexperience or confidence, or by exploiting any person's necessity, spiritual (mental) weakness or thoughtlessness, or, in general, any attempt or effort (whether successful or not), directly or indirectly to penetrate into the religious conscience of persons (whether of age or under-age) of another faith, for the purpose of consciously altering their religious conscience or faith, so as to agree with the ideas or convictions of the proselytizing party should be absolutely prohibited ...

An amendment of the Constitution of India may be sought, firstly, to clarify that the right of propagation has been given only to the citizens of India and secondly, that it does not include conversions brought about by force, fraud, or other illicit means.

China, Angola, the Arab world after Suez, this sort of attitude in India, and the like are not simply illustrations of a practical problem. They are symptoms of an intellectual, emotional, and spiritual problem in which Christians are involved. Few Western Christians have any inkling of the involvement of the Church within the object of anti-Westernism, or of the religious involvement of the resurgence in Asia and Africa of other communities. Of this resurgence we see usually only the political or economic facets, because these are the only ones that we can understand. The religious history of mankind is taking as monumental a turn in our century as is the political or economic, if only we could see it. And the upsurge of a vibrant and self-assertive new religious orientation of Buddhists and Hindus and the like evinces a new phase not merely in the history of those particular traditions, but in the history of the whole complex of man's religiousness, of which the Christian is a part, and an increasingly participant part. The traditional relation of the Christian Church to man's other religious traditions has been that of proselytizing evangelism, at least in theory. The end of that phase is the beginning of a new phase, in which the relation of the Church to other faiths will be new. But what it will be, in theory or practice, has yet to be worked out – not by the Church alone, but by the Church in its involvement with these others.

The missionary situation of the Church, then, is in profound crisis, in both practice and theory. The most vivid and most masterly summing up of this crisis is perhaps the brief remark of Canon Max Warren, the judicious and brilliant and sensitive and responsible General Secretary in London of the Church Missionary Society. His obituary on traditional mission policy and practice is in three sentences: 'We have marched around alien Jerichos the requisite number of times. We have sounded the trumpets. And the walls have not collapsed.'

We come back from the mission field to North America, and to theology. Traditional missions are the exact extrapolation of the traditional theology of the Church. The passing of traditional missions is a supersession of one phase of the Church's traditional theology. The 'ecumenical' movements have been the result in part of pressures from the mission field because there the scandal of a divided Christendom came most starkly to light. It is from the mission field also that the scandal of a fundamental fallacy in traditional theology has been shown up.

The rise of science in the nineteenth century induced a revision in Christian theology – what has sometimes been called the second Reformation. Some may think that Canon Warren exaggerates, but at least he calls attention to the seriousness of the new challenge, when he says that the impact of agnostic science will turn out to have been as child's play compared to the challenge to Christian theology of the faith of other men.

The woeful thing is that the meeting of that challenge has hardly seriously begun.

An illuminating story was told me by a Harvard friend, concerning Paul Tillich. Apparently a letter in the student paper, the *Harvard Crimson*, was able to show up as superficial in a particular case this eminent theologian's understanding of religious traditions in Asia. Some would perhaps find it not particularly surprising that an undergraduate these days should know more on this matter than a major Christian thinker. Until recently, certainly, it was not particularly expected that a man should know much, or indeed anything, about the religious life of other communities before he undertook to become a spokesman for his own. To me, however, the incident raises a significant issue. Looking at the matter historically, one may perhaps put it thus: probably Tillich belongs to the last generation of theologians who can formulate their conceptual system as religiously isolationist. The era of religious isolationism is about to be as much at an end as that of political isolationism already is. The pith of Tillich's exposition has to do with its deliberate aptness to the intellectual context in which it appears: the correlation technique, of question and answer. But that context as he sees it is the mental climate of the Western world; and he has spoken to it just at the end of its separatist tradition, just before it is superseded by a new context, a climate modified radically by new breezes, or new storms, blowing in from the other parts of the planet. The new generation of the Church, unless it is content with a ghetto, will live in a cosmopolitan environment, which will make the work of even a Tillich appear parochial.

Ever since the impact of Greek philosophy on the Church, or shall we say the forced discovery of Greek philosophy by the Church, in the early centuries, every Christian theology has been written in the light of it. Whether the Christian thinker rejected or accepted it, modified or enriched it, he formulated his exposition aware of it, and aware that his readers would read him in the light of it. No serious intellectual statement of the Christian faith since that time has ignored this conceptual context.

Similarly, ever since the rise of science, the forced discovery of science by the Church, again subsequent Christian doctrine has been written in the light of it. Formulator and reader are aware of this context, and no intellectual statement that ignores it can be fully serious.

I suggest that we are about to enter a comparable situation with regard to the other religious traditions of mankind. The time will soon be with us when a theologian who attempts to work out his position unaware that he does so as a member of a world society in which other theologians equally intelligent, equally devout, equally moral, are Hindus, Buddhists, Muslims, and unaware that his readers are likely perhaps to be Buddhists or to have Muslim husbands or Hindu colleagues – such a theologian is as out of date as is one who attempts to construct an intellectual position unaware that Aristotle has thought about the world or that existentialists have raised new orientations, or unaware that the earth is a minor planet in a galaxy that is vast only by terrestrial standards. Philosophy and science have impinged so far on theological thought more effectively than has comparative religion, but this will not last.

It is not my purpose in this essay to suggest the new theological systems that the Church will in the new situation bring forth. My task is to delineate the problems that such a system must answer, to try to analyse the context within which future theological thought will inescapably be set. Intellectually, we have had or are having our Copernican Revolution, but not yet our Newton. By this I mean that we have discovered the facts of our earth's being one of the planets, but have not yet explained them. The pew, if not yet the pulpit, the undergraduate if not yet the seminary professor, have begun to recognize not only that the Christian answers on man's cosmic quality are not the only answers, but even that the Christian questions are not the only questions. The awareness of multiformity is becoming vivid, and compelling.

Before Newton's day it used to be thought that we live in a radically dichotomous universe: there was our earth, where things fell to the ground, and there were the heavens, where things went round in circles. These were two quite different realms, and one did not think of confusing or even much relating the two. A profoundly significant step was taken when men recognized that the apple and the moon are in much the same kind of motion. Newton's mind was able to conceive an interpretation – accepted now by all of us, but revolutionary at the time – that without altering the fact that on earth things *do* fall to the ground and in the heavens things *do* go round in circles, yet saw both these facts as instances of a single kind of behaviour. In the religious field, the academic approach is similarly restless at the comparable dichotomy that for each group has in the past seen *our* tradition (whichever it be) as faith, other men's behaviour as superstition, the two realms to be explained in quite unrelated ways, understood on altogether separate principles. The Christian's faith has come down from God, the Buddhist's goes round and round in the circles of purely human aspiration, and so on. The intellectual challenge here is to make coherent sense, in a rational, integrated manner, of a wide range of apparently comparable and yet conspicuously diverse phenomena. And the academic world is closer to meeting this challenge than some theologians have noticed.

Certain Christians have even made the rather vigorous assertion that the Christian faith is *not* one of 'the religions of the world', that one misunderstands it if one attempts to see it in those terms. Most students of comparative religion have tended to pooh-pooh such a claim as unacceptable. I, perhaps surprisingly, take it very seriously indeed but I have discovered that the same applies to the other traditions also. The Christian faith is not to be seen as a religion, one of the religions. But neither is the faith of Buddhists, Hindus, Muslims or Andaman Islanders; and to think of it so is seriously to misunderstand and distort it. This is a large issue that I have treated in my book *The Meaning and End of Religion*. I believe there is no question but that modern enquiry is showing that other men's faith is not so different from ours as we were brought up to suppose.

Religious diversity poses a general human problem because it disrupts community. It does so with new force in the modern world because divergent traditions that in the past did and could develop separately and insouciantly are today face to face; and, perhaps even more important and radical, are for the first time side by side. Different civilizations have in the past either ignored each other or fought each other; very occasionally in tiny ways perhaps they met each other. Today they not only meet but interpenetrate; they meet not only each other, but jointly meet joint problems, and must jointly try to solve them. They must collaborate. Perhaps the single most important challenge that mankind faces in our day is the need to turn our nascent world society into a world community.

This is not easy. Men have yet to learn our new task of living together as partners in a world of religious and cultural plurality. The technological and economic aspects of 'one world', of a humanity in process of global integration, are proceeding apace, and at the least are receiving the attention of many of our best minds and most influential groups. The political aspects also are under active and constant consideration, even though success here is not so evident, except in the supremely important day-to-day staving off of disaster. The ideological and cultural question of human cohesion, on the other hand, has received little attention, and relatively little progress can be reported, even though in the long run it may prove utterly crucial, and is already basic to much else. Unless men can learn to understand and to be loyal to each other across religious frontiers, unless we can build a world in which people profoundly of different faiths can live together and work together, then the prospects for our planet's future are not bright.

My own view is that the task of constructing even that minimum degree of world fellowship that will be necessary for man to survive at all is far too great to be accomplished on any other than a religious basis. From no other source than his faith, I believe, can man muster the energy, devotion, vision, resolution, the capacity to survive disappointment, that will be necessary – that *are* necessary – for this challenge. Co-operation among men of diverse religion is a moral imperative, even at the lowest level of social and political life.

Some would agree that the world community must have a religious basis, conceding that a lasting and peaceful society cannot be built by a group of men that are ultimately divided religiously, that have come to no mutual understanding; but would go on to hold that this is possible only if their own one tradition prevails. No doubt to some it would seem nice if all men were Roman Catholics, or Communists, or liberal universalists; or if all men would agree that religion does not really matter, or that it should be kept a private affair. Apart, however, from those that find such a vision inherently less appealing, many others will agree that for the moment it seems in any case hardly likely. Co-existence, if not a final truth of man's diversity, would seem at least an immediate necessity, and indeed, an immediate virtue.

If we must have rivalry among the religious communities of earth, might we not for the moment at least rival each other in our determination and capacity to promote reconciliation? Christians, Muslims and Buddhists each believe that only *they* are able to do this. Rather than arguing this point ideologically, let us strive in a friendly race to see which can implement it most effectively and vigorously in practice – each recognizing that any success of the other is to be applauded, not decried.

We may move from the general human level to the specifically Christian level. Here I have something very special to adduce. It is a thesis that I have been trying to develop, and is essentially this: that the emergence of the new world situation has brought to light a lack of integration in one area of Christian awareness, namely between the moral and the intellectual facets of our relations with our fellow men.

I begin with the affirmation that there are moral as well as conceptual implications of revealed truth. If we take seriously the revelation of God in Christ – if we really mean what we say when we affirm that his life, and his death on the cross, and his final triumph out of the very midst of self-sacrifice, embody the ultimate truth and power and glory of the universe – then two kinds of things follow, two orders of inference. On the moral level, there follows an imperative towards reconciliation, unity, harmony and brotherhood. At this level, all men are included: we strive to break down barriers, to close up gulfs; we recognize all men as neighbours, as fellows, as sons of the universal father, seeking him and finding him, being sought by him and being found by him. At this level, we do not become truly Christian until we have reached out towards a community that turns mankind into one total 'we'.

On the other hand, there is another level, the intellectual, the order of ideas, where it is the business of those of us who are theologians to draw out concepts, to construct doctrines. At this level, the doctrines that Christians have traditionally derived have tended to affirm a Christian exclusivism, a separation between those who believe and those who do not, a division of mankind into a 'we' and a 'they', a gulf between Christendom and the rest of the world: a gulf profound, ultimate, cosmic.

I shall come to the theological consideration of these theological ideas in the last part of this essay. At the moment, I wish to consider the moral consequences of our theological ideas. Here my submission is that on this front the traditional doctrinal position of the Church has in fact militated against its traditional moral position, and has in fact encouraged Christians to approach other men immorally. Christ has taught us humility, but we have approached them with arrogance.

I do not say this lightly. This charge of arrogance is a serious one. It is my observation over more than twenty years of study of the Orient, and a little now of Africa, that the fundamental flaw of Western civilization in its role in world history is arrogance, and that this has infected also the Christian Church. If you think that I am being reckless or unwarranted here, ask any Jew, or read between the lines of the works of modern African or Asian thinkers.

May I take for illustration a phrase, not unrepresentative, which was under discussion recently by the United Church of Canada's commission on faith, and which ran as follows: 'Without the particular knowledge of God in Jesus Christ, men do not really know God at all.' Let us leave aside for the moment any question of whether or not this is true. We shall return to that presently. My point here is simply that, in any case, it is arrogant. At least, it becomes arrogant when one carries it out to the non-Western world. In the quiet of the study, it may be possible for the speculative mind to produce this kind of doctrine, provided that one keep it purely bookish. But except at the cost of insensitivity or delinquence, it is morally not possible actually to go out into the world and say to devout, intelligent, fellow human beings: 'We are saved and you are damned', or, 'We believe that we know God, and we are right; you believe that you know God, and you are totally wrong.'

This is intolerable from merely human standards. It is doubly so from Christian ones. Any position that antagonizes and alienates rather than reconciles, that is arrogant rather than humble, that promotes segregation rather than brotherhood, that is unlovely, is *ipso facto* un-Christian.

There is a further point at which the traditional position seems to me morally un-Christian. From the notion that if Christianity is true, then other religions must be false (a notion whose logic I shall challenge later), it is possible to go on to the converse proposition: that if anyone else's faith turns out to be valid or adequate, then it would follow that Christianity must be false – a form of logic that has, in fact, driven many from their own faith, and indeed from any faith at all. If one's chances of getting to Heaven – or to use a nowadays more acceptable metaphor, of coming into God's presence – are dependent upon other people's not getting there, then one becomes walled up within the quite intolerable position that the Christian has a vested interest in other men's damnation. It is shocking to admit it, but this actually takes place. When an observer comes back from Asia, or from a study of Asian religious traditions, and reports that, contrary to accepted theory, some Hindus and Buddhists and some Muslims lead a pious and moral life and seem very near to God by any possible standards, so that, so far as one can see, in these particular cases at least faith is as 'adequate' as Christian faith, then presumably a Christian should be overjoyed, enthusiastically hopeful that this be true, even though he might be permitted a fear lest it not be so. Instead, I have sometimes witnessed just the opposite: an emotional resistance to the news, men hoping firmly that it is not so, though perhaps with a covert fear that it might be. Whatever the rights and wrongs of the situation theoretically, I submit that practically this is just not Christian, and indeed is not tolerable. It will not do, to have a faith that can be undermined by God's saving one's neighbour; or to be afraid lest other men turn out to be closer to God than one had been led to suppose.

Let us turn, finally, to the theological problem, which the existence of other religious communities poses for the Christian (and that today's new immediate and face-to-face awareness of their existence poses urgently). This problem began, in a compelling form, with the discovery of America, and the concomitant discovery of men on this continent who had been 'out of reach of the Gospel'. In theory the peoples of Africa and Asia could have heard the Gospel story and could have believed it and been saved. If they had not become Christian, this could be interpreted as due to their cussedness, or to Christian lethargy in not evangelizing them, and so on. But with the discovery of 'redskins' in America who had lived for fifteen centuries since Christ died, unable to be saved through faith in him, many sensitive theologians were bewildered.

In our day a comparable problem is presented, and may be viewed in two ways. First, how does one account, theologically, for the fact of man's religious diversity? This is really as big an issue, almost, as the question of how one accounts theologically for evil – but Christian theologians have been much more conscious of the fact of evil than that of religious pluralism. Another way of viewing it is to phrase a question as to whether or how far or how non-Christians are saved, or know God. The diversity question has got, so far as I know, almost no serious answers of any kind. The latter has found a considerable number of attempted answers, though to my taste none of these is at all satisfactory.

On the former point I would simply like to suggest that from now on any serious intellectual statement of the Christian faith must include, if it is to serve its purpose among men, some sort of doctrine of other religions. We explain the fact that the Milky Way is there by the doctrine of creation, but how do we explain the fact that the *Bhagavad Gita* is there?

This would presumably include also an answer to our second question. Here I would like merely to comment on one of the answers that have in fact been given. It is the one that we have already mentioned: 'Without the particular knowledge of God in Jesus Christ, men do not really know God at all.' First, of course, one must recognize the positive point that this intellectualization stems from and attempts to affirm the basic and ultimate and of course positive faith of the Church that in Christ God died for us men and our salvation, that through faith in him we are saved. In the new formulations to which we may look forward, this positive faith must be preserved. Yet in the negative proposition as framed, one may see a number of difficulties, and one may suppose that the force of these will come to be increasingly felt in coming decades.

First, there is an epistemological difficulty. How could one possibly know?

If one asks how we know the Christian faith to be true, there are perhaps two kinds of answer. First, we ourselves find in our lives, by accepting and interiorizing and attempting to live in accordance with it, that it proves itself. We know it to be true because we have lived it. Secondly, one may answer that for now almost two thousand years the Church has proven it and found it so – hundreds of millions of people, of all kinds and in all circumstances and in many ages, have staked their lives upon it, and have found it right. On the other hand, if one is asked how one knows the faith of people in other traditions to be false, one is rather stumped.

Most people who make this kind of statement do not in fact know much about the matter. Actually the only basis on which their position can and does rest is a logical inference. It seems to them a theoretical implication of what they themselves consider to be true, that other people's faith *must* be illusory. Personally, I think that this is to put far too much weight on logical implication. There have been innumerable illustrations of man's capacity for starting from some cogent theoretical position and then inferring from it logically something else that at the time seems to him persuasive but that in fact turns out on practical investigation not to hold. It is far too sweeping to condemn the great majority of mankind to lives of utter meaninglessness and perhaps to hell, simply on the basis of what seems to some individuals the force of logic. Part of what the Western world has been doing for the last four centuries has been learning to get away from this kind of reliance on purely logical structures, totally untested by experience or by any other consideration. The damnation of my neighbour is too weighty a matter to rest on a syllogism.

Secondly, there is the problem of empirical observation. One cannot be anything but tentative here, of course, and inferential. Yet so far as actual observation goes, the evidence would seem overwhelming that in fact individual Buddhists, Hindus, Muslims and others have known, and do know, God. I personally have friends from these communities whom it seems to me preposterous to think about in any other way. (If we do not have friends among these communities, we should probably refrain from generalizations about them.)

This point, however, presumably need not be laboured. The position set forth has obviously not been based, and does not claim to be based, upon empirical observation. If one insists on holding it, it must be held *against* the evidence of empirical observation. This can be done, as a recent writer has formulated it:

> The Gospel of Jesus Christ comes to us with a built-in prejudgement of all other faiths so that we know in advance of our study what we must ultimately conclude about them. They give meanings to life apart from that which God has given in the biblical story culminating with Jesus Christ, and they organize life outside the covenant community of Jesus Christ. Therefore, devoid of this saving knowledge and power of God, these faiths not only are unable to bring men to God, they actually lead men away from God and hold them captive from God. This definitive and blanket judgement ... is not derived from our investigation of the religions but is given in the structure and content of Gospel faith itself. [Perry, *The Gospel in Dispute*, p. 83]

Again, a careful study by a neo-orthodox trainer of missionaries in Basle, Dr Emanuel Kellerhals, says that Islam, like other 'foreign religions', is a 'human attempt to win God for oneself ... to catch Him and confine Him on the plane of one's own spiritual life ... and for oneself to hold Him fast'. He knows this, he says explicitly, not from a study of Islam but before he begins that study, from his Christian premises; he knows it by revelation, and therefore he can disdain all human argument against it. The position seems thoroughly logical, and once one has walled oneself up within it, impregnable. Those of us who, *after* our study of Islam or Indian or Chinese religion, and after our fellowship with Muslims and other personal friends, have come to know that these religious traditions are not that, but are channels through which God himself comes into touch with these his children – what answer can we give?

One possible answer is that empirical knowledge does in the end have to be reckoned with, does in the end win out even over conviction that claims for itself the self-certification of revelation. We do not deny that upholders of this sort of position are recipients of revelation, genuinely; but we would argue that the revelation itself is not propositional, and that their interpretation of the revelation that they have received is their own, is human and fallible, is partial, and in this case is in some ways wrong.

In fact, we have been through all this before. A hundred years ago the Christian argued that he knew by divine revelation that the earth was but six thousand years old and that evolution did not happen, and therefore any evidence that geologists or biologists might adduce to the contrary need not be taken seriously. A repentant Church still claims revelation but now admits that its former theology needed revision. In the twentieth century the increasing evidence that the faith of men in other religious communities is not so different from our own as we have traditionally asserted it to be, although it is forcing some to abandon any faith in revelation at all, will in general, we predict, force us, rather, to revise our theological formulations.

Finally, even on the side of internal Christian doctrine the exclusivist position is theoretically difficult. For according to traditional Christian doctrine, there is not only one person in the Trinity, namely Christ, but three persons: God the Father, God the Son, and God the Holy Spirit. Is God not Creator? If so, then is he not to be known – however impartially, distortedly, inadequately – in creation? Is he not active in history? If so, is his spirit totally absent from any history, including even the history of other men's faith?

It may be argued that outside the Christian tradition men may know God in part, but cannot know him fully. This is undoubtedly valid, but the apparent implications are perhaps precarious. For one may well ask: is it possible for a Christian to know God fully? I personally do not see what it might mean to say that any man, Christian or other, has a complete knowledge of God. This would certainly be untenable this side of the grave, at the very least. The finite cannot comprehend the infinite.

What does one actually mean when one speaks of the knowledge of God? It has been said, and I think rightly, that the only true atheist is he who loves no one and whom no one loves, who is blind to all beauty and all justice, who knows no truth, and who has lost all hope.

Christians know God only in part. But one part of their knowing him is the recognition that he does not leave any of us utterly outside his knowledge.

It is easier, however, of course, to demolish a theological position than to construct an alternative one. The fallacy of relentless exclusivism is becoming more obvious than is the right way of reconciling a truly Christian charity and perceptivity with doctrinal adequacy. On this matter I personally have a number of views, but the one about which I feel most strongly is that this matter is important – while the rest of my particular views on it are not necessarily so. In other words, I am much more concerned to stress the fact that the Church must work, and work vigorously, and work on a large scale, in order to construct an adequate doctrine in this realm (which in my view it has never yet elaborated), than I am concerned to push my own particular suggestions. Most of all I would emphasize that whether or not my particular construction seems inadequate, the position formulated above from which I strongly dissent must in any case be seen to be inadequate also.

Having expressed this caution, I may none the less make one or two suggestions. First, I rather feel that the final doctrine on this matter may perhaps run along the lines of affirming that a Buddhist who is saved, or a Hindu or a Muslim or whoever, is saved, and is saved only, because God is the kind of God whom Jesus Christ has revealed him to be. This is not exclusivist; indeed, it coheres, I feel, with the points that I have made above in dissenting from exclusivism. If the Christian revelation were *not* true, then it might be possible to imagine that God would allow Hindus to worship him or Muslims to obey him or Buddhists to feel compassionate towards their fellows, without his responding, without his reaching out to hold them in his arms. But because God is what he is, because he is what Christ has shown him to be, *therefore* other men *do* live in his presence. Also, therefore, we (as Christians) know this to be so.

I rather wonder whether the fundamental difficulty in the formulated position, and in all similar statements, does not arise somehow from an anthropocentric emphasis that it surreptitiously implies. To talk of man's knowing God is to move in the realm of thinking of religion as a human quest, and of knowledge of God as something that man attains, or even achieves. Of course it does not state it thus, but it skirts close to implying somehow that we are saved by *our* doings (or knowings). Must one not, rather, take the Christian doctrine of grace more seriously? The question must be more adequately phrased: Does God let himself be known only to those to whom he has let himself be known through Christ? Does God love only those who respond to him in this tradition?

We are not saved by our knowledge; we are not saved by our membership in the Church; we are not saved by anything of *our* doing. We are saved, rather, by the only thing that could possibly save us, the anguish and the love of God. While we have no final way of knowing with assurance how God deals or acts in other men's lives, and therefore cannot make any final pronouncement (such as the formulator of the position stated has attempted to make), none the less we must perhaps at least be hesitant in setting boundaries to that anguish and that love.

The God whom we have come to know, so far as we can sense his action, reaches out after all men everywhere, and speaks to all who will listen. Both within and without the Church men listen all too dimly. Yet both within and without the Church, so far as we can see, God does somehow enter into men's hearts.

5

ALOYSIUS PIERIS: The Place of Non-Christian Religions and Cultures in the Evolution of Third World Theology

Aloysius Pieris (b.1934) is a Sri Lankan Jesuit who runs an Institute for the Study of Buddhism at Kelaniya, near Colombo in Sri Lanka. His collection of essays, Theology of Liberation in Asia *(Maryknoll, 1986) pleads for an indigenous liberation theology, rooted in local, eastern culture, such as the Buddhism of his native land. This was one of the three principal addresses at the Fifth Conference of the Ecumenical Association of Third World Theologians in New Delhi, 1981, which examined the theme 'The Irruption of the Third World: Challenge to Theology'.*

THEOLOGY OF RELIGIONS: CURRENT BOUNDARIES OF ORTHODOXY

Basis and Background: The Third World as a Theological Perspective

The term 'Third World' is a theological neologism for God's own people. It stands for the starving sons and daughters of Jacob – of all places and all times – who go in search of bread to a rich country, only to become its slaves. In other words, the Third World is not merely the story of the South in relation to the North or of the East in relation to the West. It is something that happens wherever and whenever socio-economic dependence in terms of race, class or sex generates political and cultural slavery, fermenting thereby a new peoplehood. Because, however, there is no people unless summoned by God, and no God worth talking about except the God who speaks through a people, all theology is about a people's God – that is, about God's people. The major focus of all 'God-talk' or theology, then, must be the Third World's irruption as a new peoplehood announcing the liberating presence of a God who claims to humanize this cruel world.

But the irruption of the Third World is also the irruption of the non-Christian world. The vast majority of God's poor perceive their ultimate concern and symbolize their struggle for liberation in the idiom of non-Christian religions and cultures. Therefore, a theology that does not speak to or speak through this non-Christian peoplehood is an esoteric luxury of a Christian minority. Hence, we need a theology of religions that will expand the existing boundaries of orthodoxy as we enter into the liberative streams of other religions and cultures.

One regrets, therefore, that the only Third World theology presently being given substance is circumscribed by the exclusively Latin and Christian context of its origin. This remark is not levelled against the Latin American model but against the antithetical attitudes it has evoked in the Afro-Asian churches, in that some 'liberationists' want to duplicate a Latin, Christian model in their non-Latin and non-Christian environments, thus driving 'inculturationists' to a defensive extreme.

In fact, at the EATWOT Asian consultation in 1979, I tried to forestall this futile debate by avoiding the liberation/inculturation schema and by defining theology as a discovery rather than an invention – that is, as a Christian participation in and a christic explicitation of all that happens at the deepest zone of a concrete ethos where religiousness and poverty, each in its liberative dimension, coalesce to forge a common front against mammon. Nevertheless, the subsequent controversy fell back upon the old paradigm and reduced religion and poverty to the categories of inculturation and liberation, respectively, though efforts were made to restore the original framework in which the *cultural* context of theology was equated with the *liberative* dimension of religiousness and poverty.

The polarization continues to this day. The reason, presumably, is that in both the First and the Third Worlds there still lurks a crypto-colonialist theology of religions (and cultures) that keeps our revolutionary rhetoric from resonating in the hearts of the Third World's non-Christian majority. This is an issue that demands frank and open discussion in all the churches.

My analysis of this question presumes that every religion, Christianity included, is at once a sign and countersign of the kingdom of God; that the revolutionary impetus launching a religion into existence is both fettered and fostered by the need for an ideological formulation; that its institutionalization both constrains and conserves its liberative force; that religion, therefore, is a potential means of either emancipation or enslavement.

But, theologically speaking – which is to say, 'from a Third World perspective' – the test case that reveals the twin aspect of sin and grace in religion is its response to the phenomenon of poverty. Poverty is itself ambivalent. It can mean dispossession forced upon the masses by the hedonism and acquisitiveness of the greedy. But it can also mean the virtue of poverty, which, according to Albert Tevoedjre's thesis, is 'the status of someone having what is necessary and not the surplus', a *conditio sine qua non* for the elimination of what I have defined here as enforced poverty.

I grant that this criterion is not universally accepted, nor is the ambivalence of the religious phenomenon comprehensively spelled out in theological circles. Thus, a certain unilateral view of religions still prevails and accounts for the polarization of the church into a Christ-*against*-religions theology and a Christ-*of*-religions theology. The rift between liberationists and inculturationists is only a recent manifestation of this polarization; there have been other versions earlier, as indicated in the Diagram overleaf.

The Liberation Thesis on Religion: Its Western and Colonialist Character

The contrast between these two perspectives (Christ-*against*-religions and Christ-*of*-religions) is quite evident even among Latin American theologies. But on the whole the perceptive pioneers, such as Gustavo Gutiérrez, and nuanced systematizers, such as Juan Luis Segundo, have always viewed religion as an ambivalent phenomenon. At the EATWOT São Paulo conference, both the enslaving and the liberating dimensions of religion (that is, Christianity) were recognized. Gutiérrez contrasted 'popular religiosity' with 'liberative faith'. Enrique Dussel therefore called for a new theory of religion.

However, there still prevails a species of Christ-against-religions theology in Latin America, which is uncritically accepted in small but vocal circles of Asian activists. That there are two major trends in liberation theology – one with a Marxist mood and method, and the other with a pastoral rootage in popular cultures – is perhaps not sufficiently appreciated here in Asia. Although I personally assess both these theologies to be basically valid, I feel compelled to question the unilateral theory of religion presupposed in the former.

CHRIST AND RELIGIONS

Historical Panorama of a Polarization

Christ-AGAINST-Religions	Christ-OF-Religions
SIXTEENTH CENTURY ONWARD	**NINETEENTH CENTURY ONWARD**
The **COLONIALIST CHRIST** of early Western missionaries conquers non-Christian religions, which are linked with the **moral poverty** of 'colonized' nations.	The **GNOSTIC CHRIST** of Indian theologians; beginning of the fulfilment theory of religions.
The medium of his action is the **Western** form of **civilization**.	The link between religion and material poverty is ignored.
LATE 1960s	**LATE 1960s**
The **NEO-COLONIALIST CHRIST** of the developmentalists conquers non-Christian religions, which are linked with the **material poverty** of 'developing' nations.	The **ASHRAMIC CHRIST** of monks and mystics, incarnated through traditional practice of religious poverty – i.e., voluntary acceptance of material poverty (renunciation, monasticism).
The medium of his action is the **Western** model of **development**.	The link between religion and structural poverty is ignored.
LATE 1970s	**LATE 1970s**
The **CRYPTO-COLONIALIST CHRIST** of the liberationists conquers non-Christian religions, which are linked with the **structural poverty** of Third World nations.	The **UNIVERSAL CHRIST** of the inculturationists, particularized in cultures through the appropriation of religious structures (idioms, symbols, moods, etc.).
The medium of his action is the **structural liberation** based on Marxist occidentalism and **Western Biblicism**.	The link between religion and liberation struggles is ignored.

The best exponent of this theory is José Miranda, a Latin American biblicist avidly read in Asia. For him religion is an evil to be destroyed, because it is an escapist objectification of the Absolute, a projection of one's own self, a justification of the status quo, a total alienation of the human person, an alibi for interpersonal justice, a cyclic view of life that stifles the voice of the Absolute in suffering humanity – and, therefore, something that negates Christian commitment. Even the more sober Sobrino speaks in the same strain, taking religion to be a degradation of faith.

This theory is certainly not of Latin American creation. As I shall indicate later, it is a blend of two European patterns of thought dating back to an era when the West was less informed than now about the complex structure and history of non-Christian cultures. How ironic that liberation-conscious Asians should subscribe to a thesis that is as colonialist as it is Western!

Why is it Western, why colonialist?

It is Western, first, because of the implied notion of 'religion'. None of the Asian soteriologies, not excluding the biblical ones, has offered us a comprehensive word for, or a clear concept of, religion in the current Western sense. Some vernacular words have no doubt acquired that meaning through use under Western impact. In earlier times, we had words only to describe the various facets of what could be designated as religion. For, in our Asian context, religion is life itself rather than a function of it, being the all-pervasive ethos of human existence. This is even more true of tribal religion, which often overlaps with 'culture'.

In the West, the word 'religion' crept into the English language, and perhaps into other modern languages as well, from the Vulgate, which rendered the Greek *threskeia* with the Latin *religio*. In James 1:26ff., one hears of 'pure religion' and in Acts 26:5 the word clearly refers to Judaism. The Latin apologists, unlike their Greek counterparts, spoke of a *vera religio* (meaning Christianity) in contrast with *falsa religio*, a conviction that grew aggressive due to conflicts with Judaism and Islam. Thus the classic Roman missiology (phases 1 and 2 in the Diagram) had set Christ against *other* (that is, false) *religions*, unlike some contemporary liberationists who have gone further and put Christ against *religion as such* (phase 3). In this lies both the continuity and the contrast between early and modern versions of this conservative evangelism!

The narrow concept of religion as advocated by the liberationists seems more Greek than Roman. Most Greek apologists were inclined to churn 'paganism' theologically and extract only its philosophy, leaving aside its religion as incompatible with Christianity. The tendency to squeeze religion out of human existence (by way of sacralization and secularization, which are two sides of the same coin) is not alien to Western tradition. Schillebeeckx has cogently argued that even the modern phenomenon of secularization took form under the sacred shadow of medieval cathedrals.

But the two forms in which this tendency influenced liberationist interpretation of religion appeared only within the last hundred years. For the philosophical rejection of (the Christian) religion characteristic of certain intellectual movements in Europe (Enlightenment, scientific revolution, rationalism) found an ideological as well as theological formulation in the two Karls of 'dialectical' fame. Marx's dialectical materialism set religion against *revolution*; Barth's dialectical theology opposed it to *revelation*. In their systems, religion was a major obstacle to liberation and salvation, respectively.

In dismissing the immanentist thesis coming down from Schleiermacher to Otto, a thesis that postulated a 'religious a priori' in the human person, Barth initiated an evangelistic theology that reduced the notion of religion to a blasphemous manipulation of God, or at least an attempt at it. The pioneering Protestant exegetical tradition – anterior to and stimulative of later Catholic biblical scholarship – was seriously infected by this bias. Kittel, for instance, referring to the conspicuous infrequency of such words as *threskeia, deisidaimonia, eusebeia,* and *theosebeia* in the New Testament, reached the conclusion that the whole concept of 'religion' (obviously, as understood in that particular theological tradition) is alien to the Bible and that in the mother tongue of the New Testament authors there was no linguistic equivalent for these Greek terms. This last remark, as already observed, is true of *all* oriental religions, and should have thrown doubt on the very concept of religion employed here!

It is, therefore, hardly surprising that many good dictionaries of biblical theology (e.g., that of Dufour or Bauer) would have no column on 'religion'. From 'redemption' they pass on to 'remnant' – indeed a symbolic *saltus*, suggesting another possible concept of religion that could be extracted from the Bible! Regrettably, it is under the aforesaid category of 'religion' that all non-Christian soteriologies are subsumed and dismissed in favour of biblical faith.

In the militant stream of liberation theology, this Barthian view of religion dovetails neatly with Marx's equally evangelistic and Eurocentric evaluation of religions and cultures. Though many a Latin American critic has succeeded in pushing the Marxian analysis to the opposite conclusion – namely, that religion could be a 'leaven of liberation rather than an opiate' – an Asian sensitivity is still necessary to monitor the Occidentalist bias of this new Marxist view. Marx, whose contribution to the liberation of Third World nations dare never be underestimated, does not, for that reason, cease to be a man of his own time and clime: a nineteenth-century European. A writer who revels in revealing the racial and class prejudices of Marx and Engels concludes:

> Their attitudes were typical attitudes of the nineteenth-century Europeans who, regardless of their ideology, thought in terms of a hierarchy of cultures with their own at the top and who occasionally used biology to provide a scientific basis for their categorization of societies into higher and lower forms.

The late Lelio Basso, the Italian Marxist theoretician, acknowledged this deficiency with laudable frankness. Let me cite a few of his well-documented observations.

In Marx's *Manifesto*, the whole idea of 'progress' and 'civilization' is simply equated with the Westernization of the East, the urbanization of the countryside, and the proletarianization of the peasantry – all in the name of socialism! And in *Capital*, the European form of capitalist industrialization is envisaged as the model for the rest of the world, an indispensable prelude to the proletarian revolution. For this reason, Engels rejoiced at the American aggression in Mexico and the subsequent annexation of rich provinces such as California. He also applauded the French acquisition of Algeria – though he did have second thoughts about it. Similarly, Marx welcomed the British conquest of India because the breakdown of the ancient Indian civilization, followed preferably by europeanization, seemed an indispensable condition for the building up of a modern industrial culture. That there could, in fact, be a non-Western, non-European way to socialism culturally based on the peasant communes of the *obscina* was of course proposed and debated at length even before the October Revolution; but in this regard, Marx, and especially Engels, did not really shed their Western chauvinism.

Lenin's postrevolutionary policies seem to have further entrenched this occidentalism in the orthodox stream of classic Marxism. After gaining power he not only tried to expedite the industrialization of the USSR (supposedly on a state basis rather than on a capitalist basis) but tried also to bring about socialism *from the top*, vertically, with little faith in the process of allowing it to emerge from the people, from below. In 'accelerating the historical process', as it is called, many extraneous elements had to be imposed on the people, with a good deal of violence to their religious and cultural sensitivities. One should not forget that Lenin (perhaps influenced by Černyševskij's ideal of destroying the Asian character of the Russian people – the *Aziatična* as it was called) introduced a steam-roller socialism that ruthlessly sought to level down the religious and cultural identities of a people. The cry for proletarian *internationalism* – valid in itself – was in practice a zeal for *occidentalism*. In this he excelled the Western missionaries of his time who preached a 'universal gospel', which in reality was their own narrow European version of it! The Brezhnev principle is a variation of this intransigent verticalism.

It is true that Lenin made many theoretical concessions to other ways of socialism as verified, for instance, in the case of Mongolia, as modern Marxist apologists observe with pride. But denying to the founders of Marxism the right to be men of their own times does not help. Would that a massive effort be made to purge Marxism of its eurocentrism and cultural colonialism! It should revise its notion of Afro-Asian religions and cultures in terms of their liberative potentialities and discover indigenous ways to socialism – the kind of aggiornamento inaugurated by Markov, Ernst and other Marxist intellectuals of the Leipzig school – vis-à-vis the precapitalist societies of Africa. Such a corrective measure, moreover, has already been anticipated in the political praxis of Africans themselves. Amilcar Cabral's Marxism is a case in point. One could also cite with some reservation Lumumba and Nkrumah. Asia has Ho Chi Minh. They wrote little and transmitted much to posterity through their praxis, which therefore serves as a *locus theologicus* for those groping for a liberation theology of religions and cultures.

This Afro-Asian critique of Marxist occidentalism is also an implicit judgement on the militant stream of Latin American theology, which maintains a methodological continuity with Western Marxism and a cultural continuity with European theology. Their Latin and Marxist idiom does not permit the ethnic identity of racial minorities to be reflected in their theology. Amerindians, blacks, and Asiatics – almost a fifth of the Latin American population – are absolute majorities in certain provinces. Has their unique community sense (e.g., the Indian *cofradías*, which are alleged to be a rich cultural alternative to Latin *hermandades*) made a visible impact on the ecclesiological revolution of basic communities?

I agree with the Marxists who hold that a conflict between ethnic struggles and class struggles could jeopardize the total liberation of a people. But this fear – if it is coupled with the Marxist tendency to confuse internationalism with occidentalism – could be an excuse for reinforcing Latinism. As a matter of fact, racism remains a contemporary problem, not a mere thing of the colonial past. Not surprisingly, even the Marxist Lipschütz, who conceded that these non-Latin ethnic groups could form self-governing 'linguistic' republics, would not think of a hypothetically socialist nation of Latin America except in Hispano-American terms, always having the Soviet model before him, a model not entirely free of Russian cultural and linguistic colonialism. It is, therefore, heartening to note that participants in the São Paulo conference did touch on this delicate question, though in the Final Document they skirted the subject, giving it only a passing nod.

Liberation and Inculturation: History of a Tension

Some theologians display an exaggerated solicitude for inculturation, because of which they stand open to severe judgement, especially when the historical context of the liberation/inculturation tension is brought into focus. The Diagram does precisely this by tabulating the three successive versions of the two christological perspectives: the Christ-*against*-religions theology and Christ-*of*-religions theology. The table is self-explanatory, and I shall here only skim over the three phases, touching down only on salient points.

Phase 1 covers the era of Euro-ecclesiastical expansionism, when the colonialist Christ was set on a warring spree against false religions in the lands now called the Third World. Not even De Nobili and Ricci contested this Christ-*against*-religions theology! They only questioned the policy of imposing Western civilization as a means of conversion, a policy that prevailed despite their protest, and persists to this day in subtle ways (phases 2 and 3). The theological breakthrough began perhaps in the nineteenth century with the epiphany of the gnostic Christ, who appeared in the works of both Hindu and Christian theologians.

Some of these Christian theologians anticipated the later official doctrine of the Lambeth Conference (1930) and the Second Vatican Council – namely, that Christ works in other religions as the final consummation of all human aspiration for redemption. Obviously this 'fulfilment theory of religions',

even in its post-Vatican II versions, is fraught with intrinsic theological difficulties that need not be discussed here. Suffice it to note that it is an abstract
theory that excludes from religious disclosure the basic theme of any genuine
theology: the poor. After all, is not the story of Jesus preeminently the story
of a God *of* the poor, a God *with* the poor, a God *for* the poor? No wonder that
in the 1960s, with the sharpening of Third World consciousness, the nexus
between the religions and the poor began to receive articulate attention.

Thus begins phase 2, with its own version of the two theological perspectives. Enter first the neocolonialist Christ in the person of the missionary
with a jeep. Western 'civilization' now yields place to Western 'development'
as the medium of Christ's saving presence. I even remember its being called
pre-evangelization! How could other religions relieve the poor in their plight
if those religions themselves are the partial cause of a people's underdevel-
opment and if technology and progress are unique Christian achievements
destined to free the non-Christian masses from their superstitious traditions?
That the non-Christian worldview could provide a saner philosophy of
development, as illustrated, for instance, by the Sarvodaya movement in its
earlier phase, or that, in the process of 'modernization', the evangelical values
of other religions and cultures were being immolated on the altar of
mammon, were still the opinions of a dissenting minority.

A counterthesis to developmentalism, however, did come from the Christ-
of-religions theology. It found an anchor in the numerous ashrams and their
equivalents already in existence for decades. They embodied the spirit of
renunciation central to many cultures, thus expressing their solidarity with
both the poor and their religions. Material progress need not necessarily
mean human development, nor is material poverty in itself human impover-
ishment. The ashramic Christ fought neither of these. His sole attack was on
that which caused such polarity: greed, the demon *within*, an enemy of all
authentic spirituality.

And there was the rub. The *organized* character of greed passed unnoticed.
While the war was waged and even won *within* the walls of ashrams, the poor –
the waste product of the earth's capital-accumulating plutocracy – continued to
grow in number and misery. Could their struggle for sheer survival succeed if
that sinful system was not a target of their struggle? Unless stained by the stigma
of solidarity with that struggle, monastic poverty will always remain a shallow
status symbol of a client-gathering guru. The claim to have renounced wealth is
vanity of vanities if those who have no wealth to renounce cannot benefit from

it. There is a precedent in Jesus, in his precursor John, and in Gandhi, his Hindu admirer, for whom voluntary poverty was not only a renunciation of mammon in the micro-ethical sphere of one's soul, but a denunciation of its stooges in the macro-ethical order of politico-religious institutions.

It is sad that whereas yesterday's feudalism turned some monasteries into oases of plenty amid deserts of poverty, pushing them into the hands of today's revolutionaries who *force* monks to practice *voluntary* poverty for the benefit of the masses (as has happened in Tibet and Mongolia), today's capitalism has entrenched some ashrams, zendos, and prayer centres in the grip of wealth-accumulating patrons who frequent them for spells of tranquility and return unconverted and unrepentant, awaiting another revolution to disrupt that unholy alliance with mammon. Have we not also heard of mystics spinning dollars by exporting meditation to the West? Like rubber, coffee and copper, our spirituality too gets processed in the West and returns with expensive price tags and sophisticated labels ('Transcendental Meditation') to be consumed locally! Who is the beneficiary? And what of the horror of caste and sexist discrimination that thrives on religious sanction? How many prayer centres have cared or dared to go against the grain? The ashramic Christ seemed no more sensitive to the demands of justice than did the neocolonialist Christ.

It is, therefore, worth noting that phase 3 dawned during a period when the pendulum of politics poised for a brief passing moment on the left extremity before it began its present rightward swing with the massive crisis in the socialist states and the rise of Reaganism. Disappointment with doctrinaire theologies and disillusionment with both the developmentalism and 'mysticism' of the previous era added fuel to the fire of mounting liberation fever in the expanding circles of Christian activists in our part of the world. It was at this time that Latin American theology (equated here with liberation theology), with ten years of maturity behind it, began to awaken the Afro-Asian 'indigenizers' from their ethnocentric stupor, just as it had earlier shocked the Euro-American theoreticians from their dogmatic slumber. It is understandable that some Asian theologians with leftist leanings began to sing the liberation song out of beat with the non-Latin rhythm of their own cultures. The 'lord of the dance' was the liberator Christ who redeemed the poor not only from their poverty but also from their traditional religions, which sustained the sinful systems. It is therefore equally understandable that the incarnate Christ of the inculturationists stood aghast on the opposite pole!

Just as one particular stream of liberation theology pursues, even today, the colonial evangelism of the past – as was shown in 'The Liberation Thesis' above – so also the bulk of literature churned out in ever proliferating seminars on inculturation does not show any significant departure from the previous era's narrow focus on religion and culture. It pays scant attention to the colossal scandal of institutionalized misery that poses a challenge to every religion.

A defensive posture adopted against the liberationist thesis may partly explain such blindness. The implications of this limitation are serious and I have spelled them out clearly elsewhere. Nevertheless, I shall resume this discussion in the second half of this chapter, after dealing with the liberative and revolutionary potentials of non-Christian religions – something that both liberationists (the school I am criticizing here) and inculturationists have failed to discern, but which is the very texture of a Third World theology of religions.

TOWARD A THIRD WORLD THEOLOGY OF RELIGIONS

Anatomy of Religion in the Third World

Every theologian should be alerted to the fact that a substantial amount of information regarding religions and cultures in the Third World is gathered, processed, and distributed by Euro-American research centres. The First World still has a monopoly on the resources required for such studies – money and media, academic prestige and personnel. Even the highly acclaimed 'participatory observation method' in anthropology has been unmasked as another arm of Western dominance.

The occidentalist bias that liberation theology has absorbed from a tradition traceable to Marx and Barth is only the tip of the iceberg. There are deeper predispositions acquired by all of us – myself included – in the course of our intellectual training: we are all dependent on these same sources for our understanding of the religious phenomenon in its global magnitude.

As Evans-Pritchard noted, generations of writers on religion (Taylor, Frazer, Malinowski, Durkheim, Freud, and their followers), in their sincere search for truth, were only reacting against the religion of their upbringing. In the face of their attempts to explain religion by explaining it away, theologians such as Barth tried to save Christianity by lifting it above the realm of religion, indirectly offering a biblico-theological prop to such antireligion theories.

C. E. Stipe has diagnosed the malaise of Western anthropologists as 'functionalism', which tends to gloss over religion as something redundant in the cultures they study. Taking the focal aspect of religion to be something outside natural, human experience, they perceive the rite, not the system of meaning and beliefs. They study social relationships without due regard to the worldview that religions provide.

An interesting case is that of Sierksma accusing Lanternari of leaving anthropology in favour of theology because the latter merely observed Christianity to be transcendent, unlike the messianic movements, more interested in human salvation on earth. Marxian interpretation of Mau Mau as purely Kenyan nationalism or Melanesian cargo cults as purely economic phenomena shares in this Western reductionism. According to Stipe, this is precisely what hinders Western anthropologists from assessing the role of religion in relation to cultural change.

Is not the same bias keeping the theologian (liberationist or inculturationist) from perceiving religion in positive terms of liberation struggles and revolutionary change? I recommend that a critical discernment be exercised in pursuing available studies on religions and that fieldwork on this subject be undertaken afresh from within the Third World perspective of peoples struggling for integral human liberation. It is with this forewarning that I wish to describe the anatomy of the religious phenomenon in the Third World.

The intricate network of religions and cultures that spreads across the Third World baffles the theologian as much as it does the anthropologist. To do more than trace its major contours would, therefore, be unpragmatic within the limitations of this chapter. Nor should I spend time on definitions of religion and culture – an academic pastime that has bred confusion in the West. We who breathe religion as our normal atmosphere would rather go by the first intuitive and experimental grasp of what it means in life. Therefore, without formulating definitions for ourselves, we can still detect the ones that are wrong!

The first observation is that religion and culture coincide fully in tribal societies practically everywhere in the Third World. Culture is the variegated expression of religion. But because religions meet each other always in and through their respective cultural self-manifestations, there result subtle differentiations between religions and cultures. Thus, one might speak about several cultures within one religion and, conversely, about several religions within one culture. The former case is exemplified in the three missionary religions: Buddhism, Islam, and Christianity (listed here in descending order of cultural differentiation). As for cultures that accommodate several religions, a whole series can be cited – for example, Buddhism and Hinduism in Nepal, Taoism and Confucianism in China, Buddhism and Shintoism in Japan, Hinduism and Islam in Java.

In some instances, the culture of one religion relates to the other as host to guest. Hence these terms possess the conceptual elasticity that the complexity of reality has bequeathed on them. For reasons that are implicit in my prefatory remarks above, I am here primarily speaking about religions as the pivotal point of reference, and obliquely about culture. This premised, let me attempt to sort out the various strands of religiousness that have been woven into the exquisite cultural fabric of the Third World. Actually one can discern at least three of them; the crisscrossing of racio-linguistic contours within the so-called scriptural religions must be mentioned first.

The so-called scriptural or book religions of the world have all taken their origin from three reservoirs of Asian spirituality, each having its own racio-linguistic idiom: the Semitic (Judaism, Islam and Christianity), the Indian (Hinduism, Jainism and Buddhism), and the Chinese (Taoism and Confucianism). These streams of religiousness have not confined themselves to the neighbourhood of their sources, but have been meandering beyond their linguistic boundaries, even across continents, thus flooding the world – Asia in particular – with a plethora of hybrid cultures.

For instance, Islam's Semitic religiousness pervades both the Malayo-Polynesian and the Indo-Aryan cultures of Indonesia and Pakistan, respectively, and also permeates many African tribes. Hinduism has a firm grip on the lives of both Dravidian and Indo-Aryan peoples of India, besides serving as the subterranean foundation for many Southeast Asian civilizations. Buddhism, which preserves its original Indian format only in Sri Lanka, has shaped several cultures by allowing itself to be shaped by them, with the result that one hears of Ural-Altaic, Malayo-Polynesian, Sino-Tibetan, Japanese and Indo-Aryan versions of Buddhist culture. Christianity too can make a few modest claims in this regard.

The second type of cross-fertilization takes place between these religions and tribal religions. As a matter of fact it coincides with the process by which, as described above, a scriptural religion acquires citizenship in another linguistic zone. Regrettably, our theological manuals that deal with non-Christian religions focus mostly on these scriptural religions, or what sociologists call 'the great traditions'. But the peasantry and the proletariat of the Third World are, for the most part, bearers of a nonscriptural or regionalized traditional religiousness either *within* the framework of a major religion (so-called popular Buddhism, popular Taoism, popular Hinduism, and, as in Latin America, popular religion) or *totally outside* any scriptural religion (e.g., tribal religions not yet proselytized by the former). This is why I urged at the Asian Theological Consultation in Sri Lanka, 1979, that due attention be paid to these religions. Their beliefs and practices have not frozen into written formulas but flow with time, thus exhibiting the *flexibility essential for social change*. This is the first corollary I wish to underline here, for future reference.

Inasmuch as all scriptural religions began as oral traditions, and traditional religions of today are bound, sooner or later, to express their sacred heritage also in written form, I prefer to use two other terms that I have already employed in other chapters of this volume: metacosmic (not to be confused with acosmic) and cosmic. The former type of religion defines its soteriology in terms of a metacosmic 'beyond' capable of being internalized as the salvific 'within' of the human person, either through the agapeic path of redeeming love or through the gnostic way of liberative knowledge – this being the major difference between the biblical religions and most nonbiblical ones. Cosmic religions, as the term indicates, revolve around cosmic powers – normally rendered as 'gods', 'deities', 'spirits' in English. They refer to natural phenomena (often personified) as well as the spirits of past heroes and one's own ancestors, not excluding 'departed souls' and 'saints' in popular Christianity. For this reason Confucianism is to be classed as a cosmic religion despite its scriptural base.

Further, wherever the two species of religiousness have merged, the common people's genius has created a synthesis that a superficial observer might mistake for syncretism. That is why Richard Gombrich has suggested the word 'accretism' to describe such mergers, for in the hybrid cultures that issue from this symbiosis, *homo religiosus* learns to align locally determined cosmic concerns (food, harvest, rain and sunshine, floods and drought, health and sickness, life and death, marriage and politics) with the soteriological orientation of his or her life toward a metacosmic Beyond. One welcomes, therefore, the bidisciplinary approach of scripture scholars (Dumont, Bechert, Gombrich, among others) who turn to anthropology in order to respect the hermeneutical reciprocity between book and beliefs, scripture and tradition, written text and living context. Popular hermeneusis of ancient lore reveals the peoples' ongoing creative response to contemporary reality. This is the second corollary I wish to put on record.

This phenomenon of accretism points also to a third corollary. No major religion could have travelled beyond its seat of origin and become incarnate in the lives of the masses had it not sent its roots deep into the popular religiousness of each tribe and race. In other words, historically and phenomenologically speaking, there cannot be a metacosmic religiousness having an institutional grip on the people save on the basis of a popular religiousness! The converse, however, is not true. For there can be and in fact there are tribal religions independent of, though open to, scriptural religions.

The patterns of mass conversion offer us a fourth and important corollary. As stated elsewhere, mass conversions from one soteriology to another are rare, if not impossible, except under military pressure. But a changeover from a tribal religion to a metacosmic soteriology is a spontaneous process in which the former, without sacrificing its own character, provides a popular base for the latter. Being cosmic religions, they are this-worldly in every sense of the term and are often drawn by some 'community advantages' to accept the institutional framework of a scriptural religion. (The latter, which generally shuns change, tends paradoxically to use its other-worldly teachings to consolidate its this-worldly institutions!)

The scheduled castes and tribes in India that have accepted Christianity, or more particularly Buddhism and Islam, on a massive scale substantiate this thesis. A better illustration is provided by the missionary conflicts between Christianity and Islam. After three and a half centuries of concerted proselytism, colonial Christianity in Indonesia collected only a little over two million converts from Islam, most of whom came from northern Sumatra, Moluccas, Ambonia and other outer islands where tribal culture prevailed. Christian 'successes' among tribal peoples of the Atlantic coast of Africa – compared with the miserable failure in Muslim Africa, except for a minor conquest among mountain tribes in Kabyles – point in the same direction.

Let me end with a fifth and final corollary. Tribal and clan societies, given their strong religio-cultural cohesion, are never immune to the danger of intertribal conflicts. Tribalism – often equated with divisive provincialism – can be exploited ideologically by the enemies of social change. The strategy of 'divide and rule' can thwart liberation movements, as will be discussed in the next section.

To sum up, I have described the anatomy of the religious phenomenon first in terms of the crisscrossing of racio-linguistic contours within scriptural religions, and, secondly, in terms of the five consequences issuing from the accretion of cosmic into metacosmic religions.

There is another interaction that deserves attention if the picture is to be complete: the interaction between these religions and various socio-political ideologies. This brings me to the core of my enquiry: religion and revolution.

The Revolutionary Urge in Religions and the Role of Ideologies

Lunacharsky, the first Soviet minister of culture, had this confession to make about religion: 'It is like a nail,' he declared, 'the harder you hit it, the deeper it goes into the wood.' By persecuting religion, revolutionaries hardly kill it but only make it more reactionary. Conversely, when challenged by an oppressive system, religion finds occasion to unleash its potential for radical change.

A true revolution cannot go against religion in its totality. If a revolution succeeds, it does so normally as a cathartic renewal of religion itself. Such a statement is based on the experience of seven decades of Marxism. Che Guevara sensed the same thing when he said: 'Only when Christians have the courage to give a wholehearted revolutionary testimony will the Latin American revolution become invincible.' With this prophecy he seems to have suggested the theme for a new chapter in the history of both Marxist ideology and the Christian religion – a chapter that Nicaragua is presently struggling at death point to write for posterity!

This is even more true of the other religions that have a more extensive hold on the Third World than does Christianity. No *true* liberation is possible unless persons are 'religiously motivated' toward it. To be religiously motivated is to be drawn from the depths of one's being. This motivation, I concede, could be occasioned by alien ideologies, as history has often attested. But the peoples of the Third World will not spontaneously embark on a costly adventure unless their lives are touched and their depths stirred by its prospects *along the 'cultural' patterns of their own 'religious' histories* – which, of course, differ widely from place to place, as was demonstrated in the previous section.

Take, for instance, the Chinese peasant culture, marked by a history of revolts, in contrast with the culture of the Guinean peasantry, which has had no such tradition – a fact explicitly noted by Amilcar Cabral, who laid great emphasis on the local cultural variants of every socialist revolution. This did not imply for Cabral that Guinea was incapable of radical change but that he had to consult his own culture rather than merely copy an alien model. Let us therefore first look at the African situation, for it offers many lessons to Third World theologians.

ISLAM AND CHRISTIANITY IN AFRICA

If Marx is rightly interpreted, the tribal communities of Africa can be classed as 'precapitalist socialist societies' in that they can reach full-fledged socialism without passing through the crucible of capitalism. Jean Ziegler, with World Bank statistics, tries to vindicate the Tanzanian experiment of Julius Nyerere in favour of this theory. But this is no easy task; both colonial and indigenous elements have left *ideological* dents in these societies. I refer to the local bourgeoisie and the feudal barons (not to mention the white settlers in Rhodesia and South Africa!) who inherited power from colonial rulers so that even progressive patriots such as Lumumba and Nkrumah could not radically change the basic character of the *nationalist* liberation movements.

Mozambique gives us the other alternative – if I may agree with Sergio Vieira, himself a member of FRELIMO (National Liberation Front of Mozambique) and a government minister. Portugal, unlike Britain, Belgium, and France, had good reasons not to give even 'flag independence' to its colonies but to cling to a fascist rule, thus inviting armed struggle. Mozambique and Angola responded. The arbitrary demarcation of the future frontiers of African 'nations' by the colonialists, which increased racial and tribal fragmentation, and the local exploitation of tribal loyalties (corollary 5, above) were attacked simultaneously in order to bring patriotism in line with intertribal proletarianism, as shown in the Mozambique people's massive self-immolation for the liberation of Zimbabwe. This is an African response to one ideology in repudiation of another. This process as illustrated in Mozambique is bound to be generally normative in the future, because Africa is, by far, the most exploited of continents.

This is the background against which the role of scriptural religions should be assessed. Of course in Africa there are only two candidates for the conversion contest: Islam and Christianity. Because the rule of the game is 'first come, first served', a tribal society that has already given its allegiance to one will not normally withdraw it in favour of the other (corollary 4). Hence, with most of tribal Africa divided between Islam and Christianity, we can expect one of three things, if not all of them: a disastrous confrontation, a defensive compromise or a daring collaboration between the two religions.

The first is *not* unlikely; the last is imperative – provided one knows wherein collaboration is desired. Let me comment on each alternative.

Why confrontation? The Christianity of the colonial masters, which still dominates the African church, is institutionally handicapped because of its history of hostilities with Islam in Europe and in the missions. It is humbled before Islam's credibility in the movement for African unity. It is hampered by its reluctance to disengage its ecclesiastical loyalties from the ideological grip of the countries of its provenance. And it is pastorally inhibited by its dread of liberation struggles. Hence, unless thoroughly revolutionized – that is to say, substituted by an indigenous alternative – it is bound to become overdefensive in the face of Islam. God forbid that it should summon all available external help to consolidate itself against its rival. Have not Rhodesia and South Africa given a precedent? The other alternative might be compromise through 'dialogue' – the dubious type of dialogue that is insidiously fostered and even financed by various ideological blocs, a dangerous compromise that blunts the liberative edge of both religions.

Common sense dictates, therefore, that the climate be created for harnessing the religious zeal of both traditions into a prophetic movement in the service of God's poor, through a socio-political collaboration in a common *theopraxis of liberation*. This obviously presupposes an unbiased Christian acquaintance with Islam.

ISLAM IN IRAN

Let Christians step back and gauge Islam's gigantic stature as it stands with self-confidence at the portals of the Third World, where it remains the most widespread single religious force to reckon with. Christians are made to believe by the media that it is also a generator of religious fanaticism and fundamentalism. Khomeini is the obvious symbol that springs to their mind. Why not focus, then, precisely on Iran and see where the fanatics come from and how a revolution is born?

Scan the last hundred years of history, pleads Eqbal Ahmed, Pakistani scholar, and you will note that the Khomeini episode is the *eighth* major battle that the Muslim nation has embarked on to defend its sovereignty against mercantile and military exploiters from the West! Religious clerics were in the thick of the struggle. Reuter's concession (1872) and the tobacco concession to Major Talbot (1895) were the first two Western manoeuvres. The third uprising was in 1905 against D'Arcy's concession to open Iran's oil resources to the West – as before, with the monarch's collaboration. This revolt succeeded in bringing about a modern constitutional government in 1906, which was soon overthrown by Czarist Russia and Britain in 1911. The opposition gathered momentum by 1919 against Lord Curzon's Anglo-Persian Treaty that would have turned Iran into a British colony, in fact if not in name. This fourth national victory lasted only two years. The British manoeuvred a coup d'etat led by Reza Khan in 1921. Thus absolute monarchy was reestablished with Khan as dictator, the father of the notorious ex-shah.

Reza Khan was praised in the Western press for ushering in 'modernization and westernization under the aegis of foreign domination,' adds Ahmed. The Nationalists did throw him out in 1941 but could not regain control of the administration, for the British maintained a regency while the future shah grew up under colonial tutelage. The Nationalists staged a return in 1950 and, after a struggle, forced new elections (under the 1906 Constitution) and established the Mossadegh government, which eventually nationalized the oil resources of Iran.

Then came Iran's nightmare: the CIA organized a coup d'etat against the Mossadegh government in 1953 and installed the shah, the tyrant who massacred nearly two hundred thousand Iranians – among them poets and writers. 'Iran's wealth was looted, transferred, and spent in the West.' Iran's Muslim masses did not simply fight the shah. They fought the superpower that forced him to be its gendarme in the Persian Gulf, sold him $19 billion worth of weapons, and supported his repressions until the last murderous days of his reign.

Who were the fanatics? Who were the liberators? Is this also the future of the ASEAN countries with a restless Muslim majority, and of Pakistan, which are all in the hands of the same powers that provoked the wrath of Iran? And what of the Soviet intervention in Afghanistan – understandable in the light of capitalist aggression, but no less abominable? Islam *is* a giant, and *not* a sleeping one.

HINDUISM IN INDIA

My third example is Hindusim – a great religion comprising many little religions, inscrutable even to the expert who can concentrate only on one little corner of the maze. With the revolutionary urge of religions as my particular focus, I can still make valid observations illustrative of principles enunciated above (especially corollaries 1, 2 and 3).

First, Hinduism can be taken as a metacosmic soteriology centred around the sacred texts of revealed and interpreted truths (*Śruti and Smṛti*). It is from within this orthodox tradition that the Indian renaissance took off as a reform movement, stimulated by the challenge of Western Christianity. Despite its social influences and theological adventures (including the discovery of the gnostic Christ alluded to above), it did not cease to be elitist.

According to one sociological survey, the offshoots of this movement have now withered into devotionalist sects. Some sects of the north and west of India have succumbed to political rightism and xenophobic chauvinism. Even god-men cults seem an apolitical middle-class phenomenon, indeed a far cry from the medieval saviour cults, which were 'liberational'. Perhaps in reaction to the onslaught of urbanization, these new cults show a marked shift from the classic concern with liberation to a mere quest for meaningfulness as in affluent societies elsewhere. Besides, the most disturbing issue of caste discrimination – a socio-economic slavery 'religiously' enforced by Brahmanic orthodoxy – is not squarely faced in these reforms.

To watch the transition from reform to revolution, one must, therefore, move away from this orthodox centre of Brahmanic Hinduism. The bhakti movement, the *Dalit Sāhitya* ('Writings of the oppressed'), and the tribal revolts represent three grades in this centrifugal trend.

The bhakti movement – initially a popular tendency on the fringes of Brahmanism – 'is the most creative upsurge of the Indian mind', which has inspired 'several social and political revolts...from Shivaji's rebellion in the seventeenth century to Mahatma Gandhi's in the twentieth.' A comparative study of two such movements in Maharashtra helps bring out the ingredients of a *religious* revolt against caste and sexist discrimination. The first is the Mahanubhava movement inaugurated by Chakradhar (1194–1276) who, in his ruthless denunciation of Brahman orthodoxy, did not spare even the Vedic scriptures. The fellowship it fostered offered equality of status to both the *śudras* and women. Chakradhar, of course, was killed for it. Yet the movement (revived only recently) could not muster popular enthusiasm, because it was conservatively monastic and relatively removed from grassroot struggles. Its message too suffered in that the mode of transmission was limited to the written word, a medium totally inaccessible to the illiterate masses.

Contrast this with the Warkari movement, which spread wider, grew deeper, and survived persecution by going underground. It was a lay initiative with a popular base and truly a movement of the oppressed: the untouchable castes. It produced a galaxy of revolutionary poet-saints, many of whom were martyred – counterparts of the Hebrew prophets. In India's religious ethos, a reformer, in order to arouse the masses, must also be a poet and a saint. The other secret of success, clearly exemplified in the Warkari movement, is the use of the oral medium for transmitting the message. Such a medium necessarily brings about a personal encounter between the mutually inspiring agents of social change: the suffering masses and the poet-saint. A vast production of oral literature and the extensive use of dance and song ensured an ongoing programme of 'conscientization'. It never petrified into a written text but ever remained fluid and flowing with the passage of time. Even the sacred lore of the ancients, whenever cited or insinuated in their freedom songs, went through a creative popular hermeneusis. In their later encounters with Islam and Christianity they also displayed a spirit of humane ecumenicity.

Circulating for two decades now, the *Dalit Sāhitya* ('Writings of the oppressed'), on the other hand, constitute an ideological departure from the bhakti movement of which it still is a historical continuation. A greater openness to other revolutionary ideologies has given teeth to this movement of popular writers, which at first had been a mere conscientization exercise within popular religion. Marx, Lenin, Mao, Che, Ho Chi Minh and Martin Luther King, Jr., figure prominently in these writings, for the Dalits feel themselves associated with the liberation struggles of all the world's oppressed. From openness to all that is liberative in other religions, there has grown a new openness to other secular ideologies. Thus the bhakti movement has lent itself to be used ideologically to destroy the oppressive religious system in which it still has its roots!

As we come to tribal India, we have not merely moved to the fringe of Brahmanic religiousness, but to *another* religious system *outside* it. The student of Indology is not often introduced to this reality. It is, no doubt, a precapitalist socialism that we meet again, in contrast with the feudalism of monastic religions (e.g., Buddhism) and of theocratic religions (e.g., Brahmanism). Yet, as in Africa, so even more in India, feudalistic tendencies are gradually seeping into tribal societies. It is said that although the tribal and the untouchable caste woman often enjoys equality with the male because of her relative economic independence, the adoption of Hindu values are tending to diminish the status of the harijan woman.

Wherever it is found, tribal society is egalitarian, free of caste and class, for it is based on a *religious socialism* that is uninhibited by puritanical mores characteristic of scriptural religions but prone to counterviolence if defence of the community requires it. No wonder, as Gail Omvedt documents, that the tribals as a whole can boast of a history of nationalist and class struggles all over Asia including India, not to speak of the bandit tradition of 'Robin Hoods' who rob wealthy landowners with the poor Indian villagers applauding as spectators.

BUDDHISM IN CHINA

Let me conclude this survey with an extensive note on Buddhism, for it is a pan-Asian religion occupying a position analogous to that of Islam in the Third World.

It is common knowledge that the Buddhist scriptures demand radical social change but lend no support to violent struggles, even though naïve theories about 'righteous killing' have been advanced in the course of Buddhist history. But tradition makes up for scripture, and it does so extravagantly! Here even orthodox Buddhism has to its credit a theory and praxis of rebellion. Some scholars warn that it is only when Buddhism as a religion is challenged in the midst of political chaos that monks come to the forefront with lay support, as in Thailand.

But what about Burma's Buddhist resurgence, which was messianically political? Initially aimed at Burmese kings, it was later directed toward their British successors. There must have been about twenty revolts from 1838 to 1928 – all inspired by the Maitreya cult: the eschatological expectation of a just social order to be ushered in with the appearance of the future Buddha. It is a belief that has scriptural foundation. Note also that it was this wave of Buddhist rebellions that brought to the surface the later independence movement with which U Nu, a philo-Marxist initially, tried his abortive experiment with 'Buddhist socialism'. Sri Lanka and Indochina have followed similar patterns. Vietnam's history of the Li dynasty and the concept of emperor-monk reflect a militantly political Buddhism that is no less virulent today.

Not surprisingly, revolutionary praxis on the fringes of the Buddhist institution shows greater radicalism. China offers us a series of persuasive examples, of which I make here a random selection. From about 402 CE there were about ten armed rebellions organized by monks, climaxing in 515 CE with that of Fa-K'ing, a revolutionary monk who, like many of his kind, married a nun. These monastic rebellions were directed against both the state and the official religious establishment. Since then there have been many messianic sects that had a popular base, clearly indicating the influence of cosmic religion over metacosmic. One such was the Maitreya sect founded in 610 CE by a Buddhist monk who declared himself emperor. This sect had incorporated into its belief system the cult of Buddha Amitābha and the desire for rebirth in his heaven known as the Western Paradise. The adherents of this sect maintained that this paradise should be created on earth, here and now, rather than in a remote future. They wished to bring about a Buddha-land, a state of peace and equity in this existence. This sect left its traces in the whole period from the seventh to the sixteenth centuries.

The White Cloud sect (between 1108 and 1300) and the Lo sect (1505–1956) were two others of the same kind. The most significant, perhaps, is the White Lotus sect (*Pai-Lien Ts'ai*, 1133–1813), a branch of which continued under the name *I-Kuam-Tao* as late as 1956 and was hunted down by the Maoist regime. The founder was a Buddhist monk named Mao tzu-Yuan (1086–1166), who was assisted by women and married monks – something that provoked the wrath of the orthodox sangha. But these movements continued to enjoy a certain amount of popular support. Mao tzu-Yuan was exiled and the movement proscribed several times; then it was once more recognized by Emperor Jen T'sing (1312–1321). Among its many revolutions, the most successful was that of 1351 under the leadership of Han Shan-T'ung, who also called himself Buddha Maitreya. This revolution succeeded in destroying the Mongol rule and established a new dynasty – the Ming dynasty. Its first emperor was Chu-Yuang-Chang, ex-Buddhist novice and a former officer of the White Lotus army. The irony was that he later turned anti-Buddhist. This movement was crushed again in 1813. The ban was removed in 1911, and a branch of it, as indicated above, was active as late as 1956.

By Marxist standards these were not real revolutions; they could at best be classed as rebellions. But they show how Buddhists could respond to the revolutionary moods and creeds of the time. In these instances, the Buddhist messianic interpretation of the scriptures and the scriptural justification of 'revolution' had come as a response to a contemporary ideology springing from the Taoist secret societies that awaited the true ruler who was to give great peace to those awaiting him, and from the Confucianist expectation of the enlightened emperor.

What I wish to underscore here is that Buddhists living in a particular historical situation may, under the influence of non-Buddhist ideologies and movements, reinterpret their scriptural sources in order to respond creatively to a contemporary need – even if it means a costly revolution. This tradition continues to this day in Chinese Buddhism.

Religion and Revolution in a Third World Theology

In scanning the wide expanse of non-Christian cultures in the Third World, I have cast a searchlight on only four areas: African religiousness (which resembles that of Oceania), west Asian Islam, south Asian Hinduism and east Asian Buddhism. Though by no means exhaustive, these four samples are illustrative of some of the major features of religiousness in the Third World and support three overall conclusions.

1. Outside the pale of Semitic monotheism, there is perhaps only one stream of religiousness (one form of Hinduism) that regards the one ultimate reality as a personal being who summons the cosmos into existence and summons human beings to a personal, redeeming encounter with the divine self. A God who is one, personal, absolute creator-redeemer of the world and of humankind is neither universally affirmed nor universally denied. Religiousness – especially in Asia – is for a greater part of humanity metatheistic, or at least nontheistic, if not, at times, explicitly atheistic. The common thrust, however, remains *soteriological*, the concern of most religions being *liberation* (*vimukti, moksa*, nirvana) rather than speculation about a hypothetical liberator. Many metacosmic religions point to a future that is attainable as the present moment of total human emancipation, putting the accent on a metapersonal Beyond, if not on an 'impersonal' but transphenomenal It: Tao, dharma, *tathatā, Brahman*, nirvana. The cosmic religions, on the other hand, look up to many gods and spiritual forces, which constitute the spectrum of a complex unity of being enveloping the whole of human cosmic existence. Even where the two forms of religion – the cosmic and metacosmic – merge, the net result is not a simple equivalent of biblical monotheism.

Hence, theology as God-talk or God's talk is not necessarily the universally valid starting point, or the direct object, or the only basis, of interreligious collaboration in the Third World. But liberation is. Soteriology is the foundation of theology. Regrettably, the contemporary theologies of religions (with Christ pitted *against* religions or niched *within* them) are devoid of any Third World perspective: they take off from textual accounts of non-Christian religiousness and ignore the historical fact that a religion's micro-ethical concern for self-purification of individuals ('cultural revolution') is often projected onto the macro-ethical level of socio-political catharsis ('structural revolution'). This is true even with those religions that are academically dismissed as 'world-denying' or escapist. Equally glossed over are the many explosive liberation myths that, in their symbolic enactments – such as dance and drama, song and ritual, parable and poetry – store the seeds of revolution in the heart of a people. Should not, then, a Third World theology of religions necessarily have a unitary perception of religion and revolution?

I submit that the religious instinct should be defined as a revolutionary urge, a psycho-social impulse, to generate a new humanity. It is none other than the piercing thrust of evolution in its self-conscious state, the human version of nature's thirst for higher forms of life. The religious quest, in other words, is an irresistible drive to *humanize* what has merely been *hominized*. As in the biosphere, where it can end up in blind alleys, so also in the *noosphere*, this evolutionary upsurge can be sidetracked to regressive states of inertia. Revolution could turn reactionary religion irreligious. But the foundation of a Third World theology of religions remains unshaken – namely, that it is this revolutionary impulse that constitutes, and therefore defines, the essence of *homo religiosus*.

This unified view of revolution, religion and cosmic evolution imparts a Third World dimension to the understanding of technology and the allied concepts of 'progress' and 'modernization', and consequently lifts the whole debate on inculturation to another plane.

2. Technology is the immediate and inevitable consequence of noogenesis or hominization. The human mind, as it emerges from the biosphere, demands more sensitive organs of perception (senses) and more effective means of movement (limbs), which the body does not provide physiologically. For the mind is capable of extending the brain, the senses and the limbs of the body by organizing external matter into sensitized and mechanized tools of knowledge and action. Technology, to be sure, is the art (*techne*) of expanding human presence and activity into space and time cognitively and conatively in order to further the psycho-social evolution of humankind. Being the natural accompaniment of hominization, however, technology too can accept or escape the impact of humanization that issues from the revolutionary upsurge of religiousness. Let me therefore recall, with parenthetical explicitations, the concept of technology I earlier proposed to the Ecumenical Association of Third World Theologians:

Technology is a [humanly] induced cosmic process, which is a conscious [i.e., self-reflective] continuation of [infrahuman] biological evolution and, like the latter [i.e., like biological evolution], becomes humanized [i.e., liberative] only by its metacosmic orientation [i.e., by the revolutionary thrust of religion toward ever nobler levels of human existence].

If, then, the law of evolution has prescribed in the book of nature the revolutionary imperative to humanize technology through religion, then a dehumanized technocracy is indeed a reversal of the evolutionary trajectory, a cosmological disaster, an irreligious undevelopment, though boorishly advertised in Asian countries as 'international culture', modernization and progress – if not also as preevangelization!

What dehumanizes technology is the sin of acquisitiveness organized into a socio-economic order of human relationships, a distorted cosmology that invariably fosters what Marx calls 'the antagonism between man and nature'. In that system, technology alienates its inseparable human partner, of whom it was meant to be the cosmic extension; it desecrates the *cosmic religiousness* of the peasant masses with the transfer of biospheric pollution from industrialized countries to the Third World, and with its acquired not innate propensity to pillage nature in order to produce the weapons of cosmic holocaust. It deflects the metacosmic orientation of nature and culture with a secularism that eclipses the 'beyond' from the 'now', and consequently engenders in the human heart a pathological obsession with cosmic need, or 'consumerism', as it is known in the cultures that first produced it. Then 'modernization' and 'progress' *must* imply the overthrow of this regressive but all-persuasive system in favour of a new order of human relationships wherein technology is not so much 'in control of' nature as 'in harmony with' its inborn thirst for humanization – that is to say, with the revolutionary dictates of religion itself.

Sexism, a sensitive issue in most religions, cannot be divorced from our discourse on technology and civilization, for there is an intimate correspondence between the anthropo-cosmic harmony advocated here and the androgynous mutuality that it presumes. If nature is an exclusively feminine symbol and if the metacosmic beyond, which is the redemptive consummation of the cosmic processes, is made to wear a masculine mask, then of course the religious enterprise of humanizing nature, civilizing technology, and divinizing the human amounts to a masculine absorption of the feminine. Woman will be the last thing to be civilized by man, says George Meredith scornfully; and also vice versa, corrects Theodore Reik.

The task of humanizing nature, which is both masculine and feminine, is founded on the reciprocal activity of men and women civilizing each other. In this area, the revolutionary impulse of all religions – save that of *some* tribal societies and *one* tiny vein in Hinduism – is ruthlessly curbed. Sexism points to an uncivilized area in religion. The new cosmological order that the Third World clamours for includes unhampered feminine participation in religion and revolution.

3. Inculturation, that infelicitous word coined in the West and reminiscent of the reductionist notion of religion running through theology, anthropology and Marxist ideology, has fortunately come to mean, in present usage, the Christian search for meaning within the *religious* ethos of non-Christian cultures. This is what compelled me to place it in the Christ-of-religions column. In this case, however, the relevant question to be asked is: Into which stream of non-Christian religiousness does Christianity hope to enter – the reactionary or the revolutionary? To allay the liberationists' misgivings about inculturation, one more crucial question has to be raised: Which brand of Christianity seeks to be inculturated, the one framed within a cosmology that is repudiated in the Third World, or the one derived from a Third World hermeneusis of the gospel?

A Third World hermeneusis vivifies the Christian kerygma by recharging the three key words around which it revolves, words now worn out by ideological misuse: *basileia* (the kingdom, or new order), *metanoia* (interior conversion to that order) and *martyrion* (overt commitment to it).

True to our non-Christian religious traditions, we can neither describe nor define the new order but can only boldly strive toward it by the *via negativa* – namely, by negating the present order not only in theory and analysis, but also in the commitment to overthrow it! The future that calls in question the present ever remains the 'unnamable' or at least the 'unmentioned presupposition' of every true revolution. For the intimate encounter with Ultimate Reality – the core of mysticism – almost overlaps with a profoundly transforming experience of present unreality. The salvific truth dawns as the unmasking of delusion. Being shines in the darkest depths of nonbeing. *Brahma/atman* is reached by piercing through *maya*. Nirvana culminates the pilgrimage of *samsara*. Life is the passage through death. Grace overwhelms where sin abounds. Revolution is born of bondage. Yahweh abides in the *anawim* (the poor). God's saving power erupts from the earth's slaving poor.

Can we touch the one without being touched by the other? Only the victim of the present order is qualified to be its judge and authorized to 'proclaim the imminent future' – which is what the kerygma means. *Metanoia*, then, is the disturbance of heart and change of life that such mysticism evokes. It is a religiously motivated desire and decision to move toward the new humanity – a 'cultural revolution' in the vocabulary of those who are allergic to the term 'religious conversion'. *Martyrion* is the concomitant growth of a collective testimony in the communities of converts, a personalized anticipation and a visible guarantee of the new order. Like the supreme martyr, Jesus, they too are the victim-judge of the existing system and the paradigm of the future they announce. This incipient 'structural revolution' is known as the church – which is good news to the poor, because the poor by birth and the poor by option constitute it.

Such basic communities are now mushrooming all over the Third World. They are not subservient to the 'international culture' of the ministerial church but are shaped by the local religiousness of the poor. As I have argued elsewhere, genuine inculturation is the fruit of ecclesiological revolution, not its seed.

Hence the embarrassing question: Is not the Third World theologian exposed to the same temptation that the Western and westernized anthropologists have succumbed to in their studies of 'primitive' cultures? These anthropologists are accused of apocalyptic megalomania in that they claim to possess a secret power of knowing these cultures 'empathetically', by reason of 'participatory observation', and to have the authority to interpret them to the ignorant West!

Inculturationists' enthusiasm for a culture from which they are estranged and liberationists' defence of the poor against those whose culture they happily share, point to a dangerous trend in Third World theology. Should not theology be the explicitation of the theopraxis of these *ecclesiolae* ('little churches') that have appropriated the revolutionary religiousness of the Third World? And should not the writing of this theology be relegated to later redactors? Did not all the sacred scriptures originate in this manner? Is this not the Third World way of doing theology?

6

LESSLIE NEWBIGIN: The Christian Faith and the World Religions

Lesslie Newbigin (1909–1998) was a leading figure in the ecumenical movement of the twentieth century. A minister of the Presbyterian, then the United Reformed Church, he became one of the first bishops of the Church of South India. His experience on the mission field and his close acquaintance with the religions of India are reflected in his numerous publications, which include The Finality of Christ *(London, 1969),* Foolishness to the Greeks *(Geneva, 1986) and* The Gospel in a Pluralist Society *(London, 1989). His critique of religious pluralism is well illustrated by the essay reprinted here.*

I. THE CHANGED SITUATION

Charles Gore and his colleagues were concerned 'to put the Catholic faith into its right relation to modern intellectual and moral problems'. They were concerned to vindicate a genuine 'development' of Christian theology that would neither lose its firm moorings in the age-long creed of the church nor retreat into a narrower and harder dogmatism, but rather 'enter into the apprehension of the new intellectual and social movements of each age' and so enable the church to 'throw herself into the sanctification of each new social order' and to show 'under changed conditions the catholic capacity of her faith' (*Lux Mundi*, preface).

While the discussions that gave birth to *Lux Mundi* were going on in Oxford, things were happening elsewhere in which these dons were not involved. In what we now see as the greatest period of their activity, mission-aries were busy in Asia, Africa and the Pacific, preaching, arguing, teaching and healing – laying the foundations for what would be hailed sixty years later, in William Temple's Canterbury enthronement sermon, as 'the great new fact of our time', the presence of the church in every part of the world, a global society made up of peoples from many cultures and drawn from many religious traditions.

The meeting of the Western religious tradition with the great religions of the East was indeed already under way. Max Müller's publication of the fifty volumes of Sacred Books of the East had begun. The mutual interpenetration of Eastern and Western cultures and religions was beginning, but – for these Oxford scholars – it was not yet visible as one of the major new realities with which Christianity would have to come to terms and which would test the meaning of its claim to catholicity. The other world religions presented no immediate challenge to English Christianity. Rather, the new challenges came from within the Western tradition.

The situation a hundred years later is very different. The explosive power of Western ideas, politics, commerce, technology and religion, penetrating into the ancient cultures of Asia, Africa and the Pacific, has not only set in motion revolutionary movements within those cultures. It has also triggered a corresponding movement in the opposite direction. Ideas and people can now move so quickly that the distances which for centuries separated the great cultures of humankind have almost been abolished. We are now acutely aware of living in a single global society. In the photographs beamed back to us from outer space we have seen what no previous generation could ever see – our planet as one fragile spacecraft, one vessel moving through the vast ocean of space, a vessel in which all who travel must learn to live together as one family if they are not to perish together in one catastrophe.

And those of us who inhabit that part of the planet which used to be called Christendom have to acknowledge our responsibility for these vast changes in the total human situation. We cannot step out of our place in history. Hendrick Kraemer's words, written thirty years ago, are still apt:

> This eastern invasion, which has been set in motion and will constantly increase in strength, is ultimately the West's own doing. The most significant point is that the West, by its contacts and by its efforts of understanding, has by its invasion of the East made the eastern cultures and religions an event of great purport in its own quest, and an important part of its own native crisis in

religion and culture. So this involvement in the eastern cultural and religious values and achievements has provided the West with ample material for its own cultural and religious doubts and self-criticism. The least that can be said about it is that the inescapable fact of the plurality of cultures and religions has not only become a weighty practical and social problem, but in the spiritual realm of either creates a spirit of relativistic indifferentism, a leaning towards the plausibility of a synthetic common denominator as the evident solution, or a propensity towards regarding the Christian heritage as irrelevant. De Lubac's words: 'Si l'Europe ne retrouve pas sa foi, alors elle est mûre pour une colonisation spirituelle', are not inappropriate.

That 'spiritual colonization' is already a reality. I am not referring to the vigorous missionary outreach of Islam in Europe, financed by the oil-rich states of the Middle East, nor to the more modest enterprises of Hindus and Buddhists in winning European converts to their faiths. I am thinking rather of the way in which that attitude to religion which is characteristic of India has (with obvious modifications) become widespread among Western Christians. It is an attitude that no longer sees religion as providing the intellectual framework within which public life is understood, but rather sees 'religions' as alternative paths to personal salvation, offering a range of options within which each person is free to choose and between which one does not argue about conflicting truth-claims.

For many centuries, and especially since the rise of Islam, the Christian West was isolated from the great religions of Asia. After that event, it was confronted by an aggressive power in which religious faith was fused with political and military organization to create a mighty imperial power. Western Christendom and Islam faced each other as rival military powers, while Eastern Christendom, except in Russia, survived only as isolated enclaves within a much more powerful empire.

After Western Christendom broke up in the religious wars of the seventeenth century, the intellectual leadership of the European nations turned from the vision of a Christian society to a new vision of a society ordered by the principles of the Enlightenment. Religious belief became more and more a matter for personal choice rather than being the generally accepted way of understanding and ordering public life. It was no longer an intrinsic element in belonging to European society. At the same time, the opening up of communications with the rest of the world vastly extended the mental horizon of the European peoples, reinforcing the tendency to see Christian belief as only one among a wide variety of options. For the savants of the late eighteenth century, China exercised a special fascination as exemplifying a high culture which owed nothing to Christianity.

Until the end of the Second World War these ideas were probably those of a minority of intellectuals in most of the European nations. For most people, Christianity in one form or another was accepted as the religion to which one naturally adhered, even if the adherence was tenuous. It was normal to be baptized, married and buried with Christian rites. 'Religious education' in the schools was based on the Bible. Since 1945 several factors have combined to change the situation: the end of the colonial empires, the migration of millions of people from the former colonies to the old metropolitan countries, the enormous increase in intercontinental air travel, and the development of radio and television networks reaching into every part of the globe. The result today is that, not for a few intellectuals but for the majority of ordinary people, Christianity is seen as only one among many religions, all worthy of respect. At the same time, the general acceptance of the idea of a secular society, of a secular style of public education, of a public life that is ordered without explicit reference to any religious beliefs, has – as its counterpart – the general relegation of religious belief to the area of private and personal choice, an area sharply distinguished from the public sphere. It is true that there are movements on what is called the 'new religious right', principally but not exclusively in the United States, to make an identification of Christian belief with certain public policies. And it is also true that there are substantial vestiges of a tribalism which conflates religious belief with ethnic allegiance (for example, in Ulster). But these are exceptions to the general rule. For most people in contemporary Western society, it would be safe to say that the following assumptions are not usually called into question: *(a)* Christianity is one religion among the many world religions, all of which are to be treated with respect because they are concerned with God and with the immortal soul; *(b)* religious belief is a matter of personal choice and everyone is entitled to have 'a faith of his or her own'; *(c)* the proper way in which religious people should behave towards one another is to be described in terms of coexistence, cooperation and dialogue, not in terms such as proselytism, evangelism, conversion or mission.

What, exactly, is new in this situation? It is not the fact that there is a plurality of religions in the world. That, apparently, has always been so. Nor is it an entirely new fact that Christians have become conscious of this plurality. From the churches of the early centuries living in the religiously plural world of the eastern Mediterranean, to the churches living and witnessing among the ancient religions of Asia today, there have always been Christians who were well aware of this plurality. What is new, at least for the churches of the old Christendom, is the widespread acceptance of religious pluralism as an ideology. Indians have traditionally seen the *dharma* as universal and eternal. Muslims have affirmed that the Qur'an is God's final and decisive word to the whole of humankind. And Christians have affirmed that Jesus is Lord of all, the light of the whole world. Today such confidence is widely regarded among British and North American Christians as a mark of ignorance or naïvety. Religious pluralism, the view that in principle and for always humankind will be religiously divided and that this is not to be deplored but to be welcomed, is something relatively new. At least the authors of *Lux Mundi* did not feel bound to consider it among the new things with which the Catholic faith must reckon. Today we can hardly avoid facing it.

II. THE CONTEMPORARY DEBATE

The contemporary debate about religious pluralism is vigorous and shows no sign of faltering. During the early part of the present century the debate was mainly among missionaries, for it was they who were in direct contact with people of other faiths. Indeed, it was largely (though by no means entirely) through the writings of missionaries that Christians in the West came to know something of Eastern religions. The Jesuits at the imperial court in China, Ziegenbalg and Plutschau in Tranquebar, and Carey in Bengal were among those who by their writings awakened European interest in Asian religions. The first two decades of the present century saw the publication of an immense amount of scholarly work, mostly written by missionaries, on the non-Christian religions. The world missionary conference at Edinburgh in 1910 gathered together and focused much of this discussion, and its volume on 'The Christian Message' gives evidence of its high quality. What triggered the most passionate debate was the publication in 1932 of the report of the Laymen's Foreign Missionary Enquiry entitled 'Re-thinking Missions'. This report, theologically directed by W. E. Hocking, looked towards the convergence of all the religions in a common way of life which could be described as the 'kingdom of God' and which Christians found exemplified in Jesus

Christ. The major response to this report came in the book of Hendrick Kraemer commissioned for the world missionary conference at Tambaram in 1938 – 'The Christian Message in a Non-Christian World'. This book, published exactly half a century after *Lux Mundi*, provided the main focus of debate for the next twenty-five years, and it was still largely a debate among missionaries and leaders in the Indian churches.

With the merger of the International Missionary Council and the World Council of Churches in 1961, the debate moved naturally into the larger context of a council of churches. It was no longer a debate conducted in the context of explicit missionary activity; rather, it was a debate about the way in which different religious communities can live and work together in the interest of the human community as a whole. The churches in the newly emancipated nations were facing the colossal task of helping their peoples to achieve national unity across the lines dividing the different religious and tribal groups that had been held together by the colonial power but must now find a new basis for unity. The debate about the relation of Christianity to the other religions had to be carried on in the new context of an urgent search for human unity. The first occasion on which the issue of religious pluralism was given a full discussion in an assembly of the World Council of Churches was in 1975 at Nairobi. The document, prepared by the section on 'Seeking Community: The Common Search of People of Various Faiths, Cultures and Ideologies', was not accepted by the whole Assembly, and it was clear that there was no common mind among the churches. Subsequent years have seen, both in the World Council of Churches and in its member churches, a struggle to articulate the nature of the relation that ought to exist between Christians and people of other faiths and ideologies, the proper role of dialogue, and its relation to the dominical commission to 'make disciples of all nations'. The debate continues, and there is little sign of consensus. A brief survey of some of the positions taken will help to introduce the theme, even though it cannot do justice to the full variety of views expressed in the debate.

III. THE EXCLUSIVIST POSITION

There are those who affirm that faithfulness to the revelation in Christ as attested in Scripture requires us to believe that all those who have not made an explicit commitment of faith in Christ are eternally lost. It is indeed not difficult to point to biblical texts that support – or seem to support – this view. Plainly, if this is the real situation of those who are outside the Christian church, then the question of dialogue simply does not arise. If a house is on fire and there are people trapped inside, one does not propose a dialogue about the different experiences of those inside and those outside. The only proper response is to rush in and rescue the victims by any means possible. If all non-Christians are in fact destined for eternal fire, then any method, however violent, that has the possibility of converting them is not only permitted but required.

The difficulties in this view are obvious. The question whether this is in fact the view that Scripture requires us to take will be considered later. The view under discussion is sometimes condemned on the ground that it would be unjust on the part of God thus to condemn those millions who, through no fault of their own, have never heard the gospel. But the argument from justice cannot stand. If it is the case (as it is) that all human beings have sinned and do sin grievously against the love of God, then punishment is not unjust. Nevertheless, if God's response to human sin is that which was revealed and effected in the ministry, death and resurrection of Jesus, it is difficult to accept this scenario. And if it is true that the faith which sets a person right with God is ultimately a matter of the heart and conscience (however necessary it may also be that the faith is outwardly confessed), can anyone other than God pronounce final judgement on whether or not this faith exists in any particular case?

Moreover, every proposal to deny all knowledge of God outside explicit Christian confession breaks down in actual missionary practice. No one can communicate the gospel without using the word 'God'. If one is talking to people of a non-Christian religion, one is bound to use one of the words that the language of that people provides to denote 'God'. Plainly the content of the word as heard by the non-Christian will have been furnished by religious experience outside the Christian faith. By using the word, the missionary is taking non-Christian experience as the starting point. Without doing this, there is no way of communicating. This fact does not by itself refute the position we are considering, but it makes it impossible to assert a total discontinuity between the gospel and the religions.

IV. THE AFFIRMATION OF PLURALISM

At the other end of the spectrum of opinions, there are those views which in one way or another affirm religious pluralism. Within this cluster of views there are differing answers to the question about the relation between mission and dialogue. John Hick is one of the most influential of those who disclaim any uniqueness or centrality for Christianity among the religions. Using his well-known analogy of the Copernican revolution in astronomy, he has argued that we require 'a shift from the dogma that Christ is at the centre to the realisation that it is God who is at the centre, and that all religions of mankind, including our own serve and revolve around him'.

There are logical difficulties in this position. The different religions are the social embodiments of different ways of apprehending the ultimate reality, the source and goal of our being – whether or not the word 'God' is used to designate that reality. In this sense, the Copernican model has a measure of aptitude. But, with all their differences, the religions make truth-claims about what that reality is. Insofar as these claims differ, one is bound to ask which of them is true or nearest to the truth. If that question is disallowed, if one refuses to ask the question about truth, one is subverting religion at its heart. Moreover, if one refuses to make judgements between the different truth-claims, one is still under the necessity of justifying that refusal, for it is itself a claim to know something about what is really the case. There can be no absolute validity about the claim that no truth-claim is absolutely valid. We have no independent standpoint from which we can compare all the different apprehensions of truth, *including our own*, with the truth itself.

In the case of Hick, however, it is clear that we are not dealing with a total relativism; far from it. The God of whom he speaks, who is the centre of this Copernican system, is not unknown. He is known as infinite and inexhaustible love. Without question, this understanding of God is part of Hick's profoundly Christian faith. 'God' who is at the centre of Hick's Copernican system is God as Hick has come to know him through the Christian tradition.

A not dissimilar position is taken by Wilfred Cantwell Smith in his 'Meaning and End of Religion'. Smith distinguishes between the experience of God which is the living heart of all religion and the cumulative tradition of credal statement, ritual, ethical behaviour and corporate life which develops through history around this central core. It is axiomatic for him that the central experience – 'religion' properly so called – is always and everywhere one. There is one reality with which the religious experience brings people into contact, whatever the 'religion' to which they adhere. It follows, for example, that condemnation of idolatry rests on a misunderstanding. No one has ever worshipped an idol. People have worshipped and do worship God –

the one God – under different forms and images. The forms are many: the reality worshipped is one.

Plainly, this position is vulnerable to the same kind of criticism as that which we have applied to Hick's. To affirm that all the different names and forms under which men and women have worshipped the Source of their being refer in fact to the same reality implies either that that reality is unknowable or else that one has access to information about it which authorizes the affirmation. In the second case, one is under the obligation to disclose the source of the information, and this will involve making truth-claims. The apostolic author who affirms that God has spoken in many and various ways through numerous messengers is in a position to make that affirmation because he relies explicitly on a claim that he believes to be true – namely, that God has spoken through his Son (Heb. 1:1–2).

The other alternative is that we conclude that God (or ultimate reality) is unknowable. The Christian tradition has always affirmed both that God's being is a reality beyond human comprehension and, at the same time, that God has so revealed his true nature that we know how to walk through this world in such a way that we are led towards the place where we shall see God as God is. This 'Way' has been disclosed, even though the end of the journey is beyond our sight (John 14:1–6). Thus, although God is not to be fully known in this life, we are given enough to know the direction of our seeking. And the seeking is both intellectual and practical. We walk by faith, not by sight; but faith is a cognitive faculty which enables us to know in which direction to walk. Walking by faith is not wandering about in a twilight where all cats are grey.

In its contemporary phase, Western culture makes a sharp distinction between knowledge and faith. Faith, since John Locke, has been understood as what we must rely on when certain knowledge is not available. Since Descartes, our culture has been fascinated by the ideal of a kind of knowledge that would be invulnerable to doubt, that would be true 'objectively' not merely in the sense of being really true but in the sense of relieving the knowing subject of any personal responsibility or commitment. In this cultural context it is easy to relegate the truth-claims of religion to the sphere of 'subjectivity', to treat them as matters on which individuals make their own personal choice while leaving others free to make theirs. Here, as a result, one does not merely acknowledge the plurality of religions as a fact; one applauds religious pluralism as a principle. But this principle is not accepted in the public world of 'facts' which are true 'objectively' and can be known to be so by the methods of modern science. Here pluralism is not accepted. Statements of 'fact' are either true or false. Of course there are differences of opinion about the facts, but these are not applauded as evidence of pluralism. They are regarded as temporary, challenging scientists to a vigorous programme of experiment and argument until agreement is reached.

Yet upon reflection we are bound to reject this bifurcation of the universe into two separate parts and of our attempts to understand and deal with it into two quite different kinds of mental activity. Philosophers and historians of science have no difficulty in showing that the entire edifice of modern scientific knowledge rests upon faith commitments whose truth cannot be demonstrated from any more fundamental certainties; and – on the other hand – the religious person in the activity of prayer, worship and practical obedience certainly believes that his or her faith is directed to a reality that is not merely 'subjective'. It is not just faith in faith. It is faith in something or someone, a cognitive faculty that is seeking contact with a reality beyond the self.

Religious pluralism as it is popular in the West today is one manifestation of this split through the heart of contemporary Western culture. It is a split, a wound, which cannot remain forever unhealed. The scientific method treated in isolation is unable to give answers to the deepest human questions about the source and the goal, the why and the wherefore of human existence. It cannot do so for the very simple reason that the enormous fruitfulness of the scientific method has depended upon the elimination of these questions from its working. The elimination is a methodological decision which has been abundantly justified, but it does not mean that the matters eliminated from consideration do not exist. It is the great world religions, the poets and the philosophers that have sought answers to these questions. Religious pluralism as an ideology implies that these questions are unanswerable. The truth-claims of the religions are taken to be merely different expressions of human subjectivity, devoid of 'objective' truth.

If C. P. Snow is right in speaking of the 'two cultures' in our society, and if W. G. Pollard is also right in saying that while the contemporary scientific culture is in the full vigour of health, the other 'culture' is merely the fragmented remains of an older culture that was once coherent but has lost its vitality, then we can understand why pluralism is rejected in the first and accepted in the second. Its acceptance is precisely the sign of intellectual exhaustion. The arduous search for reality sustains the immense labours of scientists but (it would appear) is widely abandoned in that area of human culture which is concerned with ultimate meanings.

It is illuminating to compare our present situation in respect of religious pluralism with the situation of the church in its first four centuries, making its way through the syncretistic medley of religions that was characteristic of the last days of the Greco-Roman world. The quest for ultimate truth had been widely given up as hopeless. Reality is, in the end, beyond human comprehension. The sensible person settles for the situation tartly described by Gibbon in which all religions are for the people equally true, for the philosophers equally false, and for the government equally useful. There were powerful forces tending to suck the church into this syncretistic broth. But in resisting these, the great theologians of the church devoted their intellectual energies to the task of making clear and intelligible the fact that the ultimate reality, God himself, had in fact disclosed himself, his nature and purpose, in the career of a human being whose life and work were accessible for critical study. And they did not hesitate to use this divine self-disclosure as the touchstone by which the philosophies and religions of their time were to be tested. The shape of the Christian faith was hammered out by people of brilliant intellect, living in a religiously plural world but refusing to accept religious pluralism; affirming the supremacy of reason *(logos)* over all the religious 'superstitions' of their time, but bearing witness that the divine reason had taken human form in the life and ministry of Jesus Christ.

V. 'PROVISIONAL PLURALISM'

A third position must be distinguished from that of total religious pluralism – namely, one that accepts a provisional pluralism in the context of an explicit criterion of ultimate religious truth. It is largely in this form that the religious 'colonization' of western Europe has been most effective. From the dramatic appearance of Swami Vivekananda at the World Parliament of Religions in Chicago in 1893, through the influential work of Dr Sarvepalli Radhakrishnan during the years when he was teaching in Oxford, and down to the present day, the philosophy of the Vedanta has been attractive to Western intellectuals as providing the ultimate criterion of religious truth. The word 'vedanta' – literally the end of the Vedas – points to that in which all religion reaches its true goal. That goal is the point at which all duality between subject and object disappears and one is enabled to realize the identity of the individual soul with the world soul. This realization can come only at the end of a long and hard road of spiritual discipline, and few reach the end. But this road defines the religious quest.

Scholars of the strictest school of the Vedanta usually distinguish three stages in the journey, or three circles in the inward spiral. The first is the way of duty, of good works – the *karma marga*. Beyond this is the way of faith and devotion, the *bhakti marga*, the stage at which one relies on no good works but wholly on the grace and mercy of a loving personal God, to whom one clings with total devotion. But even this does not take one to the end of the journey. That is reached only by following the way of wisdom, the *gnana marga*, a way of total renunciation, a 'journey inwards' to the still centre of the soul where all duality disappears and the soul is at one with the ultimate reality.

From this perspective it is clear that the various religions of the world, and the various religious experiences of men and women, are understood and evaluated according to the progress they have made along this path. Evangelical Christianity, for example, will be seen as an example of the *bhakti* stage in the journey. It will not be condemned as false. It will be accepted as a genuine and valid expression of a certain stage in growth towards the truth. The Christian will be gently encouraged to move beyond the place he or she has reached towards the centre point where all are one because the All is One. Here the names and forms and events that belong to the various world religions disappear in the white light of truth, for indeed they were only shadows. Here any claim for final validity on behalf of one of these names or forms is ruled out. An assertion by the Christian that Jesus is the truth by which all else is to be tested must necessarily be uncompromisingly rejected. All forms of religion, from the most 'primitive' to the most sophisticated, can be accepted and welcomed. In that sense one can speak here of religious pluralism. But it is not an absolute pluralism. There is one criterion by which all truth-claims in the field of religion can be and must be tested.

There is another, and quite different, kind of 'provisional pluralism' which comes not from an Eastern but from a Western source. It was influentially represented in the famous 'Laymen's Report' to which reference has already been made. Here also religious plurality is accepted as a fact and the variety of religions is welcomed, but there is a criterion by which they are judged. This is implicit in the fact that the report looks toward a convergence of the religions in the idea and practice of the way of life that is described as the kingdom of God and that is defined by the example of Jesus. Unlike most of those who have discussed the problem of religious pluralism, the Laymen's

Report does not concern itself mainly with the question, 'Who can be saved?' It is concerned, rather, with the question, 'How can the nations move towards a tolerable world order?' It sees Western science and technology as being, in spite of their Western provenance, essentially universal. There is no cultural imperialism involved in their worldwide spread. But as far as religion is concerned, Christianity will not make its contribution to the coming world order by trying to displace the other religions by its missionary effort. Rather, it must join with them in a common quest which will require all the religions, including Christianity, to 'reconceive' themselves in a single world faith capable of obtaining a beneficent world order. The character of this world order, however, will be determined by Jesus' teaching about and manifestation of the kingdom of God.

There is thus a provisional religious pluralism which (as in the case of the Vedanta) precludes the attempt to convert people from one religious allegiance to another. But it is not an absolute pluralism, for there is a criterion by which the religions are evaluated and a goal towards which they must all be summoned to strive.

These two varieties of 'provisional religious pluralism' face different kinds of difficulty. Certainly the position of the Vedantin cannot be logically faulted. Much of human history testifies to its enduring power. Even though the number of those who have the spiritual stamina to win through to the deepest levels of 'realization' is small, the idea that a pure mysticism of this kind is the real heart of religion is widespread. Moreover, it fits well with the dominant scientific culture of the West, since it eliminates the idea of a personal God, creator and sustainer of the cosmos, whose will determines what is right and what is wrong in human conduct. Mystical experience is a very widely attested fact in many cultures, and there are no grounds on which the truth of this testimony can be questioned, however it may be explained. But the claim that mystical experience is the central clue for understanding the whole human situation is a claim of faith. Its truth cannot be demonstrated. It must take its place along with the other faith commitments that lie at the root of the other world religions and ideologies. There are no grounds upon which this claim can assert priority over the others.

It is often remarked that in interreligious discussions Western thinkers tend to argue disjunctively in terms of 'either–or', whereas Eastern thinkers are more inclined to say 'both–and'. This difference is sometimes treated as though it was merely a matter of cultural conditioning in which questions of truth are not involved. But profound issues of truth are involved. It is indeed true that, as a result of honest dialogue, two opposed positions are seen in a new light to be different aspects of one truth. But that larger truth must itself be open to critical question in the light of other apprehensions of reality. The Vedantin who tends to take the 'both–and' position to its greatest lengths does so on the basis of his belief in the ultimate identity of all things, as expressed in the slogan *tat tvam asi*. That is itself a truth-claim that can be questioned. In pure monism there is no room for 'either–or', but (in spite of John A. T. Robinson) one must make up one's mind as to whether or not monism gives a true account of reality.

The view that is exemplified in the Laymen's Report has considerably less credibility than has the Vedanta as a way of dealing with religious pluralism. No doubt there is a natural tendency to judge a religion by the kind of life (personal and social) that it engenders, and there is dominical authority for this. But there are two obvious difficulties. The first is that one has to ask for the source of the criterion by which a certain kind of society is judged to be desirable. The source will be found in one or other of the great religions or ideologies. One has to ask, 'Why should we desire the kind of society that the report looks forward to?' The reader of its pages fifty years after they were written can easily see that its vision of the 'kingdom of God' was remarkably similar to the generally accepted goals of progressive capitalism at that point in history.

The second difficulty is that it is not in the nature of genuine religion to accept a merely instrumental role in relation to social goals. The devout worshipper seeks to give praise and honour to God *because he is God*, not because it is a way of securing a better society. At a later stage I shall have to criticize a type of argument that concentrates exclusively on the question or individual salvation. The Laymen's Report escapes this criticism. But it is also necessary to say that a view which considers only the role of religion in shaping society cannot be finally acceptable.

VI. 'ANONYMOUS CHRISTIANITY'

Another way of dealing with the plurality of religions has been that taken by a number of Roman Catholic scholars, of whom Karl Rahner has been the most influential. He has set out his views in four theses, which may be summarized as follows: (1) Christianity understands itself as the absolute religion, being founded on the unique event of the incarnation of God in Jesus

Christ. But since this event occurred at a certain point in history, we have to ask about God's relationship to people who lived before that event or before that event was brought to their notice. Moreover, this question will not just be about individuals considered without reference to their religious affiliations but about the religions themselves. 'Man, who is commanded to have a religion, is also commanded to seek and accept a social form of religion.' (2) It follows that non-Christian religions, even if they contain error (as they do), are lawful and salvific up to the time at which the gospel is brought to the attention of their adherents. The gospel requires us to assume that God's grace is offered to all, and that 'in a great many cases at least' it is accepted. But after the point at which the gospel has been preached, the non-Christian religion is no longer lawful. (3) The faithful adherent of a non-Christian religion may and must therefore be regarded as an 'anonymous Christian'. He or she can be saved through the faithful practice of the other religion. But the one who accepts the gospel 'has a greater chance of salvation than the anonymous Christian'. (4) The other religions will not be displaced by Christianity. Religious plurality will be a continuing fact, and conflict will become sharper with the passage of time.

This way of dealing with religious pluralism is of course unacceptable to devout non-Christians. Hindus, Buddhists and Muslims are not impressed by the information that they are already Christians without having made a decision to that effect, any more than a Christian is persuaded to the view that he or she is a Hindu on the way towards the truth. But what is to be said from the standpoint of Christian theology about this proposal? At this stage in the discussion perhaps six points may be made.

1. We must surely believe that God, who has revealed himself in Jesus Christ, is indeed gracious to all, that his love is always directed to all that he has made, that in truth every human being exists from moment to moment by God's grace, and that we must expect to find evidence of this fact in all of human life. God, who is the Word, is the light that illumines every human life (John 1:9).

2. We need not, however, and we should not accept Rahner's assertion that it is human religion that is the sphere of God's gracious dealing with all people. This is simply taken for granted in his writing, but it must surely be rejected. There is much in the Gospels to suggest that it is not in religion but in the ordinary human relationships of loyalty, trust and kindness that the light of God is to be discerned. In the final judgement the sheep and the goats are

separated on grounds that have nothing to do with religion (Matt. 25:31 ff.). And in the Fourth Gospel, from which I have just quoted, it is made clear not only that the light of God's truth shines on every human being but also that the light shines in the darkness and that it is among the men and women of religion that the darkness is at its most profound. That God deals graciously with every human soul is something that (in the light of Christ) we must affirm. But that this dealing is primarily or exclusively by way of the person's religion is something that we have good grounds for denying. Here we follow the example of one of the earliest theologians to make use of the thought of the Johannine Prologue in expounding the gospel for a world of religious pluralism. Justin Martyr in his *Apology* claims the great philosophers such as Socrates and Plato as among those who walked in the light of God's Word but condemns the religions of his time as irrational superstitions or as the work of demons.

3. Rahner affirms that religions are necessarily social and that we must therefore trace the salvific work of grace not only in the lives of individual adherents of these religions (a work which some have thought to be in spite of rather than by means of this adherence) but in the religions themselves. The religions as such, he argues, are salvific, or rather are the unwitting bearers of the saving work of Christ. On this we must make both a positive and a negative comment. Positively, we must affirm in the light of Scripture that salvation is a making whole and therefore a corporate affair. It is not only the reconciliation of women and men with God and with one another; it is also the reconciliation of the whole cosmos ('all things, whether on earth or in heaven', Col. 1:20) in Christ. To think of salvation purely in terms of the destiny of the individual soul is therefore to violate the basic meaning of the word. But, having fully accepted that salvation is necessarily social, we have to ask why the social element is to be identified with social organizations of religion. There are other societies that can become bearers of the grace of God – families, guilds and societies of all kinds, schools and universities and, of course, the state which is (according to Paul) a servant of God for our good (Rom. 13:4).

4. The fourth point can be introduced here but must be developed later after other positions are reviewed. It is characteristic of Rahner, as of many other participants in this discussion, that they fix attention almost exclusively on the fate of the individual soul. They ask, 'Can the individual non-Christian be saved?' and answer (in Rahner's case), 'Yes, through faithful

adherence to his or her religion.' At this point in the discussion the individual is abstracted from the whole society and the whole history without which no human life can be understood. Salvation is now treated in terms of an atomic individualism. The biblical vision of the consummation of the whole human and cosmic story has been lost. It would be helpful to refer here to the main concern of the Laymen's Report about the role of the religion in the future development of the human story. With all its defects, to which we have drawn attention, this is an attempt to do justice to the biblical truth that salvation is to be understood in terms of the human story as a whole and can not be rightly conceived in terms of the destiny of each soul considered as a separate individual. Rahner, Hans Küng and others are critical of Protestant theologians who are reluctant to pronounce firm judgements on the fate of individual non-Christians. We shall look at this criticism later. But it is reasonable at least to formulate another question: Ought we to concentrate on the question, 'Can the individual non-Christian be saved?' or on the question, 'Where can we find the revelation of God's nature and purpose which can guide the human race as a whole in its shared journey?' We are obviously touching here very difficult questions about the relation of the individual story to the total human story and about the relation of the kingdom of God to history. At this stage it is enough to point out that Rahner's way of putting the question is not the only possible one.

5. Rahner sees the non-Christian religions as salvific up to, but only up to, the point at which the gospel is presented. Once the reality of God's incarnation in Christ has been clearly presented, no other religion is lawful. Salvation now depends absolutely on acceptance of the gospel. The one who rejects it has rejected salvation. If this is so, it would almost seem better that the missionary should not go, since his or her going precipitates such a terrible crisis. It is indeed true that, according to the Fourth Gospel, the coming of Jesus does precipitate this crisis: 'If I had not come and spoken to them, they would not have sin; but now they have no excuse for their sin' (John 15:22). Does every preaching of the gospel where it has not been preached before precipitate such a crisis? Rahner says that one who has accepted the gospel has, 'other things being equal, a still greater chance of salvation than someone who is merely an anonymous Christian', but the one who has rejected it has no chance at all. How does Rahner reconcile this with Paul's argument in Romans 9–11 that the Jews who have most emphatically rejected the gospel are, nevertheless, destined for salvation? It

seems clear that the picture is more complicated than the one that Rahner has drawn.

6. Finally, and very briefly, if the devout adherents of non-Christian religions are already on the way to salvation as anonymous Christians, it is very hard to see why it is precisely they who are generally most hostile to the preaching of the gospel, while those who profess no religion are often those most open to it. Why is it that the most devout and zealous upholders of the religion of Israel were those who were most determined to destroy Jesus? If, as we have argued, there can be no total discontinuity between non-Christian religion and the gospel, equally there can be no simple continuity. The situation is more paradoxical.

VII. 'THE CHRIST PRINCIPLE'

We may look briefly at two scholars who, while unambiguously affirming the centrality and decisiveness of the Christ-event, also take a generous view of the world's religions but are not preoccupied with the question, 'Can the individual non-Christian be saved?'. Kenneth Cragg has been for many years an outstanding interpreter of Islam to Christians and of the gospel to Muslims. In his recent book *The Christ and the Faiths*, he widens his field of study to include Judaism, Buddhism and Indian religion. He is concerned primarily with the conditions for fruitful coexistence, cooperation and mutual understanding between the great world religions. While clearly affirming the unique responsibility of the church to live by and to bear witness to the saving revelation of God in Jesus Christ, and while delineating sharply the areas of incompatibility between each of the other four religions and Christianity, he is eager also to explore the areas where mutual hospitality is possible, where Christians can accept and acknowledge insights from the other religions and vice versa. Basing his thought on the Gospel incident in which Jesus rebuked his disciples because they had rejected those who healed in Jesus' name but were not part of their company (Luke 9:49–50), Cragg argues that there are many who, outside the church, do the works of Jesus, and that we must believe that they are accepted by him. As a missionary with a lifelong commitment to the task of commending the gospel to Muslims, Cragg has no doubt about the unique and inescapable responsibility of the church to bear witness to Jesus. But he would wish the church so to extend its vision of God's universally gracious work as to include in Christian worship acceptable passages from the scriptures of the world religions.

With regard to this proposal, I think that the question has to be asked whether this does not confuse the issues between the 'Christ-principle' and the 'Christ-event'. If at the heart of the Christian testimony there is the affirmation that God has chosen a certain people and a certain history to be the bearers of the divine purpose and therefore the clue to all human history, it must be asked whether the church's witness will not be radically confused by the substitution of something else than the Old Testament in its liturgy. Will it mean that the story that continues from the Old Testament through the present experience of the church becomes merely the narrative representation of a body of ideas rather than the actual history which is the clue to all history? If it is true that this history is the clue to all history, then it is understandable that there are reflections of it in all the strands that make up the human story as a whole. But these reflections cannot replace the central story. Obviously, to raise this question is not to pass any judgement on the truth value of the religious literature which might be proposed for inclusion in place of the Old Testament in the church's liturgy.

M. M. Thomas of India is, like Kenneth Cragg, clear and unambiguous about the centrality and decisiveness of Jesus and at the same time generous in his approach to the other religions. His major concern in his many writings has been with the problem of maintaining a free and open secular society which can cope with religious plurality and moderate interreligious conflict. He differs from the writers so far considered in that it is fundamental to his position that secular ideologies are included along with religions in his effort to understand the scope of the gospel and the role of the church. He is clear that the ultimate truth is in Jesus Christ. But he is concerned to deal responsibly with the penultimate issues that statesmen have to wrestle with, especially in a vast country like India where the struggle for human community is made more difficult by the rivalry of religions and ideologies. In his most recent book he affirms the central role of the eucharistic community which binds together those totally committed to Christ, but he wants to keep its frontiers open to other communities, both religious and secular, in which the 'Christ-principle' is honoured even though the name of Jesus is not acknowledged. Here, in welcome contrast to the over individualism of much of the literature on religious pluralism, salvation is seen in terms of the healing of the entire human community and not merely in terms of the destiny of the individual soul after death.

The difficulty with the position of M. M. Thomas, attractive as it is, lies (I think) in the relation of the penultimate to the ultimate. It is right to recognize that ultimate religious commitments can negate the proper (if penultimate) concern to secure human unity in a religiously plural society. But the commitment to a society in which all are free to practise their religion and yet are bound together in a common commitment to human values must, in the last resort, rest upon some ultimate belief about human nature and destiny. We have seen in contemporary Western societies how quickly the secular society can become the pagan society in which the ultimate commitment is to a hedonistic and destructive individualism. People of different ultimate commitments can and should cooperate in securing penultimate objectives (such as national unity), but, by definition, the ultimate commitment must govern everything.

VIII. 'BIBLICAL REALISM'

The name that dominated discussion of this topic in Protestant circles for almost a quarter of a century from the Tambaram conference of 1938 was that of Hendrik Kraemer. His famous book *The Christian Message in a Non-Christian World*, written for that conference, was a sustained rebuttal of the theology represented by the Laymen's Report. Kraemer was deeply influenced by, but not uncritical of, the theology of Karl Barth. He followed Barth in refusing to regard the Christian faith as merely one example of the larger phenomenon called 'religion'. It must, of course, be remembered that when Barth made his famous equation 'Religion is unbelief', he was not thinking primarily, if at all, of the world religions, with which he had little direct contact. He was speaking about the religion that he knew all around him and in which he had been nurtured, the religion of Protestant Europe. He was rejecting Schleiermacher's understanding of religion (including Christianity) as essentially an aspect of human experience. He was affirming the gospel as news about a unique action of the sovereign lord God.

Kraemer followed Barth in this, but declined to follow the latter's refusal to discuss the ways in which God works outside the unique revelation in Christ. However, Kraemer was clear that the work of God in human experience outside the direct range of the gospel is to be evaluated in the light of the unique revelation in Christ, not the other way around.

Kraemer used the phrase 'biblical realism' to describe his approach. He insisted that while religion is a very widespread feature of human experience, and while Christianity as it exists in history shares many of the characteristics of a religion, the gospel is the announcement of a unique event, something (to use his favourite phrase) *sui generis*, something that cannot be put in a class along with other events. It cannot be treated as one example of a class of things called 'religion'. That God, the source of all that is, was incarnate in the human being Jesus, suffered, died and rose again, is an event, a fact of history, which is – quite simply – unique. There are, of course, in many cultures myths of dying and rising gods; but in respect of none of these can one speak of a date in history. There is no place in such myths for words like those which affirm that the death of Jesus happened 'under Pontius Pilate'. In this unique event, Kraemer affirmed, God 'opened a way of reconciliation where there was no way before'. This event, therefore, calls for a response from every human being.

The well-nigh universal fact of human religion represents the human seeking for God, and God's grace is certainly at work in this seeking. Kraemer had no desire to deny the universal graciousness of God towards all people. But what was important for him was the fact that the church has been charged with the unique and unsharable responsibility of making known to all peoples the mighty event in which reconciliation is offered to the whole world. Kraemer was a profound and loving student of the religious life of humankind. He gave much time to deep-going dialogue with devout representatives of other faiths. But, with all this, Kraemer insisted in all of his writings that the gospel is the announcement of that one, unique and decisive event in which a holy God has reconciled a sinful world to himself, and that it is the duty of the church to bear witness among all the nations to that event.

The earlier discussions of Kraemer's position centred on the question of continuity or discontinuity between the gospel and the world's religions. Recent discussion has been dominated by the question to which Rahner devotes his main attention – namely, the question of the salvation of the non-Christian. In a recent survey of the whole debate, Gavin D'Costa divides the possible positions into three: 'pluralist' (represented by Hick), 'exclusivist' (represented by Kraemer), and 'inclusivist' (represented by Rahner). In classing Kraemer as exclusivist, D'Costa – like many others before him – assumes that Kraemer regards all who have not accepted the gospel as lost. Kraemer nowhere says this; it is assumed to follow from his affirmation of the uniqueness of the gospel event. It is certainly true that Kraemer refused to recognize any of the world religions as ways of salvation alternative to Christ.

He did not, however, draw the conclusion that all non-Christians are eternally lost. Is this merely a failure of logical rigour? I do not think so. The assumption that this is the only possible conclusion arises (I think) from the fact that the whole discussion is dominated by the question about the salvation of the individual soul. As always, everything depends upon how we formulate the question. If we insist that the Bible must answer our questions in the way we formulate them (whether about the destiny of the soul or about the future of our society), we shall find ourselves faced either with silence or with contradiction. If, on the other hand, we suspend our questions and try to listen to the way in which the Bible puts the issue, I think we may find that we are not shut up to what seem like impossibilities. We must suspend the argument for a moment and try to attend to the way the Bible portrays the human situation.

IX. THE DRAMA OF SALVATION

At the risk of distortion, let me try to suggest in five affirmations the main lines of the biblical picture, the central plot in the drama of salvation.

1. The whole cosmos and the whole human family is the creation of a wise and loving God, held in being from moment to moment by God's overflowing goodness. God's grace is without limit. God's tender mercies are over all God's works. God has never left himself without witness. There is no human being in whose consciousness there is not some trace of God's presence and goodness.

2. There runs through all being a dark mystery, a perversion, an apostasy, which results in the alienation of human being from its source. The depth of this alienation is crucially and decisively exposed in the events that are recorded in the New Testament. In the events of the ministry and death of Jesus it is seen that humankind, even in the highest of its achievements, is at enmity with the source of being. The depth and the horror of this mystery are shown in the fact that those human achievements which reflect the universal goodness of God – the religion and morality, the law and the political order, which claim to represent God's purpose of righteousness – are the weapons turned against the incarnate Lord to destroy him.

3. This apostasy, this rejection of the truth of human being, is carried through in actual historical events at particular times and places. God's dealing with it is also, necessarily, a matter of particular events in history. It is a matter of names, times and places. It is a matter of one people among all the

peoples – Israel. Eventually it is a matter of one human being among all that people – Jesus. It goes, necessarily, by the way of election – of one chosen and called for the sake of the many. It has the necessary particularity which is the stuff of human history. And as the story unfolds, it becomes more and more clear that the purpose of election is fulfilled in the suffering of the elect. One people is called to bear the sin of many. Finally one man dies, the Elect, to bear and bear away the sin of the world.

4. The crucified is raised from the dead. To chosen witnesses (election again!) he reveals himself as the one who has finally overcome the dark power that holds the world in thrall. He sends them out to be his witnesses and tells them that they will be authentic witnesses as they share his conflict. In sending them, 'he showed them his hands and his side' (John 20:20). The victory over sin and death which they are to proclaim and to embody is one that lies on the other side of death and the grave. It is a consummation that will gather into one glorious event both the story of every human soul and the story of all the nations. Living in the world where the power of sin and death is still at work, they will be corporately a sign, because a first fruit, of that consummation. They will not become a new imperial power bringing the world under their control; as the suffering servant of God, they will be the sign of a kingdom which is God's alone and which is to come. They will also be a learning community, not pretending to possess all the truth, but having the promise that, as they bear witness among all the nations, the Spirit will lead them into all the truth.

5. This community is therefore no triumphant company of the saved surrounded by the multitude of the lost. It is the sign and first fruit of God's purpose to save all. Does that eliminate judgement? Are all in the end necessarily saved? There is no such assurance. The New Testament, in many different strands of its teaching, affirms that there is a final judgement, that it is indeed possible to miss the way and to be lost, that God's judgement is a reality which will have to be faced. Three things are clear in the New Testament teaching about this judgement; (a) The judgement will be in accordance with what each one has done. Not those who say 'Lord, Lord', but those who do the will of God will be accepted; (b) the main thrust of the warnings about judgement is directed against those who are confident that they are safe; (c) the one thing that can certainly be said is that there will be surprises. The first will be last and the last first. Those who thought they were safely inside will find that they are

left out, and the outsiders will find to their surprise that they are accepted. The warning is therefore clear: 'Do not pronounce judgement before the time, before the Lord comes' (1 Cor. 4:5). To the very natural question, 'Lord, will those who are saved be few?' Jesus answers with a sharp switch from speculation about other people to the urgent challenge facing the self; 'Strive to enter by the narrow door.'

X. HOPE FOR A DIVINE CONSUMMATION

This very brief reminder of the main lines of the biblical teaching is given simply to put into its right context the question that has dominated recent discussion about religious pluralism. That question has been about the possibility of salvation for the non-Christian. That question has to be put alongside the other one that has played a much smaller role in the discussion, the question, 'What belief holds out hope for the future of the human race?' We have noticed that this question appears in the Laymen's Report and in the work of M. M. Thomas. It is surely an equally legitimate question if one is looking at the matter from a biblical perspective. The centre of attention in the Bible is not the destiny of the human soul considered as an atomic entity; it is the completion of God's whole purpose in a consummation which gathers up the story both of the human soul and of the cosmos. To think only in terms of one or the other of these questions is to be headed for an impasse. Human being cannot be understood except in terms of sharing in a story along with other human beings and in the context of the created world. If everything is subordinated to the question of the destiny of the individual soul, the story of the race and of the cosmos becomes a tale without meaning. But if everything is concentrated on a vision of the future within history, the individual (who will be dead before it is realized) is marginalized. To those who affirm, like Kraemer, the unique and decisive character of the Christ-event, the question is always asked: 'What, then, is the fate of those who lived and died before that event, or before they had the opportunity to know of it?' If one is thinking entirely in terms of the salvation of the individual soul, then the question seems to lead inevitably to an exclusivist position. How, then, does it come about that Paul is sure that Israel, who has emphatically rejected the Christ, will nevertheless be saved (Rom. 11:26)? The answer is that he is not thinking in these terms. Nor, of course, is he thinking in terms of an intrahistorical utopia. He is thinking of an event that is beyond history, an event of which the resurrection of Jesus from the dead is the sign and pledge, an event in the light of which both the long story of Israel and the nations, and also the story of each human soul, will find its meaning.

There is, of course, an immensely strong and ancient religious tradition, most typically represented in the religious life of India, which affirms that the ultimate meaning of life will be found by looking away from the events of history to that inner 'cave of the heart' where the immortal self knows itself to be one with the universal self. From this point of view it is absurd to suggest that an event at one particular time and place could be decisive for salvation. In that case, one will not look to religion for the vision and the motive power to create a just and peaceful human society. One will not expect human history to contain the clues to eternal reality. There is indeed a massive logic and an enduring attraction in this position, and there are many who affirm that this is the real essence of the religious truth.

The Christian gospel is not an answer to the problems of the meaning of human life formulated in either of the two ways we have been looking at. It is the witness of a community to the fact that in specific ways at particular times and places God, the author of all being, has so acted as to break the power that binds us in sin and death and opened for us a path that leads to the glorious consummation of all human and cosmic being. For those who have been called to be part of this community and commissioned to be bearers of this witness, it is simply unthinkable that one should keep silent about it, and unthinkable that one should be willing to allow this witness to be listed as merely an expression in story form of one of the varieties of human religious experience. It must be shared as the clue both to the whole human story and therefore to every person's story. It *can* be told, because every human language contains words that bear witness to the fact that every human being already has – however deeply buried or however gravely distorted – some witness in heart and conscience to the reality of God. If this were not so, the story could not be told. The story invites that radical conversion, that U-turn of the whole being, which is called repentance. It invites belief and a response of grateful obedience. It does not propose a masterful programme of world domination. It does not promise that, within history, the followers of Christ will be the masters and teachers of the human race. It is not an invitation to a theocratic imperialism as the clue to the human story. Nor does it offer to the individual a guarantee of personal salvation apart from continued participation with Jesus in the warfare of the kingdom of God against the powers of evil. There is no private salvation apart from active involvement in the ongoing work of Christ in the world. The apostle who is sure that nothing can separate him from the love of Christ also knows that he must accept the discipline of a Christian soldier, lest having preached to others he himself should be disqualified (Rom. 8:38–39 and 1 Cor. 9:24ff.).

The gospel is not an answer to the question which we put either in terms of personal salvation or in terms of the human future. It is the announcement of a sovereign work of God which sets aside these self-centred questions and directs attention to God and his glory. It invites us to a life of worship and obedience that is wholly directed to God, a life that finds its central direction in the prayer that Jesus taught his disciples: 'Our Father in heaven, your name be hallowed, your kingdom come, your will be done on earth as in heaven.' With its central point of reference in the crucified and risen Jesus, it promises a continuing share in the tribulations which are the experience of those who stand with him at the frontier between the reign of God and the power of Satan. In those tribulations they have his peace. And if it is asked, 'What motive is there for the work of missions if in the end the non-Christian may be saved and the Christian may be lost?' the answer is simple. It is that we want to be where Jesus is, and he himself said on his way to the cross, 'Where I am, there shall my servant be' (John 12:26). As we share with him in his warfare, we share also in the foretaste of his victory.

Here lies the possibility of a kind of life that makes sense both of one's personal story and of the story of the human race. Indeed the one cannot be meaningful except as part of the other. And when it is objected (as repeatedly happens) that to propose one name, the name of a human being who happened to live at a particular time and place and as part of one particular culture, as the name in and through which all human being is to find fulfilment is arrogant imperialism, we must put the counterquestion: 'If not this name, then what other?'. And if the reply is, 'We must give equal honour to many names,' the next question must be: 'Is the human story a unity or not? Are there many conflicting stories? Is there in the end no unifying meaning which makes sense of the human story as a whole? Or are we left finally in a twilight where there is no sure landmark and we must all go our separate ways?'

The gospel of God's free and sovereign grace carries with it the invitation to believe that there is in truth one story, not the story of the triumph of modern civilization with its science and technology (as the Laymen's Report suggested), not the story of religion. It is a real story which looks towards a real ending at which it will all make sense. Because it is the real story, it contains the names of people and places and the dates of crucial events. But that does not entail the exclusion of those who lived without knowledge of it. According to the New Testament, the whole human race from its beginning is involved. The men and women of faith in all ages were looking to Christ. They are not lost. With us they still look forward to his coming in victory, for it was God's purpose that they without us 'should not be made perfect' (Heb. 11:40). Equally we shall not be made perfect without the generations yet to come. It is one story with one goal. While we are on the way, we do not see the end: we walk in the faith that at the end we shall see and understand. But we do not abandon the faith that there is one story and that we have the clue to our journey when we take our bearings from that story which has its centre in Jesus Christ.

XI. AN ECUMENICAL FAITH

The century since the writing of *Lux Mundi* has seen the rise of the ecumenical movement. The fact that the present volume brings together contributions from beyond the Anglican communion is as natural for us in 1988 as it would have been questionable to the original authors in 1888. A way of thinking that is popular today suggests that the time has come to extend the ecumenical movement beyond the confines of the Christian churches to include all the religions. We are often urged to accept this 'wider ecumenism'. Certainly if 'ecumenism' is only a matter of interchurch relations, then it has no right to the name. The *oikoumené* is the whole inhabited earth and embraces all peoples. That is why it is important not to forget that the origins of the modern ecumenical movement were in the missionary enthusiasm which dared to claim the whole world for Christ and dared to use the slogan 'The Evangelisation of the World in This Generation'. It is plain, therefore, that to accept religious pluralism as a principle of action – to propose that theology must henceforth be centred not in Christ but in the general religious experience of the human race – would not be an extension of the ecumenical movement but a reversal of it. A movement of mere theological relativism would never have developed the power that this one has done. This one was born out of a fresh conviction about the absolute supremacy of Jesus Christ. It was born at the missionary frontiers where Christians met those who did not know Christ, at the point where the stark realization of the difference between Christ and no-Christ made all the differences between Christians seem small. The greatness, the finality, the absoluteness of what God had done in Jesus Christ for the salvation of the whole world radically relativized the differences between the Christian confessions of him. The World Council of Churches could not have come into existence and could not have survived without its christological basis. The churches that constitute it, divided as they are in their conceptions of what is essential to the being of the church, could accept common membership only because these differences – great as they are – are displaced from the centre of attention by the absolute claim of Jesus Christ.

To accept religious pluralism would be to reverse this movement. It would be to relativize that which alone has enabled the churches to relativize their own differences – namely, the absolute Lordship of Jesus Christ. One must therefore ask: 'What is the absolute in relation to which Jesus is relativized? Is it "religion" in general?'. If that is the answer, the further question has to be pressed: 'What, in the medley of human religious ideas, is the criterion of truth?'. Or is the absolute the absolute necessity for human unity? Then one has to ask: 'Where is the centre around which the conflicting wills of people and nations are to find reconciliation?' As André Dumas has pointed out, every proposal for human unity that does not point explicitly to the centre around which this unity is to be created has as its hidden centre the beliefs and interests of the one who proposes it. The word 'imperialism' is the word we normally use to describe proposals for human unity that do not originate with ourselves. The Christian church points unambiguously to Jesus Christ as the one whom God has set forth to be the given centre of human unity, the one who 'through the blood of his cross' can reconcile all people and all things. One can, of course, reject this. One can treat this as a mythological way of describing one of the varieties of religious experience and give it a place in a syllabus for the comparative study of religions. But one certainly cannot claim that to do so is to extend the ecumenical movement.

To deny religious pluralism and to affirm the centrality, the decisiveness, the absoluteness of this one name, is to affirm that – in the last analysis – the human story is one story, not a medley of different stories. It is to affirm that we belong together in one history and that this history has a shape, a meaning, a goal. But that affirmation can be made without incurring the accusation of imperialism only because it is made, not in the name of the Christian church, but in the name of the one who reigns from the tree, the one who has made peace by the blood of the cross, the one who alone has broken the power of sin and death and pierced the barrier that divides the time of our human history from the eternity of God in whom is our home.

The 'cash value' of these theological statements is only to be realized in the actual mission of the church as it refuses to be domesticated within any one culture but presses beyond every frontier to the ends of the earth and the end of time. To affirm the centrality of Christ, the cruciality of his incarnation, ministry, death and resurrection for the entire human story, is now an act of faith. Faith will vanish into sight only at the end when he is confessed in every tongue and in the idiom of every culture, when all the nations bring their distinctive treasures into the city where he reigns. The church *in via* does not possess the fullness of the truth (John 16:12ff.). That is why, as the writers of *Lux Mundi* affirmed, there must be development in the church's doctrine. But (as the Johannine text just referred to reminds us) authentic development takes place in a missionary context. Every translation of the gospel into a new language involves necessarily some development. Jesus' promise to lead the church into the fullness of the truth is part of the missionary commission. The church is not led into the fullness of the truth simply by theological reflection. It is led as it allows the Holy Spirit to challenge the world's assumptions about sin and righteousness and judgement as it moves into one human culture after another.

The biblical paradigm for this development is provided (as has often been pointed out) in the story of the conversion of Cornelius and its sequal (Acts 10:1–11:18). That event was not only the conversion of Cornelius – the recruitment of a pagan household into the church. It was also the conversion of the church to a much fuller understanding of its nature and mission. But this was not the result of some kind of synthesis between the religious experiences of Peter and Cornelius. It was not that, by sharing their different religious insights and experiences, they arrived at a fuller apprehension of the truth. It was that, by a sovereign action of the Holy Spirit, two things happened: Cornelius and his household became part of Christ's ongoing mission, and the church was led to a fuller understanding of the nature of that mission. The *occasion* was Peter's faithful word of witness to the gospel (Acts 10:36–43). The active agent was the Holy Spirit leading the church one step along the road to the fullness of the truth, which is not something that happens apart from the gathering of the fullness of the nations. Once again we are reminded that we, the church at any one time and place, cannot be made perfect without them, all the nations. The uniqueness and universality of what God has done in Christ is to find its expression through mission to all the nations. Christ, who is the light of the world ('Lux Mundi'), leads us into the fullness of the truth as we follow him in his mission to all the nations and so learn that he is 'Lumen Gentium', the light whose one glory is to be reflected in the manifold richness of a multicultural world, the world of all the nations. The true pluralism will not look for a plurality of divergent human stories but to the plurality of many different gifts in the one body of him 'in whom all the fullness of God was pleased to dwell' and through whom God is pleased 'to reconcile to himself all things, whether on earth or in heaven, making peace by the blood of his cross' (Col. 1:19–20).

7

HANS KÜNG: Is There One True Religion?
An Essay in Establishing Ecumenical Criteria

Hans Küng (b. 1928), the Swiss Roman Catholic theologian, was, for many years, Professor in the Catholic faculty of theology at Tübingen. Among his best known books are Infallible? An Inquiry *(English trans., London 1971),* On Being a Christian *(English trans., London 1977) and* Does God Exist? *(English trans., London 1980). His licence to teach having been withdrawn by the Vatican in 1979, he became Professor at the Institute for Ecumenical Research in the same University, and has published many books on Christianity and other religions and on global ethics.*

It is easy to insist that no critical ecumenical theology today is thinkable apart from the dimension of the world religions, but this desire is hard to realize. After concentrating in the sixties and seventies on the internal Christian ecumene, while always trying to keep the world religions in view, I myself found I had some radical new learning to do. It is a wearisome job to make oneself knowledgeable about the various religions with their complex history.

To be sure, I became increasingly aware that discussion with the other world religions is actually essential to survival, necessary for the sake of peace in the world. Are not the most fanatical and cruel political struggles coloured, inspired, and legitimized by religion? How much would the affected peoples have been spared, if the religions had been quicker to recognize their responsibility for peace, love of neighbour, and nonviolence, for reconciliation and forgiveness, if they, instead of helping to foment conflicts, had resolved them? Thus any ecumenical theology today has to acknowledge its *share of responsibility for world peace.* There can be no peace without peace between the world religions. And there can be no peace between the world religions without peace between the Christian churches. The Church's ecumene is an integral part of the world ecumene: ecumenism *ad intra,* concentrated on Christendom, and ecumenism *ad extra,* oriented to the whole inhabited earth, are interdependent.

But the confrontation between the world religions goes beyond the issue of peace. It calls decisively for a clarification of the *question of truth.* Much as the material analysis of the various religions, much as comparison of religions can make convergencies and divergencies apparent, the question of the truth must still be raised continually and inexorably. Is there one true religion or are there several? Is there a system of criteria for justifying the claims to truth of the individual religions? What does a critical ecumenical theology say nowadays about the problem of the 'true religion'? The following remarks are aimed at this basic question of interreligious ecumenical dialogue.

No question in the history of the churches and the religions has led to so many disputes, bloody conflicts, and indeed 'wars of religion' as the question of truth. Blind zeal for truth has brought on unrestrained injury, burnings at the stake, destruction, and murder at all times and in all churches and religions. Conversely, fatigued forgetfulness of truth has as its consequence disorientation and anomie, so that many people no longer believe in anything at all. After a history of bloody conflicts the Christian churches have learned to blunt the edge of the dispute over truth and to arrive at common answers in the ecumenical spirit. These answers, of course, should at long, long last be followed by practical consequences. The same pattern has yet to be seen in the relations of Christianity to the other religions. Still, some people ask: Is there any theologically responsible way that allows Christians to accept the truth of the other religions without giving up the truth of their own religion and, with that, their own identity?

I. ONE OR SEVERAL: A PRAGMATIC SOLUTION?

Nevertheless others ask, conversely: Is this still a question at all for us, the descendants of the Enlightenment? Aren't we fighting rearguard actions in intellectual history because we are still afraid of the diffusion of our own identity? Hasn't a pragmatic solution been found long since? 'Of these three religions only one can be the true one,' Sultan Saladin had claimed in

Lessing's famous 'dramatic poem' *Nathan the Wise*, and turning to Nathan, he added, 'A man like you does not remain standing where the accident of birth has flung him: or if he remains, he remains because of discernment, reasons, the choice of what is better' (act 3, scene 5).

But what is discernment based on? What are the reasons for choosing what is better? Lessing's solution is contained, as we all know, in the parable of the three rings: If – and this is the assumption – the theoretical clarification of the question of truth fails, if 'the right ring cannot be proved true', what rule holds then? The answer: only practical experience. Let everyone 'strive ... in accordance with his uncorrupted, unprejudiced love!' That is, let the power of the genuine ring prove itself 'with meekness, with cordial peaceableness, with benefaction, with most heartfelt acquiescence in God', Thus proof comes only through devout humanity in life itself. For our problem this means that every religion is genuine, is true, insofar as it practically and factually gives proof of the 'miraculous power' to make a person welcome 'in the eyes of God and man', Doesn't this point of view, as clear as it is simple, spare us the trouble of posing the fatal question of truth?

In this century it was above all the Americans Charles Sanders Peirce, William James, and John Dewey who proposed a pragmatic solution to the quest for truth. In looking at the truth of religion, pragmatism simply asks how a religion, on the whole, 'works', what practical consequences it has, what its actual value is for the shaping of one's personal existence and life together in society – in history, here and now.

No one could deny that such a concept of the function and utility of religion contains much that is right. In religion don't theory and practice overflow into one another? Doesn't there have to be practical proof of what a religion 'is good for', in keeping with the words of Scripture, 'By their fruits you shall know them'?

The question is only, Can truth be simply equated with practical usability? Can the truth of a religion be reduced to usefulness, helpfulness, and the satisfaction of needs? Can it be sacrificed in case of emergency to tactical necessity, or even surrendered to commercial or political exploitation? And might not a religion that is seldom practiced still be true? Might not a programme that is forever being violated nevertheless make sense? Might not a message that finds little or no faith still be a good one?

In any case we need to reflect here whether there is not a deeper understanding of pragmatism than its utilitarian variety reveals, a pragmatism that is not a mere reduction of religion to practical reality, but its reconnection to the practice of a truly good life. Still in any case the questions arise: By what criteria should such complex phenomena as the major religions be judged? Should we characterize the effects over millennia of Buddhism in Asia or Catholicism in Europe as good or bad? Don't all contemporary religions have their credit and debit sides? And doesn't such a way of looking at things continually seduce the observer into comparing the high ideals of one's own religion with the more lowly reality of the others; for example, comparing real Hinduism or real Islam with ideal Christianity?

Thus the question, 'What is the true religion?' must be returned to those who asked it. Back in the very beginning of his classic treatment of *The Varieties of Religious Experience* (1902) James argued that a usable criterion for judging authentic religion was not only the 'ethical test' but – along with immediate certainty – the 'philosophically demonstrable reasonableness'. But what does 'philosophically demonstrable reasonableness' mean in this context? Evidently, for all one's orientation to praxis there is no getting around the question of truth. In order to prepare a constructive answer here, I would like to undertake in the second part an examination of four basic positions.

II. FOUR BASIC POSITIONS

a) *No religion is true.* Or, *all religions are equally untrue.* I have no intention of repressing the atheistic position here – though with its various critiques of religion it is certainly not my topic. Still it implies a permanent challenge for all religions. Normally, the lamentable condition of any religion itself provides reason enough for suspecting that its teachings and rites are aimed into the void, that religion is nothing but projection, illusion, empty promises; in short, that there is nothing to the truth of this religion, indeed to the truth of all religion ...

Now I cannot and do not wish to prove that religion is actually aimed at a reality, indeed the first-and-last, realest reality. But for their part the atheistic opponents of religion have no proof that religion is simply a venture into nothingness. Like God, this nothingness is nowhere to be found. Pure, theoretical reason, bound up as it is with this world, cannot reach far enough to answer this question. On that point Kant was right once and for all. Putting it positively, in the famous, crucial question of the truth of religion, we are dealing with no more and no less than the *great question of trust* of our life: in the face of all the obvious absurdity of this world to say *Yes* nevertheless, in a tested, illusion-free, realistic act of trust, Yes to the primal Ground, Mainstay, and Meaning of the world and humanity that is accepted in the major religions. This is a thoroughly rational Yes, insofar as it has to show for itself, if not strict proofs, at least good reasons.

Anyone who says *No* will have to take responsibility for that in the eyes of history. It is the primal, ancient religious history of humanity, which can be traced back at least as far as the burial rites of Neanderthal man, that the arguments of atheism (which are closely connected to specifically Western culture and intellectual history – Nietzsche's 'God is dead' presupposes 2,500 years of Western metaphysics) greatly relativize. It makes no difference whether one considers the human race (diachronically) in its many thousand years of history or (synchronically) in its global extension: One will never find a tribe that lacked faith in some sort of transcendence. From the global perspective, atheism among the masses is a typically Western 'achievement', even though it has spread to the East. It is thus the affair of a cultural minority in this century.

b) *Only one single religion is true.* Or, *all other religions are untrue.* The *traditional Catholic position* – prepared in the early Christian centuries by Origen, Cyprian, and Augustine, and defined as far back as the Fourth Lateran Council (1215) – is widely known: *'Extra Ecclesiam nulla salus!'* Outside the Church there is no salvation. Fifty years before the discovery of America the ecumenical council of Florence (1442) unequivocally stated, 'The holy Roman Church ... firmly believes, confesses, and proclaims that no one outside the Catholic Church, neither heathen nor Jew nor unbeliever nor schismatic will have a share in eternal life, but rather is condemned to the eternal fire prepared for the devil and his angels, unless he joins it [the Catholic Church] before his death.' Doesn't that settle once and for all the claim of the other religions to truth and salvation? That is how it was, it seemed, at least from the fifth to the sixteenth centuries.

As early as the age of the discovery of new continents Catholic theology tried to come to a *new understanding* of that uncompromising 'Outside the Church' doctrine, which meant for the most part to reinterpret it and, finally, to turn it inside out. It was never openly corrected because it was 'infallible'. Of course, as early as the Council of Trent theologians like Bellarmine and Suárez recognized an unconscious 'longing' (*desiderium*) for baptism and the

Church as sufficient for salvation. And in the seventeenth century Rome condemned the principle cited by the rigorous French Jansenists, *'Extra Ecclesiam nulla gratia'* (Outside of the Church there is no grace). In 1952 the Roman 'Holy Office' (Congregation of the Faith) felt itself obliged, paradoxically enough, to excommunicate a campus chaplain, Fr Leonard Feeney, who with the old Church Fathers and the Council of Florence asserted that all people outside the visible Catholic Church were damned. Once again without making any formal correction the Second Vatican Council finally declared, invoking God's all-embracing salvific will and plan of salvation in its Constitution on the Church (1964): 'Those individuals, who for no fault of their own do not know the Gospel of Christ and his Church, yet still search for God with an upright heart and try to fulfil his will, as recognized in the commands of conscience, in deeds prompted by the working of his grace, can attain eternal salvation' (article 16). And in the Declaration on the Non-Christian Religions the appreciative description of the other religions culminates in the sentence, 'The Catholic religion rejects nothing of all that which is true and holy in these religions' (article 2).

This means, the traditional Catholic position is today no longer the official Catholic position. Even the non-Christian religions can be – since people are, after all, bound to the historical and socially constructed forms of religion – ways to salvation. Perhaps not normal, 'orderly' ways, but nonetheless perhaps historically 'extraordinary' ways. As a matter of fact contemporary Catholic theology distinguishes, thanks to this about-face, between the Christian way of salvation – the 'ordinary' way – and the non-Christian way of salvation – the 'extraordinary' way (sometimes, too, between 'the way' and the various 'paths').

However one may judge this theological solution and terminology, the important thing is that for the first time in its history the Catholic Church has formally expressed itself *against* a narrow-minded, arrogant *absolutism*, which posits its own truth 'absolutely'; that is, 'loosed from' the truth of the others. It has backed off the standpoint of exclusivity that condemns the non-Christian religions and their truth *en bloc* and opens the door wide to every kind of apologetics, inability to learn, and dogged insistence on being in the right. It has moved away from the dogmatism that fancies it has the whole truth a priori in its possession, and holds out for the other positions only condemnations or demands for conversion. No, contempt for other religions is now to be followed by respect for them, neglect is to give way to understanding, proselytizing by study and dialogue.

Thus the Catholic Church took a step as much as twenty years ago that many *Protestant theologians* still hesitate to take today. Still on the path laid out by the younger Barth and dialectical theology – and often without careful knowledge and analysis of the world religions – they can only go about dogmatically with that Protestant claim to truth: by which 'religion' is nothing but 'natural theology' and so a 'power trip', a sinful revolt against God, unbelief pure and simple. For its part, they say, Christianity is no religion at all, because the Gospel is the end of all religion. I think that, to my taste, such 'dialectical theology' would have to be more dialectical.

No, the world religions must neither be dogmatically condemned nor, as other theologians have done, simply ignored. A noble-minded *Ignoramus* ('we don't know') is all the *more* irresponsible. And if Protestant theology has no answer to the question of the salvation of the majority of the human race, then has it any reason to wonder that people today, as Voltaire in his time, pour out their scorn at the presumptuousness of the 'one holy Church' or content themselves with enlightened indifferentism? That is why the ambivalent attitude of the World Council of Churches is completely unsatisfactory: Neither in its 'Guidelines for Dialogue with Individuals of Different Religions and Ideologies' (1977/1979) nor at the latest plenary assembly in Vancouver (1983) did it ever manage to answer the question about salvation outside the Christian churches. Conflicting viewpoints on the part of the member churches prevented it.

There is no missing the fact that nowadays the problem is being posed more intensely. After the discovery of the giant continents outside of Europe the world religions were first and foremost an external, *quantitative* challenge for Christendom. But they have now become an internal, *qualitative* challenge not just for some enlightened spirits but for the Christian churches themselves. It is no longer just the fate of the world religions that stands in doubt as it did in the 'Christian' colonialist epoch. The fate of Christianity itself is at stake in an epoch of postcolonialism and postimperialism.

And the question now is, If Christian kerygmatics today, unlike the earlier kind, has come to see the riches, instead of the poverty, of the world religions, what does *it* have to offer? If Christian theology recognizes manifest light everywhere, to what extent will it bring 'the Light'? If all religions contain light, why should Christianity in particular be *the* truth? If salvation can already be found outside the Church and Christianity, why should there be a Church and Christianity at all? A simple answer to this question is provided by the third position:

c) *Every religion is true.* Or, *all religions are equally true.* Anyone who really knows the world religions will hardly claim that they are all alike. That would be to flatten the key differences between the basic types of mystical and prophetic religion, and to suppress all the contradictions between the individual religions. It would be to overlook the fact, as Wilfred Cantwell Smith in particular has stressed, that even individual religions do not simply remain the same in the course of history, but develop and become more complex – often astonishingly so.

But don't we have to distinguish *objective* religion (the often contradictory myths and symbols, doctrines, rites, and institutions found in the various religions) from *subjective* religion, piety, the fundamental religious experience of the Universal One and Absolute, which we meet at the primal roots of every religion? Still, recourse to a fundamental religious (mystical) experience, supposedly everywhere the same, does not solve the question of truth. Why? Because religious experience never comes in isolation. Religious experience is a priori interpreted experience, and for that reason it is stamped by the religious tradition in question and by its different expressive forms.

But there is even more to it than this. Anyone who claims that all religions are in principle equally true, is excluding from the domain of religion – of all things – the human capacity for error and moral mistakes. But why shouldn't the old saying that 'To err is human' also hold for religion? Is there a religion that has not been poured into the mould of human forms? Could it be that all religious statements, all myths and symbols, all revelations and professions of faith, and finally all rites and customs, authorities and phenomena in Hinduism, Buddhism, Islam, Judaism and Christianity are true and valid in the same way, are equally valid in the full sense? No, the reality of the person having an experience in no way guarantees the reality of what he or she experiences. There is a difference between religious and pseudoreligious experiences, and we cannot place magic or the belief in witches, alchemy or native belief in miracles and all sorts of foolishness on the same level as belief in the existence of God (or the reality of Brahman), in salvation and redemption. There can be no talk about 'religious experiences' being equally true.

Just as everything isn't simply the same, neither is everything simply equal – not even in one's own religion. 'Anything goes', 'Everything is possible' just cannot silence the basic questions of human life about *truth* or ultimate reliability and commitment. Or could it be that in the religious sphere everything is legitimate because it does happen ('the power of the factual') and may possibly come along in picturesque garb (religion dressed as folklore)? If it is the 'truth' and only the truth that, according to the Gospel of John, 'makes us free', we have to push our questioning further.

Along with exclusivist absolutism we must also avoid the crippling *relativism* that makes all values and standards a matter of equal indifference. That also holds, by the way, for Lessing. For the discretionary pluralism that was slowly emerging in his time, but is now modern and intellectually popular, the pluralism that approves without making distinctions between one's own and other religions, has no more right to invoke Lessing than the indifferentism for which all religious positions and decisions are the same and spares itself the trouble of 'discerning the spirits'.

d) *Only one religion is true,* Or, *all religions have a share in the truth of the one religion.* If the standpoint of exclusivism, which recognizes no truth outside its own, is just as unacceptable as the relativism that relativizes all truth and makes all values and standards a matter of equal indifference, that approves and upholds one's own and the other religions without making any distinctions, it would seem that the standpoint of generous, tolerant *inclusivism* is the real solution.

We meet this approach above all in *religions of Indian origin*. All empirical religions represent only different levels, partial aspects of the inherent, universal truth. The other religions are not untrue, just provisional. They have a share in the universal truth. By invoking mystical experience one can claim such a 'higher kind of knowledge' for one's own religion. The result is that every other religion is de facto reduced to a lower or partial knowledge of the truth, while one's own religion is elevated to a supersystem. Every other religion is integrated into one's own as a preliminary stage or partial truth. Any special, peculiar claim it might have is denied. What looks like tolerance proves in practice to be a kind of conquest by embracing, a cooptation by admission of validity, an integration through relativization and loss of identity.

A variety of this inclusivism can be found – paradoxical as that may sound – *in Christianity too*. Karl Rahner's theory of the 'anonymous Christian' is in the final analysis still dependent on a (Christian) *standpoint of superiority* that sets up one's own religion as the a priori true one. For, according to Rahner's theory, which attempts to solve the dilemma of the 'Outside the Church' dogma, all the Jews, Hindus, Muslims and Buddhists are saved not because they are Jews, Muslims, Hindus and Buddhists, but because in the final analysis they are Christians, 'anonymous Christians', to be precise. The embrace here is no less subtle than in Hinduism. The will of those who are after all not Christians and do not want to be Christians, is not respected but interpreted in accordance with the Christian theologian's interests. But around the world one will never find a serious Jew or Muslim, Hindu or Buddhist, who does not feel the arrogance of the claim that he or she is 'anonymous' and, what is more, an 'anonymous Christian'. Quite apart from the utterly perverse use of the word 'anonymous' – as if all these people did not know what they themselves were – this sort of speculative pocketing of one's conversation partner brings dialogue to an end before it has even got under way. We must not forget that followers of other religions are to be respected as such, and not to be subsumed in a Christian theology.

What, then, is required of a Christian's fundamental attitude toward the world religions?

- Instead of indifferentism, for which everything is all the same, somewhat more *indifference* toward supposed orthodoxy, which makes itself the measure of the salvation or perdition of mankind, and wants to enforce its claim to truth with the tools of power and compulsion;
- instead of relativism, for which there is no absolute, more sense of *relativity* toward all human establishing of absolutes, which hinder productive co-existence between the different religions, and more sense of *relationship*, which lets every religion appear in the fabric of its interconnections;
- instead of syncretism, where everything possible and impossible is mixed and fused together, more will to achieve a *synthesis* in the face of all denominational and religious antagonisms, which are still exacting a daily price in blood and tears, so that *peace* may reign between religions, instead of war, hatred and strife.

Given all the religiously motivated intolerance, one cannot stop demanding tolerance and religious freedom. But at the same time too there must be no betrayal of freedom for the sake of the truth. The *question of truth* must not be trivialized and sacrificed to the utopia of future world unity and the religion of world unity. As a threat to cultural and religious identity, a religion of world unity would be feared in the Third World, where the history of colonization, and the history of the missions that is part and parcel of it, are still by no means forgotten. On the contrary, as Christians we are challenged to *rethink* the question of truth in the spirit of a freedom rooted in Christianity. For, unlike arbitrariness, freedom is not just freedom *from* all ties and obligations, something purely negative. It is at the same time positive: freedom *for* new *responsibility* – toward our fellow men and women, toward ourselves, toward the Absolute. True freedom, therefore, is freedom for the truth.

III. THE KNOTTY QUESTION OF A CRITERION FOR TRUTH

We could go on with long and complicated discussions on the question of what truth is, and take a position on the various contemporary theories of truth (the theory of correspondence, reflection, consensus, coherence, etc.) But the question of the true religion must remain firmly planted in the foreground. The following initial thesis will serve as a presupposition for everything I shall now have to say about the possible *untruth* in religion: Christians have no *monopoly on the truth*, although they also do not have the right to renounce *their profession of faith in truth* by adopting some sort of discretionary pluralism. Dialogue and witness are not mutually exclusive. Confessing the truth includes the courage to sight untruth and speak up about it.

It would, of course, be a crude prejudice to identify the boundary between truth and untruth in advance with the boundary between one's own and whatever other religion. If we stay sober about this, we shall have to grant that the *boundaries* between *truth and untruth* also pass *through one's own religion.* How often are we not right and wrong at the same time. That is why criticism of another position can be justified only on the basis of vigorous self-criticism. Only then can an integration of the values of others be justified as well. This means that *in religion, too, not everything is equally true and good.* There are also things that are untrue and not good in teachings on faith and morals, in religious rites and customs, institutions and authorities. Needless to say, this also holds for Christianity.

With good reason *criticism by the world religions of Christianity* is clear and pointed. Christians have too little awareness of how often, despite its ethic of love and peace, Christianity, in its actual appearance and activity, strikes the adherents of other religions as exclusive, intolerant and aggressive;

- it strikes other religions not as integral, but – because of its other-world-liness and hostility to the body and secular life – as internally torn;

- it strikes them as almost morbidly exaggerating the consciousness of sin and guilt of human beings, who are supposedly depraved at the core, in order to bring their need for redemption and dependence on grace all the more effectively into play;
- it strikes them as, besides, using its Christology to falsify the figure of Jesus – seen in the other religions almost universally in a positive light – by making him exclusively divine (the Son of God).

Whatever is valid in this criticism, one thing is clear: The question of the truth of any religion aims at more than pure theory. The nature of truth is never established only in systems of true statements about God, man and the world, never only in a series of propositional truths, as opposed to which all others are false. Truth is always at the same time also a *praxis*, a way of experience, enlightenment and proven worth, as well as of illumination, redemption and liberation. If, accordingly, religion promises an ultimate, all-encompassing sense for our living and dying, if it proclaims supreme, indestructible values, sets up unconditionally binding standards for our acting and suffering and provides a spiritual home, then this means: The dimensions of the *True (verum)* and the *Good (bonum)*, of the meaningful and the valuable, overflow into one another in religion; and the question of the truth (understood more theoretically) or meaningfulness of religion is at the same time the question of its goodness (understood more practically) or valuableness. A 'true' Christian or Buddhist is the 'good' Christian or Buddhist. To that extent the question 'What is true and what is false religion?' is identical with the other, 'What is good and what is bad religion?'

The basic question, then, about the true religion has to be framed differently: How are we to manage to distinguish between true and false, valuable and valueless, in the religions themselves? Here we may think not only of the Hindu caste system, the Shaktist form of Tantric Buddhism with its dubious sexual practices, of the 'holy wars' and cruel forms of punishment in Islam, we must also recall phenomena in Christianity such as the Crusades, the burning of witches, the Inquisition, and persecution of the Jews. Thus we can easily see how thorny and difficult the question of the *criteria for the truth* is, if they are not to arise simply from subjective whim or to be sticks for hitting other people over the head with.

Of course – and this is a point we shall have to return to – no religion can entirely dispense with applying its *quite specific* (Christian, Jewish, Islamic,

Hindu, Buddhist, etc.) *criteria of truth* to the other religions. But in each religion believers should realize that these criteria can be relevant, in the first instance, only for themselves; they cannot be relevant, much less obligatory, for the others. For if the others, whoever they may be, should likewise insist on their own criteria for truth, the prospects for genuine dialogue automatically disappear. Thus, for example, the Bible can fulfil its criteriological and liberating function only in discussions between the Christian churches, or at most in discussions between Christians and Jews. But in conversation with Muslims and still more with Hindus and Buddhists a direct appeal to the Bible as a criterion of truth would be out of place. What is the alternative then, if in religious dialogue Christians may no longer simply call upon the Bible (or Muslims upon the Qur'an, or Hindus on the Gita, or Buddhists upon the Sutras) as the irrefutable authority, so as to be in the right, in the truth vis-à-vis the others? In all caution let me *attempt* another approach and offer it for discussion. We shall go through a sort of inward spiral, in three stages of argument: from the ethical in general to the religious in general and only from there to Christianity in particular.

IV. THE HUMAN ELEMENT: GENERAL ETHICAL CRITERION

When we compare our religion with the other, but also when we reflect upon the misuse of our own religion, the question arises for all religions of the criteria for the true and the good: of *general* criteria, which can be applied analogously to all religions. This is important, it seems to me, not least of all for questions of international law. Neither the descriptive discipline of religious studies (which has little interest in normative criteria, but itself presupposes definite notions – often without scrutinizing them – of humanity, nature, history, the divine – for instance, tacitly preferring the 'mystical'), nor Christian theology (which hitherto has scarcely made serious comparisons of itself with other religions and has for the most part evaded this difficult problem) has done the required criteriological work. But it is precisely this lack of theory that challenges one to offer a suggested solution – no more than that.

The inevitable starting question here must be, Can all means be sanctified by religious ends? Thus, in the service of religious devotion is everything allowed – including the misuse of economic power, of sexuality, or aggressiveness? May something be a *religious commandment* that evidently harms, injures, perhaps even destroys human beings? There are examples in abundance in every religion: Can human sacrifices be justified because they are offered to a god? May children be slaughtered for reasons of faith, may widows be burned, heretics tortured to death? Does prostitution become divine worship because it takes place in a temple? Can prayer *and* adultery, ascesis *and* sexual promiscuity, fasting *and* drug consumption be justified in the same way, if they serve as means and paths to 'mystical experience'? Are charlatanism and bogus miracles, every possible kind of lying and deception allowed, because they are done for a supposedly 'holy' purpose? Is magic, which aims to compel the deity, the same as religion, which implores the deity? Are imperialism, racism, or male chauvinism to be affirmed where they appear with religious underpinnings? Can one even have nothing to object against a mass suicide like the one in Guyana because it was religiously motivated? I would say no.

Institutionalized religion – whichever one – is not a priori 'moral' in each and every thing; and some collectively ingrained mores need scrutiny too. That is why, along with the specific criteria, which every religion has for itself, the *general ethical criteria* need to be discussed more than ever today. In this context we cannot, of course, get into the increasingly more complex hermeneutical questions regarding the basic forms of contemporary ethical reasoning (empirical, analytical, or transcendental-anthropological argumentation) and the validation of norms. An orientation to the human element, to what is truly human, means in any case – let me say this to avoid misunderstandings beforehand – no reduction of the religious to the 'merely human'.

Religion has always shown itself to be most convincing where it succeeded (long before all modern strivings for autonomy) effectively to bring out the human element against the background of the Absolute. One need mention only the Decalogue, the Sermon on the Mount, the Qur'an, the sermons of the Buddha and the Bhagavadgita.

On the whole, of course, Christianity itself, which so long resisted freedom of religion and conscience, profited from the fact that humanism (though certainly often secularized and hostile to the Church) separated itself out from the Christian faith, criticizing religion and spreading its sphere of influence through the modern process of emancipation. This humanism called upon the (often rather unchristian) churches in a new way to translate into reality what were basically primal Christian values, such as freedom, equality, fraternity and 'human dignity'. For it was precisely by being religiously and ecclesiastically emancipated in modern autonomy that *the human element* could once again find a home in the domain of Christianity – before all other religions.

Conversely, Christianity, religion as a whole, can – particularly in a time of disorientation, the atrophy of human ties, a widespread permissiveness and a diffuse cynicism – establish for the conscience of the individual (more so than all psychology, pedagogy and even positive legislation) why morality is more than a question of personal taste and judgement or social convention: why morality, ethical values and norms oblige us *unconditionally* and so *universally*. In fact, only the Unconditioned itself can oblige unconditionally, only the Absolute can bind absolutely, only religion can unconditionally and universally create and at the same time concretize an ethic, as it has indeed been doing for thousands of years, sometimes badly, sometimes well.

In any case, there is no mistaking the fact that in the question about the human element in other religions as well a process of reflection has been set in motion. Thus, the question of *human rights*, for instance, is being intensively discussed in Islam, especially since it has become increasingly clear that the *sharī'a*, Muslim law, often flagrantly contradicts the General Declaration of Human Rights of the United Nations (1948). This is particularly the case with respect to legal equality for women (laws on marriage, divorce, inheritance and work) and for non-Muslims (prohibited from certain professions, etc.), all of which naturally implies probing questions directed at the Qur'an itself. There are grounds for hope that in the question of human rights and general *ethical criteria* – despite all the difficulties – an elementary basic consensus on the 'key premises of human life and fellowship' (W. Korff) might take shape, with time, between the world religions, a consensus equal to the demands of a modern, humane consciousness. These are *guiding convictions* of key human values and key demands that certainly first forced themselves upon human consciousness in the course of historical evolution, but then – exactly like the Copernican world picture – achieve lasting, irreversible, unconditional validation, indeed often get codified into law (as 'human rights' or 'basic rights'), even though they continually need to be given fresh shapes.

In any case we cannot miss the progress that has been made toward more humanity within the various religions – for all the time gaps in awareness. One thinks, for example, of the abolition by Roman Catholicism of the practises of the Inquisition – the stake and the rack – which were customary well into modern times; or of the humane reinterpretation of the doctrine of the 'holy war' and reforms in the penal code in the more progressive Islamic countries; or of the abolition of human sacrifice and suttee, which, although they had been rejected from the first by Indian Buddhists and Christians, were practised in isolated regions of India up until the English occupation. Numerous examples from the Far, Middle, and Near East have convinced me that in the future a strongly growing awareness with respect to human rights that need safeguarding, the emancipation of women, the realization of social justice and the immorality of war is likely to be observed in all the world religions. The worldwide religious movement on behalf of peace has, in particular, made strong progress. All these religious motivations and movements – something we have become conscious of not least of all in connection with Poland, Iran and Afghanistan – point to the presence of a political-social factor that must be taken very seriously. Hence my question: Should it not be possible, *invoking our common humanity*, to formulate a general ethical *criterion* that is based on the *human, the truly human element*, concretely on human dignity and the *basic values* related to it?

A new *reflection on the human* is at work in the world religions. A particularly clear example of this is the declaration of the 'World Conference of Religions for Peace', held in Kyoto, Japan, in the year 1970: 'When we were together to deal with the overriding theme of peace, we discovered that the things which unite us are more important than the things which separate us. We found that we have in common:

- a conviction of the fundamental unity of the human family, of the equality and dignity of all men and women;
- a feeling for the sacrosanctness of the individual and his conscience;
- a feeling for the value of the human community;
- a realization that might is not the same as right, that human power cannot be self-sufficient and is not absolute;
- the faith that love, sympathy, selflessness and the power of the mind and inner truthfulness have, in the end, greater power than hatred, hostility and self-interest;
- a feeling of obligation to stand on the side of the poor and oppressed against the rich and the oppressors;
- deep hope in the ultimate victory of good will.'

The basic question in our search for criteria thus reads: What is *good* for the individual? The answer: What truly helps him or her to be a human being. Accordingly, the basic ethical norm is: Man should live in a human, not an inhuman, fashion; he should realize his humanness in all his relationships. The moral good is what allows human life in its individual and social dimension to succeed and prosper in the long run, what makes possible the optimal development of the person in all his layers and dimensions. Accordingly, human beings should realize this humanity in all its strata (including that of the instincts and emotions) and dimensions (including their connection to society and nature) as individuals and as a community. But that means at the same time that humanness would fail at its core, if the dimension of the 'trans-human', the unconditioned, all-embracing, Absolute were denied or faded out. Humanness without this dimension would be a mere torso.

According to the basic norm of genuine humanity, *good* and *evil*, true and false, can be distinguished. We can also distinguish what is basically good and evil, what is true and what is false in *any individual religion*. This criterion might be formulated with regard to religion as follows:

a) *Positive criterion*: Insofar as a religion *serves* the virtue of humanity, insofar as its teachings on faith and morals, its rites and institutions *support* human beings in their human identity, and allows them to gain a meaningful and fruitful existence, it is a *true* and *good* religion.

In other words:

Whatever manifestly protects, heals, and fulfils human beings in their physical and psychic, individual and social humanness (life, integrity, justice, peace), what, in other words, is humane and truly human, can with reason invoke 'the divine'.

b) *Negative criterion*: Insofar as a religion *spreads inhumanity*, insofar as its teachings on faith and morals, its rites and institutions *hinder* human beings in their human identity, meaningfulness, and valuableness, insofar as it *helps to make them fail to achieve* a meaningful and fruitful existence, it is a *false* and *bad* religion.

In other words:

Whatever manifestly oppresses, injures and destroys human beings in their physical and psychic, individual and social humanness (life, integrity, freedom, justice, peace), what, in other words, is inhumane, not truly human, cannot with reason invoke 'the divine'.

For all the doubtful individual cases, there is no lack of manifest examples – as I merely hinted at before – of good *and* evil, true *and* untrue in the previous history of either Hinduism or Buddhism, Judaism, Christianity or Islam. Wherever religion is the force that lowers the dignity of the individual or of a race, class, caste or sex, wherever individual persons or whole groups are exposed to physical, psychic, or mental injury or even destruction, then we are dealing with a false and bad religion. We must consider here that it is precisely in the realm of religion that my self-realization and the self-realization of others, along with our common responsibility for society, nature and the cosmos, are inseparably joined.

Hence all religions must take thought anew for the demands of human nature: This element of the human that has been given to all men and women is a general ethical criterion that holds for every single religion. But the religions must continually remember – and here we go on our spiral inward – their *primal, peculiar 'essence'*, as it shines forth in their origins, in their normative scriptures and normative figures. And they will continually be reminded by their critics and reformers and prophets, by their wise men and women, wherever it is a religion is being untrue to or violating its 'essence': the original 'essence' peculiar to every religion, its normative origin or canon (its 'standard'), is a general criterion for religion by which each can be measured.

IV. THE AUTHENTIC OR CANONICAL: GENERAL RELIGIOUS CRITERION

Given religious attitudes and developments that have gone wrong, given religious decadence and deficiencies in its own back yard Christian theology in particular has always brought the *criterion* of the origins or canon into play. This is not because the older is necessarily the better. The old is no better a priori than the new. But because the *original* or *canonical* from the beginning was the normative factor: primitive Christianity, the primal testimony of the Bible; Christ the author and original of Christian faith. Christians measure themselves against their origins, but they are often so measured by non-Christians: 'You invoke the Bible and Christ – and you act like this?!' The Bible, particularly the New Testament, serves Christianity as a *canon*, as a normative standard.

And isn't the Torah the normative factor for Jews, as the Qur'an and the figure of Muhammad (as the embodiment of the Islamic way) is for

Muslims, and the teaching (*dharma*) and figure of the Buddha is for Buddhists?

But what does it mean, then, in the search for criteria, when, for example, Shaktist Tantrism (for all its striving after salvation) still contradicts, in some essential features, the monastic life that the Buddha said should be aimed at? What about its consumption of alcohol and its sexual practices? To what extent is this Tantrism still (or was it ever) Buddhist? At this point internal Buddhist criticism sets to work: The great majority of Buddhists would likely agree with Christians that sexuality certainly has its own value and place, but precisely for that reason it does not belong in the practice of meditation or worship, especially not in a cultic practice where partners are inter-changeable, where religion can no longer be distinguished from sexuality nor sexuality from religion, and the door is flung wide open to a promiscuous misuse of both.

With the criterion of the authentic (original) or canonical (normative), therefore, we have not just a Christian criterion, but a *general religious criterion*, which is applicable, at least in principle, to other religions as well: a religion is measured here by its *normative doctrine or practice* (Torah, New Testament, Qur'an, Vedas) and sometimes too by its normative *figure* (Christ, Muhammad, the Buddha). This criterion of 'authenticity' or 'canonicity' thus can be applied not just to Christianity, but to all the major religions – *mutatis mutandis,* of course: modified according to each religion, a process that is easier with some religions (Hinduism, say) than with others. It seems to me that this religious criterion, in a time of great social change and rapidly progressing secularization, offers heightened meaning for the basic orien-tation of the non-Christian religions too. What is 'essential', what is 'permanent', what is 'obligatory', and what is not? The religion's identity is at stake. People in religion are in agreement that the primal religious legacy should not be sold at bargain rates to the modern world; rather, it should be made to bear fruit once more in that world. And so reflection on the original (authentic) or normative (canonical) has given unusually strong impulses to reform movements (which keep breaking out in all great religions): religious re-formation as thinking one's way back to the original form *and* at the same time re-novation as renewal for the future.

How often has it not been until the criterion of authenticity or canonicity was applied that the *primal and peculiar features* of a religion could be clearly seen.

This convincingly answers the question of what – in theory and practice – true Christianity is and is not, and the same for true Judaism, true Islam, Buddhism, and finally even true Hinduism. To be sure, this feedback from the origin or canon – event, person, or scripture – has a quite different meaning in the historically oriented religions, but it is also by no means unknown in the mystically oriented religions.

To give only a brief hint:

1. *True Hindu religion* is in principle only the religion that is based on the revealed scriptures of the Vedic seers. As dissimilar as the religions and their gods, especially in India, can be, and as great as the tolerance of the Hindus is too, because Buddhism (like Jainism) rejects the Vedas it cannot be the true religion for Hindus. And *it* is rejected (as, still more, Indian Islam is rejected). A similar statement could be made about the canon of the monotheistic religions of India such as Vishnuism or Shivaism.

2. *True Buddhism* can only be the religion that takes its refuge in the Buddha, who set the 'wheel of teaching' in motion, and in the 'teaching', the 'dharma', and thus in the 'community', the 'sangha'. As great as the differences may be between Theravāda Buddhism and Mahāyāna Buddhism, and as numerous as the different Buddhist 'sects' may be, religions that reject the Buddha, the *dharma* and the *sangha* (the community of monks) are not accepted as the true way.

3. *True Islam*, finally, is only the religion that can be based on the Qur'an revealed to Muhammad. As momentous for religion and politics as the differences, say, between Shiites and Sunnites were and are, both lean on the Qur'an, for whom it is God's word. Whoever departs from it, stands outside the true religion and falls victim to 'excommunication'. Similar things can be said – despite all its dogmatic tolerance and the different interpretations of the Law – about *Judaism*.

4. Far more unequivocably than with the mystical Asian religions, obviously, we can with the historical religions, particularly *Christianity*, answer the question of what true religion is in terms of their *origin*. And with that – we are going on the inward spiral for a second time – the general religious criterion of truth has been concretized in a *specifically Christian* criterion of truth, to which there may be a corresponding specifically Jewish, Islamic, Hindu or Buddhist criterion.

VI. ON THE SPECIFICALLY CHRISTIAN CRITERION

What have we achieved so far? According to the *general ethical criterion* a religion is true and good to the extant that it is *humane*, does not oppress and destroy humanity, but protects and advances it.

According to the *general religious criterion* a religion is true and good if and insofar as it remains true to its own *origin* or *canon*: its authentic 'essence', its normative scripture or figure, which it continually invokes.

According to the *specifically Christian criterion* a religion is true and good if and insofar as it allows us to perceive the spirit of Jesus Christ in its theory and practice. I apply this theory *directly* only to Christianity, in posing the self-critical question whether and to what degree the Christian religion is at all Christian. *Indirectly* – and without arrogance – the same criterion can certainly also be applied to the other religions: for critical clarification of the question whether and to what degree one also finds in other religions (especially Judaism and Islam) something that we would label as Christian.

If we wish to come to a solution concerning the central question of the true religion, we absolutely must *distinguish between an inner and an outer perspective*. One can see Christianity, like every other religion, entirely *from the outside*, as a 'neutral observer', as a student of religion, as a non-Christian or an ex-Christian – without any special obligation to the Christian message, tradition, or community. Christianity then fits into its place among the world religions and must satisfy the general ethical and religious criteria for truth. In this perspective there are *many true* religions.

But this reflection 'from the outside' (as a sort of 'foreign policy') does not exclude the *internal* perspective (as a sort of 'domestic policy'). And for the individual it is completely honourable and serious to integrate both perspectives. Think about it: this inner-outer relationship holds not only for religion. An international lawyer too, when he compares, as an expert, various national constitutions with one another or tries to reach an accord on a given critical point in international negotiations, sees his national constitution (and his state), as it were, 'from the outside'. 'From the inside', however, he sees the same constitution (and his state), when he feels obliged as a loyal citizen among other citizens of the state precisely to this constitution (and no other) and conscientiously stands by it. In this sense nobody can simply be a one-dimensional person. Reality is more complex than this.

If now as a Christian (and as a theologian) I look upon Christianity *from within* – as every non-Christian does with his or her own religion – if I then speak as a follower of this religion, this message, this tradition or community, then Christianity is for me, as every other religion is to its adherents, more than a system to which I can draw near in a purely intellectual sense. Then Christianity is, like every religion (in contrast to every philosophy), at once a message of salvation and a way to it. I am met here not only by a philosophical-theological chain of arguments that demand my consideration, but by a religious challenge and, in the case of Christianity, a prophetic message that demands that I take an altogether personal position, that I 'follow'. Only in this way is this religion rightly understood at all. If then, from this point on in my remarks I speak in the language of the religious profession of faith, then this is not because out of fear of 'final consequences' I am falling back again on my religion, but because I am working from the assumption that no one can grasp a religion in its depths unless he or she has affirmed it from within, with ultimate existential seriousness. Only when *a* religion has become *my* religion, does the conversation about truth take on exciting depth. What is at stake here for me, then, is truth, *my faith*, just as Judaism and Islam for the Jew and the Muslim, Hinduism and Buddhism for the Hindu and the Buddhist, is at stake – is *his* religion, *his* faith, and so *the* truth. In my religion and in the other religions as well, the issue is not a general, but an existential truth: '*tua res agitur*'. In this sense there is for me – as for all other believers – only *one true religion*.

That means that in the search for the true religion no one may simply abstract from his own life history and experience. There is no such thing as a theologian nor a student of religion, neither a religious nor a political authority, that stands so far above *all* religions as to be able to judge it 'objectively', from above. Anyone who thinks he can stand in a 'neutral' position above all traditions, will get nothing done in any of them. And whoever refuses (to borrow an image from Raymondo Painkkar), while looking out of *his* window to take in the *whole* picture, to speak with the others who are looking out of *their* windows; whoever thinks he can float above everything and judge it, has obviously lost his footing. He will easily melt his waxen wings, as Icarus once did, in the sun of truth.

Thus I profess my faith in my historically conditioned standpoint; this one religion is *for me the true religion* for whose truth I can cite good reasons, that may possibly convince others. For me Christianity is the path that I take, the religion in which I believe I have found the truth for my living and dying. Still at the same time it is true that the *other* religions (which for hundreds of millions of persons are the *true* religion) are for that reason still *in no ways untrue religions*, are by no means simply untruth. Not only do they have a great deal of truth in common with Christianity. They also each have their own truth, which we do not already have ('anonymously' or 'implicitly'). Now it must be left to the Jewish, Muslim, Hindu or Buddhist theologian (philosopher) to explain exactly why he is a Jew, Muslim, Hindu or Buddhist. The Christian theologian for his part must at least be able as a matter of principle to name the specific Christian criterion and to try to answer the question of what concretely distinguishes Christians from non-Christians, what should distinguish them, what makes Christians Christians.

Why then am *I* a Christian? It would be worth a separate essay to present, in a new context of comparative religion, the reasons I have for not being a Hindu or Buddhist, nor a Jew or a Muslim, but a Christian. Let me just suggest the bare essentials here. I am a Christian because I – as a consequence of the Jewish, and in anticipation of the Islamic, faith in God – trustingly and altogether practically commit myself to the fact that the God of Abraham, Isaac (Ishmael) and Jacob has not only acted in the history of Israel (Ishmael) and spoken through its prophets, but that he has made himself known in an incomparable and, for us, decisive way in the life and work, suffering and dying of *Jesus of Nazareth*. The very first generation of his disciples was convinced that despite his death of shame on the gallows of the cross Jesus did not remain in death, but was taken up into God's eternal life. He stands now for God himself ('on the right hand of God') as God's definitive envoy, as his Messiah or Christ, as his word made flesh, as his image and likeness, as (to us an ancient royal title of Israel) his son. Thus, in brief, I am a Christian because and to the degree that I believe in this Christ and – though of course the times have changed – I try practically to emulate him (along with millions of others, each in his own way), and I take him as the guide for my path in life. Hence, in accordance with the words of the Gospel of John, he is for us, *the* way, *the* truth and *the* life.

But this also means, speaking self-critically to Christians, that Christians *do not believe in Christianity*. As a religion, with its dogmatics, its liturgy and discipline, like every other religion a highly ambivalent historical phenomenon. Karl Barth has quite rightly stressed this. It is therefore untenable to define Christianity as the 'absolute religion', in the way Hegel thought he could do this. As a religion Christianity appears in world history just as relative as all other religions.

No, the only absolute in world history is the Absolute itself. For Jews, Christians and Muslims, of course, this one Absolute is not ambiguous and vague, wordless, without a voice. It has spoken through the prophets. For believing Christians it is also not faceless, without a countenance. No, it became manifest in the relativity of the man Jesus of Nazareth. For believers – and only for them – he *is* the Word and Image, he is the Way; for others, he is at least the invitation to enter upon this way. That is why Christians do not *believe* in Christianity but *in the one God*, who after sending man prophets and enlightened messengers sent this person, Jesus, as *his Christ*, his anointed envoy. Jesus Christ is for Christians the *deciding regulative factor.*

And insofar as concrete Christianity testifies to this one God and his Christ, it can – in a derivative and limited sense – be called for believers themselves *the true* religion, whatever Karl Barth may say. But insofar as concrete Christianity continually deviated from this one God and his Christ, from this, its deciding regulative factor, it was also continually *untrue* religion. It also needed, even *after* Christ, the *prophetic corrective*, the prophets in the Church and – we see this today ever more clearly – the prophets and enlightened ones outside the Church as well, among whom the prophet Muhammad and the Buddha should no doubt be included *par excellence.*

Once again, the decision for the one God, who is not only the God of the philosophers and the learned (the God of the Greeks) and the God of Abraham, Isaac and Jacob (the God of the Jews), but finally and ultimately the God of Jesus Christ (the God of the Christians), represents a *faith-decision* at its deepest level. This is a rational act of trust: this faith-decision is by no means purely subjective and arbitrary, but is altogether *rationally responsible.* I have presented elsewhere what can be said in detail for making this decision to be a Christian – in comparison with Judaism, Islam, Hinduism and Buddhism. As Christians we cannot – unless we simply wish to issue dogmatic postulates – avoid the trouble of justifying in a substantial, empirical manner the significance of Jesus Christ. Referring to a dogmatically affirmed doctrine of the Trinity and Divine Sonship is of little help here. Nowadays we must be able to show concretely in a new way that and why we are Christians – even in critical comparison with other great religious figures – in terms of this figure and his message, his way of life and his destiny. And, to do this, scholarly research on religion is indispensable. What is needed is not the separation of theology and religious studies (as with Karl Barth), but not their identification either (which de facto reduces theology to the study of religion or vice versa), but their critical cooperation.

I would like to have at least called attention here to one aspect, but a thoroughly central aspect, of Jesus of Nazareth, that shows us something in a striking fashion: for Christian faith the *specifically Christian* criterion coincides not only with the *general religious* criterion of the origins, but finally with the *general ethical* criterion of the human element. The spiral endures. For what is the purpose – as a consequence of the proclaiming of the Kingdom and Will of God – aimed at in the Sermon on the Mount and all of Jesus' behaviour? Nothing more or less than a new, *true humanity*: the Sabbath, the commandments for the sake of man, and not the other way around.

This new true humanity means a *more radical way of being human*, which is manifested in *the fellowship of solidarity* even with one's opponent. From the perspective of Jesus, the real, true person, this more radical humanity of the Sermon on the Mount – now seen against a completely different world horizon – would have to be put into practise as a fellowship of solidarity with the men and women in the *other religions* as well. A fellowship of solidarity, therefore,

- that not only renounces religious wars, persecution and Inquisitions, and practises religious tolerance, but that also in relations with the other religions replaces collective egoism (ecclesiocentrism) with philanthropy, the solidarity of love;
- that, for this reason, instead of adding up the debts of history owed by the religions, practises forgiveness and dares to make a new beginning;
- that does not simply abolish the religious institutions and constitutions (which often separate people), but relativizes them for the good of humanity;
- that instead of an open or concealed power struggle between the religious-political systems strives for successive reconciliation. No, there should be no unified religion for the whole world, but peace among the religions as a prerequisite for peace among the nations.

This means that the more humane (in the spirit of the Sermon on the Mount) Christianity is, the more Christian it is; and the more Christian it is, the more it appears to the outside as a true religion. And with that the three criteria of truth should now be developed, and we can summarize the crucial points in a concluding section:

VII. ON THE WAY TO EVER GREATER TRUTH

By now it ought to have become clear: if we wish to answer the question of what is good for the individual – not only pragmatically or positivistically, but fundamentally; not only abstractly-philosophically, but concretely-existentially, and not only psychologically-pedagogically, but in an unconditionally binding and universally valid way, then we cannot get around religion – or put in its place quasi-religion. But conversely every religion will have to let itself be measured by the general ethical criterion of the human element and for that reason will not be able, given modern conditions, to dispense with the findings of psychology, pedagogy, philosophy and jurisprudence. This is no vicious circle here, but, as so often, a dialectical interrelationship:

1. *True humanity is the prerequisite for true religion.* This means that the human element (respect for human dignity and basic values) is a minimal demand levelled at every religion: at least humanity (the minimal criterion) must be given, where one wishes to translate genuine religious feeling into reality.

2. *True religion is the perfecting of true humanity.* This means that religion (as the expression of an all-encompassing meaning, of highest values, of unconditioned obligation) is an optimal prerequisite for the realization of the human element. It is precisely religion (a maximum criterion) that must be present where people wish to realize the values of humanity on the basis of an unconditional and universal obligation.

What, then, is the true religion? I have tried to give a differentiated answer to this complex question with the greatest possible conceptual clarity and theoretical exactness, with the help of three dissimilar and yet dialectically interwoven criteria – the general ethical, the general religious and the specifically Christian, as well as the two dimensions, the external and the internal. My answer also includes the answer to the question, Is there true religion? In summary we can say:

● Seen *from the outside,* from the standpoint of religious studies, there are *different true religions*: religions that for all their ambivalence correspond, at least in principle, to the ethical and religious criteria we have set up: various ways of salvation to the one goal, ways that in part intersect and that can in any event reciprocally benefit each other.

• Seen *from the inside*, from the standpoint of the believing Christian oriented to the New Testament, there is for me *the true religion, which for me, since I cannot possibly take all paths at the same time, is the path that I try to take*: Christianity, insofar as it bears witnesses to the one true God in Jesus.

• This (for me, for us Christians) one true religion in no way excludes the truth in *other religions*, but lets them have a positive validity. The other religions are not simply untrue, but neither are they unconditionally true, but *conditionally* ('with reservations' or whatever) *true religions*, which, so far as they do not contradict the Christian message on decisive points, can by all means complete, correct and enrich the Christian religion.

From these long and complex remarks it should have become clear that a maximum theological openness to the other religions forces one to suspend neither his faith conviction nor the question of truth. We should struggle – in 'fraternal emulation' (Vatican II) – over the truth. But one final limitation, which affects all religions, has to be made. There are not just the two 'horizontal' dimensions (external–internal), but also a third dimension (a 'vertical' one, so to speak): *for me* as a believer, *for us* as a community of faith, Christianity, *so far* as it attests to God in Christ, is certainly the *true* religion. But no religion has the *whole* truth, only *God alone* has the *whole truth* – Lessing was right about that. Only God *himself* – as we have always mentioned – *is the* truth.

And for that reason one final point here: Christians cannot claim to comprehend him, the incomprehensible One, to have grasped him, the unsearchable One. Even in Christian faith, according to Paul, we recognize the truth itself, which is God, only as in a mirror, in puzzling outlines, fragmentarily, in certain aspects, always dependent upon our quite specific standpoint and place in time. Yes, Christianity too is '*in via*', on the way: *Ecclesia peregrinans, homines viatores*. And we are not on the way alone, but with millions upon millions of other human beings from every possible religion and denomination, who are going their own way, but with whom the longer we travel together the more we will be in a *process of communication*, where one should not dispute about Mine and Yours, my truth/your truth; but rather where one should be endlessly ready to learn, should make one's own the truth of the others and ungrudgingly communicate one's own truth.

But whither, some will ask, *will all this lead?* History is open toward the future, and open-ended too is interreligious dialogue, which – unlike interdenominational dialogue – has only just begun. What the future of the Christian religion, which is for me the true one, will bring, we do not know. Nor do we know what the future will bring to the other, non-Christian religions. Who knows what the Christology, the Qur'anology, or the Buddhology, like the Church, the *Umma*, the *Sangha*, of the year 2087, will look like?

As far as the future goes, only one thing is certain: at the end both of human life and the course of the world Buddhism and Hinduism will no longer be there, nor will Islam nor Judaism. Indeed, in the end Christianity will not be there either. In the end no religion will be left standing, but the one Inexpressible, to whom all religions are oriented, whom Christians will only then completely recognize – when the imperfect gives way before the perfect – even as they themselves are recognized: *the* truth face to face. And in the end there will no longer be standing between the religions a figure that separates them, no more prophet or enlightened one, not Muhammad and not the Buddha. Indeed even Christ Jesus, whom Christians believe in, will no longer stand here as a figure of separation. But he, to whom, Paul says, all powers (including death) are subjected, 'subjects himself, then, to God' so that *God himself (ho theos)* – or however he may be called in the East – may truly be not just in all things but '*everything to everyone*' (1 Cor 15:28).

8

PAUL KNITTER: Christian Theology of Liberation and Interfaith Dialogue

Paul Knitter (b. 1939), Professor of Theology at Xavier University, Cincinnati, is one of the few Roman Catholic theologians to have adopted the pluralist position in the theology of religions. In No Other Name? A Critical Survey of Christian Attitudes Toward the World Religions *(1985) and in other works, he suggests that there is a 'liberative spirit' discernible, though differently expressed, in all the religious traditions of the world.*

RESPONSE TO CRITICS OF PLURALIST THEOLOGY

In what follows, I hope to respond to the critics of a pluralist theology by drawing on the method and content of liberation theology. My hopes are to serve the cause of pluralism by bringing together two of the most disturbing and promising theological movements within the Christian communities – the theology of liberation and the theology of religions. Their encounter, maybe even their marriage, can bear much fruit for the Christian churches and for the world.

Liberation: A New Hermeneutical Context for Dialogue

Our contemporary world offers what can be called a new 'hermeneutical kairos' for interreligious encounter – that is, a situation that casts both its shadows and its lights on all corners of the globe and in doing so makes a new encounter of religions both *necessary* and *possible*. We call it a 'kairos' because it is a unique constellation of events that constitutes both new opportunities and responsibilities; it is 'hermeneutical' because it enables followers of different religious paths not just to feel the need for each other but to understand *and* to judge each other. It is a global situation of crisis that transcends differences of culture and religion and so touches all peoples.

The many expressions of this transcultural crisis might be summarized in a trinity of oppressions that grip and torment our globe: *socio-economic oppression* which affects the majority of the world's population and is often based on class/race or sex; *nuclear oppression* which, despite the thawing of the cold war, still menaces humanity with an arsenal that, at the press of a few buttons, could annihilate life as we know it; *ecological oppression* which is already, slowly but surely, annihilating the ability of the planet to sustain life. All of these forms of oppression are well known and well documented, constituting as they do, a part of the cultural consciousness of people throughout the world.

In differing ways, all these forms of oppression call for *liberation* - that is, for new freedom, for new hope against forces that today, more than ever, are threatening not just the quality but the very existence of the human project and the planet. Gordon Kaufman summarizes the new 'common human experience' confronting all religions:

> Throughout the world there appears to be a growing passion to reconstruct the present order into one more truly humane. That is the great aspiration of our time − underlying much of the unrest of our world − whether we are Christians or Buddhists, Americans or members of the so-called third world, communists or adherents to Western-style democracy. How shall we build a new and more human world for all of the peoples of the world? That is our most important question.

And what Kaufman goes on to say about Christian theology would apply even more compellingly to interreligious dialogue: 'A theology [or dialogue] that makes an essential contribution to our humanization is the only sort we can afford today.'

If the need for liberation is a reality that can be felt by religious believers transculturally − that is, no matter what their culture or their religion − then I am suggesting that a soteriocentric, or liberation-centred, approach to interreligious understanding can provide the basis for responding to the critics of a pluralist theology of religions who argue that pluralists are creating a non-existent common centre for dialogue or that they are imposing their own centres on others. Here we have a common starting point for interreligious dialogue that is not imposed by any one religion on the other, for it is 'imposed' on all of them by the reality of the world in which they live. On the basis of their shared concern for confronting the suffering that racks our world, on the basis of a shared commitment to oppressed persons or to the oppressed earth, followers of different religious paths have the basis on which they might construct what Mark Kline Taylor calls the 'shaky common ground' of mutual understanding and mutual criticism.

But more needs to be said about how such a soteriocentric process of mutual understanding among religions works.

How a Liberation-Centred Dialogue Works

A soteriocentric dialogue would not begin simply with a conversation of words or study. It would, rather, enter the so-called 'hermeneutical circle' at the point recommended by liberation theologians – that is, *shared liberative praxis.* What liberation theologians have said of Christian theology can be applied to interreligious dialogue: dialogue, like theology is always a 'second step'. The first step is action, doing – some form of shared efforts to bring about an end to suffering, oppression, hunger, death. This will require that participants in interreligious dialogue first roll up their sleeves together, first identify together what they see as suffering, first try to undertake some form of analysis together by which they might grasp the cause of the specific suffering or oppression, and then act together, risk together, struggle together. How this is done will vary, of course, from situation to situation.

But such praxis, by its very nature, calls for reflection. In the light of praxis and of efforts to work with and for the suffering, believers return to their tradition, their scriptures, their doctrines – in order to understand them, revise them, appropriate them anew. But the reflection we are talking about here will be done not only in separate religious camps; it will be done interreligiously, together. In such a context followers of different religious ways can understand not only themselves, but each other anew. In the fervour of the insights, questions, commitments, frustrations of their shared praxis, they can now make known to each other what it is that motivates them and sustains them and guides them. Now, for example, Christians can communicate to Buddhists what the kingdom of God means and how it grounds their praxis. And Buddhists can make clear how the experience and reality of

Sunyata liberates them for involvement in their world without clinging to this world. Traditional symbols or beliefs will be discussed not as abstract notions but as statements or claims that have been born in and are constantly revivified and reviewed within a *way of life* – a praxis of liberation.

This soteriocentric model for dialogue is based on an epistemology that would merit the approval not only of contemporary philosophers but also of Muhammad and Buddha and Jesus. For in all religions, I believe, praxis grounds theory; doing the truth is necessary for knowing it; faith or conversion precedes clear understanding; one must come and follow in order to see; one must practise the Eightfold Path in order to know the Four Noble Truths. Or in more contemporary parlance: we will know the world only by acting to transform it. And if adherents of the different ways can share this effort to transform the world, they will be able, perhaps as never before, to enter into and understand and be changed by each others' religious histories.

This praxis will be more than a matter of simply identifying ethical concerns common to our different religions. It will imply a shared conversion to those who are suffering, to the oppressed. To be truly committed to the struggle with and for those who are suffering is a process by which our whole being is shaken, challenged and redirected. Out of this shared, existential commitment and conversion we can all the more adequately and effectively give witness to and understand each others' religious beliefs. Before we have actually begun the explicit dialogue, we will have been changed together. Conversion precedes understanding.

A Soteriocentric Core in All Religions?

For many, I am sure, a shadow of suspicion continues to follow this proposal for a liberation-centred model of dialogue. Is our proposal another, even more subtle and nobly decked imposition of a Western plan of what's best for the world? Does it make the concerns of Christian liberation theology the prerequisites for dialogue? Does it cast other believers, not as anonymous Christians, but, even more slickly, as anonymous co-workers for the kingdom of God? These are valid, demanding questions.

Because I take them seriously, I have tried to be clear that I am *proposing* or *suggesting,* not imposing or presuming, a liberation-centred dialogue among religions. I am aware that it is a Christian proposal which stands in need of criticism and clarification. But I trust that it is, basically, a model which can win the approval of a significant number of believers in all the major religious communities of our day. I believe that concern for liberation and for the promotion of human welfare in this world constitutes, if I may use a highly suspect term, what may be called a *soteriocentric core* within the history of religions. Whether this is so can be known, of course, only in the dialogue itself. But for the moment, let me offer some considerations why I feel it is worthwhile to talk about and search for this core.

To assert that all religious soteriologies begin by identifying a dissatisfying or broken state of human affairs which they then try to repair may sound sweepingly simplistic. But it is, fundamentally, true. And it does imply that all religions, in a vast variety of ways, do seek to fix or promote human welfare. Gordon Kaufman, who admits his lack of detailed knowledge of other religions, feels justified in claiming that 'Every religious tradition promises salvation in some form or other, i.e., promises true human fulfilment, or at least rescue from the pit into which we humans have fallen. Every religious tradition thus implicitly invokes a human or humane criterion to justify its existence and its claims.' Therefore, Kaufman feels assured that in proposing 'humanization' as the criterion for interreligious understanding and assessment, he is not fostering 'western spiritual imperialism' but is appealing to a 'universalistic criterion' implicit in all religions. Aloysius Pieris, who knows much more about Asian religions than Kaufman, is less cautious when he asserts that the 'religious instinct' behind all religious traditions can be 'defined as a revolutionary urge, a psychosocial impulse, to generate a new humanity it... is this revolutionary impulse that constitutes, and therefore defines, the essence of *homo religiosus*'.

Yet, it is also undeniable that in the symbolism and doctrine of many religious traditions certainly of Christianity, there is a flight from the world and from responsibility and concern for it, either through an eschatological vision of our true home in the next life or through a dualistic retreat into a spiritual-mystical centre insulated from the sufferings of this vale of tears. Can there be a soteriocentric dialogue with such other-worldly spiritualities? There are no ready-made answers to that question. For the moment, I would suggest that the insights of Marjorie Hewitt Suchocki into the genesis and significance of such other-worldly visions could be fruitfully explored. Suchocki holds that these escapist moves were not part of the earliest stages of religious history but arose, as it were, as coping mechanisms when a religious community found itself in what seemed to be a hopeless situation – when, for instance, the socio-economic structures, often defended by political-military powers, or the devastating forces of nature made it seem impossible to realize the religious vision of betterment in this world. The focus was then shifted to a better 'life beyond', and such other-worldly adaptations eventually became frozen into belief systems.

Suchocki suggests that the qualities of the 'other worldly realm' or of the 'mystical-monastic community' are what the particular tradition originally intended for *this* world, and it is these visions that can form the basis or starting point for shared liberative praxis leading to a soteriocentric dialogue. Suchocki's case is bolstered by the sociologists and historians of religions who have revealed how the apparently other-worldly images of popular religion are often packed with hidden, transformative power for this world. James Cone argues that this was true of black slaves in the United States when he reminds us that 'black eschatology' is not 'merely compensatory' and 'language about God, and heaven does not always lead to passivity'. Rather,

> Liberation as a future event is not simply *other* worldly but is the divine future that breaks into their social existence, bestowing wholeness in the present situation of pain and suffering, and enabling black people to know that the existing state of oppression contradicts their real humanity as defined by God's future... the statement about heaven becomes revolutionary judgement against the system of oppression. The future becomes a present reality in the slave's consciousness, enabling him to struggle against the white system of injustice.

What looks like religious opium can well be revolutionary dynamite.

We can go a step further in trying to describe the ingredients of this common soteriocentric core. If it is true that all religions begin with an 'evil' or dissatisfying state of affairs which they then try to fix, it also seems that there is among a number of religious traditions a differently coloured but clearly identifiable consensus as to the diagnosis of and remedy for such evil. According to the myths, doctrines and moralities of most religions, humankind's woes flow from a pool of disunity and dis-ease fed by a false notion of the self; to remedy the situation we must dry up or replace the contents of that pool. In many different ways, all (or most) religions seek to convert the energies of one's self from a centripetal to a centrifugal movement and so to broaden the focus of concern from me or us (egocentricity) to you or them (altruism).

Most religions share a vision of mutuality. Every religion, it would seem, seeks to place its followers in contact with a Reality, or to provide them with an exercise, whereby they can break the bonds of ego-clinging in order to embrace and be part of and so be transformed by that which is other. In so doing, the religions promote 'that limitlessly better quality of human existence which comes about in the transition from self-centredness to Reality-centredness'. All religions, therefore, can be seen as 'forms of resistance' to the confines of the status quo and as visions of liberation. They free our stolid imagination and sagging energies to dream and work for undreamt of possibilities of human freedom and human society.

Here a caveat is necessary. What has just been stated is the ideal, what the religions propose 'in theory'. It is not their historical track record. This must be admitted. There is within all religious traditions what Paul Tillich has called 'the demonic' – the possibility, indeed the propensity, to be turned in the direction opposite the altruistic vision of its founder or original witness. Within every religion there is not only Dr Jekyll but Mr Hyde, not only 'the culture of utopian peaceableness', but also the 'culture of violence and war'. In our post-modern consciousness, we realize, perhaps more clearly than ever, that the religions' vision of love and liberation has been turned into the ideological weapons of dominance and conflict. And so we make our claims for a soteriocentric core humbly and soberly and cautiously.

But again, we must sound the warning of too quickly, too conclusively, and therefore too imperialistically defining the soteriocentric core within religions. Though I am proposing such a core, I remain in full (though somewhat nervous) agreement with David Tracy's declaration:

> There are family resemblances among the religions. But as far as I can see, there is no single essence, no one content of enlightenment or revelation, no one way of emancipation or liberation, to be found in all that plurality...there are different interpretations of what way we should follow to move from a fatal self-centredness to a liberating Reality-centredness ...The responses of the religions, their various narratives, doctrines, symbols, and their often conflicting accounts of the way to authentic liberation are at least as different as they are similar. They are clearly not the same.

Around the soteriocentric core, there grows a stubborn, prolific plurality – a plurality that contains not only variety but contradiction. Such a plurality must be accepted and confronted – not only to show proper respect but to ensure creative encounter. To sweep away or step on differences hurts not only the other but our own possibilities for growth. A soteriocentric dialogue, therefore, does not ignore plurality of difference or opposition.

Christocentrism Revised and Reaffirmed

With a soteriocentric approach, pluralist theologians are also able to respond to the concern of critics that pluralism waters down the centrality of Jesus Christ in traditional Christian belief and practice. In a pluralist theology of religions, such critics complain, christocentrism seems to be an anathema. Not really. If from the pluralist perspective I am advocating, we can speak about a certain development in Christian theology of religions from ecclesio-centrism (in which membership in the church is necessary for salvation) to christocentrism (in which the anonymous or cosmic presence of Jesus Christ is necessary for salvation) to theocentrism (in which the universal action of the theos of the New Testament is necessary for salvation), and now to sote-riocentrism, such a development means a *sublation* (Aufhebung) of what went before, not a denial. The importance of the church, the centrality of Christ, the universality of God are not at all denied or watered down in a soterio-centric theology of religions; but they *are* understood differently in the broader context of soteria or, in biblical terms, of the *Basileia tou Theou.*

More specifically, in regard to christology, a soteriocentric approach affirms the centrality of Christ insofar as it recognizes that one always confronts and understands the other from one's own perspective. Here the anti-foundationalists are right; we cannot climb out of our own perspectival skins to a skinless, disembodied universal viewpoint. This means that Christians remain incorrigibly and happily christocentric. Their under-standing of liberation or human welfare is and remains the kingdom vision of the Nazarean. But as Wilfred Cantwell Smith has pointed out, the more one consciously admits and makes use of one's own christocentric perspective, the less an impediment it can become to truly meeting other perspectives. The more one learns about other religions from one's own perspective, the more one realizes the limitations of one's own perspective. As the Johannine Jesus tells his followers, 'the Father [and the Father's kingdom] is greater than I' (John 14:28).

Religiously or existentially, in a soteriocentric dialogue and theology of religions, one is both genuinely committed to one's own perspective and at the same time truly open to the possible truth or challenge contained in others' perspectives. One's own perspective – Christ for the Christian – is, in a paradoxical but real sense, both absolute *and* relative. The Christian is committed to the Gospel vision of justice and the kingdom with full energies and with a devotion that would, if need be, embrace martyrdom; yet at the same time, the Christian recognizes the relativity of any view of the kingdom or of salvation. To be absolutely committed to what one recognizes to be relative is, as Langdon Gilkey maintains, a religious paradox that somehow can be lived even though we cannot 'explain' it theologically.

Here is the crucial difference between christocentrism as it has usually been understood and christocentrism in a liberation-centred model. The Christian view of 'soteria' is not understood, as Jesus Christ has been in the past, as the only or the final or the normative perspective on what it is that human beings are or can be. Christ remains a universally normative, a tremendously important, manifestation of what the human condition can be, but he may not be the only. And so we Christians follow him with full but open devotion. Our 'Absolute' is not Christ, or even God. It is, rather soteria – human salvation, especially for those who, because of injustice, are most in need of salvation. And because soteria is indeed our *Absolute*, we will humbly recognize that while we affirm it and commit ourselves to it, it will always be more than what we know. Such an apparently 'relativistic' understanding of soteria is, I suggest, entirely consistent with biblical eschatology: we can know and realize the Kingdom of God *now*, but its fullness is *not yet* here. We cannot, therefore, make absolute claims about what we are absolutely committed to.

Just how one works out the balance between absolute commitment and the recognition of relativity, just how one decides whether the perspective on human welfare or emancipation of another religion complements and fulfils or interrupts and obliterates one's own perspective cannot be known until one engages in shared liberative praxis and dialogue. Only in the sticky, ever shifting process of dialogue does soteria or shared concern for human welfare become the common shaky ground on which we grow in mutual understanding and commitment.

A soteriocentric christology reflective of a soteriocentric theology of religions would suggest to the critics of pluralism a different hermeneutical key for interpreting central New Testament affirmations about Jesus. From a soteriocentric perspective, titles such as 'the only begotten Son of God' and 'one Mediator' were not meant to supply the early community with definitions of Jesus' ontological status by which the first Christians could then rule out all other contenders; the language of such titles was not primarily dogmatic or philosophical. It was, rather, performative – *action language* – meant to call the disciples of Jesus and all peoples to commit themselves to the work of love and justice, to live as Jesus lived, to devote themselves to realizing the Kingdom. The purpose of 'professing' is to follow, not the other way around. Fidelity to the NT confessions about Jesus, therefore, essentially means acting with and like Jesus, not insisting that he is above all others. In fact, the only way we can really know what our christological professions and titles really mean is by following Jesus and working for justice and love. As the liberation theologians tell us, orthopraxis (working for the Kingdom) should take first place to orthodoxy (making confessional or theological statements about Jesus' nature) – though the two aspects of religious life cannot be separated; orthodoxy is meant to serve and foster orthopraxis; orthopraxis calls for orthodoxy.

With such a soteriocentric christology, we Christians can be genuinely open to other religions and disposed to authentic dialogue. If fidelity to our traditional confessions is primarily a matter of following Jesus the prophet-servant of the Kingdom, we will be, at least theoretically, open to the possibility of other prophets. What matters most is that the Kingdom be promoted, not that Jesus maintain the primacy. Therefore if in the dialogue we encounter other prophets who are promoting human welfare and salvation – even in ways utterly unexpected and different from what we have seen in Jesus – we will rejoice and learn and cooperate. 'Seek ye first the Kingdom of God, and all else will be added' (Matt. 6:33) – including a clearer understanding of other religions.

9

JOHN HICK: The Theological Challenge of Religious Pluralism

John Hick (b.1922), for many years H.G. Wood Professor of Theology at Birmingham and Danforth Professor at the Claremont Graduate University in California, is the leading exponent of the philosophy of religious pluralism. In such books as Problems of Religious Pluralism *(London and New York, 1985) and* An Interpretation of Religion *(London and Yale, 1989) he has argued that all the world religions constitute differently configured human responses to the same Ultimate Reality lying beyond all representation in human terms.*

In our own time a new challenge to the structure of Christian belief has come from our awareness, not merely of the existence of the other great world faiths – there is nothing new about that – but of their spiritual and moral power. The challenge is to the traditional assumption of the unique superiority of the Christian gospel, or faith, or religion. If I am right, we are in the early stages of an adjustment that may take another fifty or more years. This is the transition from a view of Christianity as the one and only true religion to a new Christian self-understanding as one true religion among others. This will certainly mean a considerable restructuring of Christian theology.

I shall for the most part confine what I say here about other religions to the *great world faiths*, meaning those traditions that have existed for upward of a thousand years, which have profound scriptures and have produced great saints and thinkers, and which have provided the foundations of civilization for many millions of people. Oral primal traditions, and the many smaller and newer religions, and also the modern secular faiths, are not intrinsically less important, but in the case of the great world religions one can assume a certain common background of knowledge that can facilitate discussion. If we can achieve a viable Christian view here, it will then be easier to cope with the further problems posed by the yet wider religious life of the world.

Christians have, of course, always been aware of other religions. However, during the second half of the twentieth century a new kind of awareness has developed. The cause that I would single out here has been the large-scale immigration from the East to the West, bringing millions of Muslims, Sikhs, Hindus, Taoists and Buddhists into a number of European and North American cities. The population of the Los Angeles area, for example, includes the third largest Jewish community in the world, the biggest Buddhist temple in North America, supported by a large Buddhist population, and quite large Muslim and Hindu, and smaller Sikh and Taoist, communities. And when one meets some of one's neighbours of these other faiths, and gets to know individuals and families, and is invited to their weddings and festivals and community events, one discovers that, while there are all manner of fascinating cultural differences, Muslims and Jews and Hindus and Sikhs and Buddhists in general do not seem to be less honest and truthful, or less loving and compassionate in family and community, or less good citizens, or less religiously committed, than are one's Christian neighbours in general. The ordinary people of these other faiths do not generally seem to be better human beings, morally and spiritually, than Christians, but neither do they seem to be worse human beings. Further, reading a fair amount of the literature of these other faiths, and encountering several outstanding individuals of the kind whom we call saints, confirms the impression that these other traditions are, to about the same extent as Christianity, contexts of a salvific human transformation from natural self-centredness to a new orientation centred in the divine or the transcendent. And, although this is another dimension of the subject which there is not time to go into here, I think we have to conclude that the civilizations in which these faiths have been expressed, although very different, have been more or less on a par with Christendom as regards their moral and spiritual fruits.

I appreciate that these last statements can be contested. Indeed, probably most Christians assume as a matter of course that Christian religious life and Christian civilization exhibit a manifest superiority. Rather than debate this here, I would like to focus attention on the procedural issue. Just as it has been asked whether Christianity stands or falls by historical evidence concerning the truth of the Gospel accounts of Jesus, so also it can be asked whether it stands or falls by historical evidence concerning the moral quality of Christian civilization. And I image that just as there have been theologians (such as Kierkegaard, Barth, Tillich, Bultmann) for whom knowledge about the historical Jesus does not affect the core of their faith, so also there will be theologians for whom the superiority of Christianity is accepted a priori, without depending on historical evidence.

Indeed, such an a priori judgement comes very naturally to us all. It is where we most naturally start. But it evokes a 'hermeneutic of suspicion', arising from the fact that in perhaps ninety-nine per cent of cases the religion to which one adheres (or which one specifically rejects) is selected by the accident of birth. When someone is born into a devout Muslim family in Pakistan or Egypt or Indonesia, it will nearly always be a safe bet that he or she will become a Muslim, either observant or nonobservant. When someone is born into a devout Christian family in Italy or Mexico, it will nearly always be a safe bet that he or she will become a Catholic Christian, again either observant or nonobservant. And so on. And of course it normally seems obvious that the religion that has been part of one from infancy is normative and basically superior to all others.

This relativity of religious conviction to the circumstances of birth and upbringing is so obvious that we seldom stop to think about it. But it nevertheless has immense significance. If there is a religious 'plus', a spiritual gain, advantage, benefit, in being a Christian rather than a Jew, Muslim, Hindu or Buddhist, then there is a corresponding 'minus', a spiritual loss or disadvantage, in being a Buddhist, Hindu, Muslim or Jew. It then becomes a proper question why only a minority of the human race, have been awarded this religious 'plus'. For if the 'plus' is a reality, divine providence has favoured those born into a Christian society over those born in non-Christian countries. And the greater the religious 'plus' for Christians, the greater the 'minus' for everyone else and the greater the discrimination that needs to be accounted for in our theology. Should we conclude that we who have been born within the reach of the gospel are God's chosen people, objects of a greater divine love than the rest of the human race? But then, on the other hand, do we not believe that God loves *all* God's creatures with an equal and unlimited love?

There is obviously a problem here, and yet it is very rare to find it discussed. I am aware of only two responses to it. One is to stress the imperative of evangelization, the duty to bring all humankind to enjoy the religious 'plus' of knowing Christ. But the general failure of the Christian mission to Jews, Muslims, Hindus and Buddhists leaves the original problem very largely intact. (The Christian population of the entire Indian subcontinent, for example, after two hundred years of fairly intensive missionary activity, is about 2.5 per cent.) The other response is the horrific suggestion, based on the concept of middle knowledge – the idea of a divine knowledge of what everyone would freely do in all possible circumstances – that God knows concerning all those who lack any real access to the Christian gospel that they would reject it if they heard it. They thus deserve the religious 'minus' under which they suffer, which, according to the evangelical Christian philosophers who propound this theory, consists of eternal damnation. This theory declares completely a priori that each one of the hundreds of millions of men and women in each generation who have lived without knowledge of the Christian gospel are depraved sinners who would have rejected it if they had heard it. This is a priori dogma carried to terrifying lengths.

Suppose, then, we accept (1) that most of us are not Christians as a result of a deliberate choice resulting from a comprehensive study and evaluation of the religions of the world, but because we were born into a Christian rather than some other society; and (2) that the moral and spiritual fruits of faith seem to be more or less on a par within the different world religions. The question that I am then raising is: How should this affect our inherited Christian belief-system?

It might at this point be said that our belief-system has already been adjusted to take account of all this. The older exclusivist position was, in its Roman version, that outside the church there is no salvation or, in its Protestant version, that outside Christ (that is, outside a personal faith in Christ as our Lord and Saviour) there is no salvation. But through the discussions and debates of the last thirty or so years a new majority consensus has emerged, which is generally known as Christian inclusivism. This is both continuous and discontinuous with the previous exclusivism. The continuity is in the claim that salvation is, exclusively, Christian salvation, made possible solely by the atoning death of Jesus. The new element however, the discontinuity, is in the claim that this Christian salvation is not limited to Christians but is available to all human beings without restriction.

I should perhaps remind us at this point that the question of salvation for non-Christians as well as Christians is distinct from the question of universal or restricted salvation, which is not the issue here. The inclusivist position is that all who are saved, whether they constitute the whole human race or only part thereof, are saved by Christ, but that this is not dependent on their accepting Jesus as their Lord and Saviour, at least not in this life.

INCLUSIVIST TYPE OF THEOLOGY

This inclusivist type of theology of religions takes three forms. The first (in the arbitrary order in which I shall discuss them) is based on the idea developed within Catholic thinking of implicit faith, or the baptism of desire, the idea that at least some individuals of other faiths, and indeed of no faith, may be so rightly disposed in their hearts that they *would* respond to the Christian gospel if it were properly presented to them. But they have in fact never encountered it, or only in inadequate ways, and have thus had no real opportunity to respond to it. Such people, who may be said to have an implicit faith in Christ, have been dubbed by Karl Rahner anonymous Christians. Only God knows who they are; but we can at least know that non-Christians who in their hearts sincerely desire to know the truth and to serve the good are not excluded from salvation by the fact that, through no fault of their own, they are not presently Christians. This was the view of some of the early church fathers concerning persons who lived before Christ. But Rahner and others have now gone farther in applying this principle to people of the other world religions since the time of Christ. Not only those who lived BCE (Before the Common Era), but also non-Christians today, may be anonymous Christians.

The second form of inclusivism holds that salvation does require a conscious personal faith in Christ but that although this is not possible for hundreds of millions in the present life, it will be possible in or beyond death. Thus the devout Muslim living, let us say, in Pakistan and insulated from the gospel by a powerful Islamic faith, will encounter Christ after or in the moment of death and will thus have an opportunity to receive salvation.

Among contemporary Catholic theologians perhaps the most explicit recent expression of this idea is Father J. A. Dinoia's 'Christian theology of religions in a prospective vein'. Father Dinoia, who is the secretary for doctrine and pastoral practice of the National Conference of Catholic

Bishops in the United States, rejects Rahner's suggestion that some non-Christians can now, in this present life, be accepted as having an implicit faith in virtue of which they are anonymous Christians. 'Rather,' he says, 'than attributing an implausible implicit faith in Christ to the members of other religious communities, theology of religions in a prospective vein contends that non-Christians will have the opportunity to acknowledge Christ in the future. This opportunity,' he says, 'may come to them in the course of their present lives here on earth or in the course of their entrance into the life to come.' And he invokes the doctrine of purgatory, adding that the interval in which the necessary purification or transformation takes place 'may be thought of as instantaneous and coterminous with death'. Thus, he says, 'The doctrine of purgatory permits Christians a wide measure of confidence about the salvation of non-Christians.'

Among Protestant theologians George Lindbeck is probably the most influential proponent of what he calls 'an eschatologically futuristic perspective'. Like Dinoia, he is critical of the Rahnerian idea of implicit faith. He speaks of 'the temptation to religious pretentiousness or imperialism implicit in the notion that non-Christians are anonymously Christians', and says that, 'saving faith cannot be wholly anonymous, wholly implicit, but must be in the same measure explicit: it comes, as Paul puts it, *ex auditu*, from hearing'. His alternative theory is eschatological. 'The proposal is,' he says, 'that dying itself be pictured as the point at which every human being is ultimately and expressly confronted by the gospel, by the crucified and risen Lord. It is only then that the final decision is made for or against Christ; and this is true not only of unbelievers but also of believers. ... Thus it is possible to be hopeful and trusting about the ultimate salvation of non-Christians no less than Christians.'

The difference between the theories, on the one hand of the prospective or eschatological salvation of non-Christians, and on the other hand of their present anonymous salvation, is however not as great as it might seem. For Rahner also presumably holds that ultimately the implicit faith of the anonymous Christian will become explicit. I shall therefore not play these two kinds of inclusivism off against each other but shall bracket them together in the composite view that (1) salvation is in Christ alone, and (2) non-Christians may nevertheless receive this salvation by being related to Christ either implicitly in this life and explicitly beyond it or, as an alternative version, only explicitly and beyond this life.

It is to be noted that this kind of inclusivism, in either form, does not regard other religions as such as channels of salvation, but is a theory about individuals within them. A third form of inclusivism, however, validates those religions themselves as alternative mediators or contexts of salvation; and this is a large step closer to the position at which I think we must eventually arrive. But before coming to that, let me comment on the individualistic inclusivism of the 'anonymous Christians' and the eschatological salvation theories.

The appeal of inclusivism is, of course, that it retains the unique centrality of Christ as the sole source of salvation, and yet at the same time avoids the morally repugnant idea that God consigns to perdition the majority of the human race, who have not accepted Jesus as their Lord and Saviour. It is thus a comfortable and comforting package, enabling Christianity to go on regarding itself as superior while at the same time being charitable to the people of other religions.

But there are nevertheless two problems. One is its sheer arbitrariness. I referred earlier to the 'hermeneutic of suspicion' evoked by the presumed centrality and normativeness of the religion into which one was born. If I, who was born in England and who as a student experienced an evangelical Christian conversion, had instead been born in India or Egypt or Tibet, my religious awakening would almost certainly have taken a Hindu or a Muslim or a Buddhist form. Of course this is a misleading way to put it, because it would not then be the same I, since we are all so largely formed by our surrounding culture, including our religious culture. But when someone, anyone, is born as an Indian or an Egyptian or a Tibetan the belief-system that he or she internalizes will very likely not be Christian but Hindu, Muslim, or Buddhist, as the case may be. And just as it seems obvious to most devout Christians, without any argument being needed, that their familiar Christian set of beliefs is true and any incompatible beliefs therefore false, so likewise it seems obvious to devout people of the other world religions that *their* inherited beliefs are true and any incompatible beliefs false. They can also, if they wish, fit sincere and devout Christians into their own belief-system as anonymous Hindus, Muslims, or Buddhists, or as to be converted to one of those faiths beyond death, as indeed some of the thinkers of these traditions do. But is not the sheer arbitrariness of this procedure, whoever is using it, glaringly evident?

One can of course 'bite the bullet' and say, Yes, it is arbitrary; but why not? It so happens that the beliefs that were instilled into me by my Christian upbringing are true, while those instilled into Hindus, Muslims, Buddhists and so on, insofar as they are incompatible with mine, are false. As Karl Barth wrote, 'The Christian religion is true, because it has pleased God, who alone can be the judge in this matter, to affirm it to be the true religion.' This is a theological cover for the fact that, having been brought up as a Christian, Barth assumed that Christian revelation is revelation and that other 'revelations' are not. And if this seems unilaterally dogmatic in a way that is difficult to defend rationally, one can add that happily the situation is not as harsh as it might seem, because we can believe that God is also able in the end to save by some indirect route those who presently lack the one true revelation.

This kind of armour-plated belief-system is logically invulnerable. What we normally do when faced with someone else's armour-plated conviction is to look at its practical fruits. In the case of major world religions, we have to make discriminations, recognizing both good and evil elements. Some Christian beliefs, for example, have in the course of history proved extremely harmful to others. Thus the belief that the Jewish people are guilty of deicide authorized the medieval persecution of the Jews and created a prejudice that continued in the secular anti-Semitism of the nineteenth and twentieth centuries, culminating in the Nazi Holocaust of the 1940s. The belief, during the European wars of religion, that Protestants, or Catholics, are heretics who have forfeited divine grace, validated slaughter on a massive scale. The belief that white Christian colonists stood on superior religious ground to that of the pagan natives of what today we call the third world, and were accordingly justified in conquering them, validated their enslavement and the exploitation of their natural and human resources. The belief that, because Jesus and his apostles were all men, women cannot serve the church as ordained priests, still continues to validate the ecclesiastical oppression of women. And similar discriminations have to be made within each of the other great world faiths. The belief that the caste system of India is divinely ordained; the belief that God has given the entire area of Israel and Palestine to the Jewish people; the belief that God demands the death of Salman Rushdie, are obvious examples of beliefs that validate evil. Thus while claims to be the sole possessors of the truth may start out as pure and innocent, they can all too easily become a cloak for human prejudice and self-interest, and their arbitrariness properly evokes, as I have suggested, a 'hermeneutic of suspicion'. In the case, to take recent examples, of such cults as the People's Temple of the 1978 Jonestown mass suicide, or the Branch Davidians of the

1993 Waco massacre, or the Order of the Solar Temple of the 1994 Swiss mass suicide, the fruits were manifestly evil, and we condemn their arbitrary dogmatism.

The other main criticism of Christian inclusivism turns on what we mean by salvation. If this means being forgiven and accepted by God because of the atoning death of Jesus, then salvation is by definition Christian salvation and it is a tautology that Christianity alone knows and proclaims its possibility. Either an exclusivist or an inclusivist theology of religions then becomes virtually inevitable. But suppose we think of salvation in a much more concrete and empirically observable way as an actual change in men and women from natural self-centredness to, in theistic terms, God-centredness, or in more general terms, a new orientation centred in the Ultimate, the Real, as conceived and experienced within one's own tradition. Salvation in this sense is the central concern of each of the great world religions. Within Christianity it is conceptualized and experienced as the state in which Paul could say, 'It is no longer I who live, but Christ who lives in me' (Gal. 2:20, RSV). Within Judaism it is conceived and experienced as the joy and responsibility of life lived in accordance with God's Torah. Within Islam it is conceived and experienced as a personal self-surrender to God in a life lived according to God's revealed commands. With Advaitic Hinduism it is conceived and experienced as a transcending of the ego and discovery of unity with the eternal reality of Brahman. Within Buddhism it is conceived and experienced as a loss of the ego point of view in a discovery of the Buddha nature of the universal interdependent process of which we are all part. And in each case this transformation of human existence from self-centredness to Reality-centredness is reached by a moral and spiritual path. The Golden Rule is taught by all the great traditions, as are love and compassion, justice and fair dealing, and a special concern for the vulnerable – in the societies within which the scriptures were produced, the widows and orphans. Within Buddhism, for example, much of the Noble Eightfold Path to enlightenment is ethical, including among its requirements kindness, truthfulness, abstaining from stealing, from dishonesty, from cheating, from illegitimate sexual intercourse, from intoxication and from earning one's living by trading in arms or by killing animals. And each of the other world religions has its own overlapping though not identical moral requirements.

So if we understand by salvation the transition to a life centred in the Divine, the Ultimate, the Real, we can properly look about us for the signs of it. To what extent is this transformation actually taking place among Christians, among Jews, among Muslims, among Hindus, among Buddhists? I suggest that, so far as we can tell, it is taking place to much the same extent within each of these traditions. It is true that we have no organized evidence or statistics to establish this. But we can properly put the issue the other way round. If anyone asserts that Christians in general are morally and spiritually better human beings than Jews, Muslims, Hindus, or Buddhists in general, the onus is on them to produce the evidence for this. It cannot simply be affirmed a priori, without regard to the concrete realities of human life.

My conclusion, then, so far is that the salvific transformation seems to be taking place more or less equally within all the great world religions, including Christianity, and that for any one of them to assert that it alone is the source of this change within all the others is an arbitrary claim that cannot be refuted but on the other hand cannot be rationally justified.

But there is also a third kind of inclusivism. This goes farther than the other two in speaking, not only of non-Christian individuals, but of the other world faiths as such. It sees the divine Logos, or cosmic Christ, or Holy Spirit as at work within these other religious histories. It holds that God, whether as second or third member of the Holy Trinity, has been and is savingly present within them. There are different ways of developing this thought. One is the Christocentric version, which gave rise to the idea of the unknown Christ of Hinduism, and likewise by implication the unknown Christ of Islam and so on. Since Hinduism and Buddhism (and also Taoism, Confucianism, Zoroastrianism and Jainism) all long predate Christianity, the Christ who has been at work within them from the beginning cannot be the God-man Jesus, but must be the cosmic Christ or eternal Logos who later became incarnate as Jesus of Nazareth. And so we are in effect talking about a worldwide and history-long divine presence to and within the religious life of humanity, while insisting that this be named and thought of in exclusively Christian terms. The inevitable criticism of this insistence is, once again, its arbitrary and religiously imperialistic character. To claim that Christ is the real though hidden source of saving grace within other religions is a way of asserting the unique centrality of one's own tradition. The hermeneutic of suspicion that I referred to earlier is inevitably brought into play here.

The other version is the much more radical idea that the same God who saves Christians through their response to the incarnate Christ also saves

Jews through their response to the Torah, and saves Muslims through their response to the Qur'an, and saves Hindus through their response to the Vedic revelation and the various streams of religious experience to which it has given rise, and saves Buddhists through their response to the Dharma. This view validates the other world religions as alternative channels or contexts of divine salvation. One can then stress their complementarity, and the possibility that they may in the future converge as a result of friendly dialogue.

There are two comments to be made about this more promising theory. The first is a clarification. The test question for this position is whether it involves a renunciation of the missionary ideal of converting Jews, Muslims, Hindus, Buddhists to Christianity. Does it entail the conclusion that there is an equal possibility of salvation within whichever of the great world religions one has been born into, so that there is no salvific 'plus' in being a Christian rather than a Jew or a Muslim, for example? If it does not accept this implication, then it is only an elaborate manoeuvre for preserving belief in the unique superiority of Christianity. But if it does entail a renunciation of that supposed religious superiority, it then comes close to the kind of pluralism that I want to recommend.

There is, however, at this point a qualification to be made to the idea that no religious 'plus' is involved in being born into one rather than another of the great world faiths. Each tradition has its own distinctive religious 'pluses' and 'minuses', for each is a different and unique mixture of good and evil. But this fact does not amount to one of these complex mixtures being superior as a totality to the others. If any of them claims this for itself, that claim must be established by objective evidence. Nevertheless, for the individual who has been spiritually formed by a particular tradition, that tradition does normally have an overall 'plus'. For our religion creates us in its own image, so that it fits us and we fit it as no other can. It is thus for us the best, truest, most naturally acceptable faith, within which we rightly remain. This is the point made by Ernst Troeltsch, at the beginning of the modern discussion of the problems of religious plurality, when he said, 'We cannot live without a religion, yet the only religion that we can endure is Christianity, for Christianity has grown up with us and has become a part of our very being.' There are, of course, and will always be, individual conversions in all directions, for individual reasons. But broadly speaking we do best to live within the religion that has formed us, though with an awareness that the same holds for those who have been formed by a different tradition from our own.

My other comment on the idea that the Christian God is at work saving people through the medium of each of the world religions is that it does not take adequate account of the nontheistic traditions, most particularly Buddhism. If we are to proceed inductively from the actual religious experience of humanity, rather than deductively from an arbitrarily adopted premise, then we must see theism as one form, but not the only form, of religious thought and experience. And if we accept that the fruits in human life of Buddhist faith are on a par with the fruits of the monotheistic faiths, we have to expand our theory to take account of this fact.

Such an expanded understanding of religion has been forming in many minds during the last seventy or so years and has come to be known as religious pluralism. This is the view that the great world faiths, both theistic and nontheistic, are different culturally formed responses to the Ultimate, and thus independently valid channels or contexts of the salvific human transformation. The general conception is ancient and widespread – from the basic Vedic declaration that 'the Real [*sat*] is one, but sages name it variously', to the edicts of the Buddhist emperor Ashoka affirming and supporting all the religions of his empire; to the Sufis of Islam, with Rumi, for example, saying of the religions of his time, 'The lamps are different, but the Light is the same'; to the Christian Nicholas of Cusa's statement that 'there is only one religion in the variety of rites'. The problem comes when we try to spell out this basic insight in a philosophically coherent way. Some who take a broadly pluralist view think that it is not possible, or not necessary, or not desirable to spell it out. There are indeed many good Christians who in practise treat people of other religions on the implicit basis that it is perfectly acceptable in the sight of God for them to be, and to remain, Jews, Muslims, Hindus or Buddhists, but who shrink from making explicit the implications of this. If they are ecclesiastical officials, they probably do so to avoid controversy and division within the church. If they are lay people, they probably shrink from it because it would be unacceptable to the church leaders. All this is readily understandable. We are in an interim situation in which theological theory lags behind our practical religious insights. But it is the task of Christian theologians and philosophers to think through the implications of these insights. And so as a contribution to this I will now very briefly outline a positive suggestion.

A POSITIVE SUGGESTION

This rests on two basic principles. One is the view, widespread in philosophy since Kant, and confirmed by cognitive psychology and the sociology of knowledge, that consciousness is not a passive reception of the impacts of our environment but always an active process of selecting, ordering, integrating and endowing with meaning in accordance with our human systems of concepts. I suggest that this applies to awareness of our divine, or supranatural, environment as well as of our physical environment. The other basic principle is consequent on this: the distinction between something as it is in itself, independently of human observation, and as it appears to us, with our specifically human perceptual equipment and conceptual resources. This also, I suggest, applies to our awareness of the Ultimate.

To avoid using a string of alternative terms, such as the Divine, the Transcendent, the Ultimate, Ultimate Reality, the Real, I shall arbitrarily employ the last. The distinction then is between, on the one hand, the Real in itself and, on the other hand, the Real as variously conceived and experienced and responded to within the different world religions. These fall into two main groups. One group thinks of the Real in personal terms, as a great transcendent Thou, further specified as the Adonai of Judaism, or more complexly as the Holy Trinity of Christianity, or as the Allah of Islam, or as the Vishnu or Shiva of theistic Hinduism, and so on. The other thinks of the Real in nonpersonal terms, as Brahman, or the Tao, or the dharmakaya, and so on. According to this pluralistic hypothesis, the status of the various God-figures is as *personae* of the Real, that is, the Real as variously perceived by the personifying human mind, while the various nonpersonal absolutes are *impersonae* of the Real, that is, the Real as variously manifested in nonpersonal terms to a nonpersonifying religious mentality. Both are joint products of the universal presence of the Real above, below, around and within us, together with the distinctive set of concepts and accompanying spiritual practices of a particular religious tradition.

The Real in itself lies beyond the range of our entire network of concepts, other than purely formal ones. We therefore cannot experience it as it is in itself but only as we conceptualize it in our human terms, organizing its impact on us in a particular form of religious experience. The religious traditions thus stand between us and the Real, constituting different 'lenses' through which we are aware of it. As Thomas Aquinas wrote, in a foreshadowing of the Kantian insight, 'Things known are in the knower according to the mode of the knower.' And in relation to the Real or the Divine the mode of the knower is differently formed within the different religious traditions.

Here, then, are the bare bones of a pluralistic hypothesis. It is open, as probably all large-scale hypotheses are, to a variety of objections, and I will now in conclusion look briefly at a few of these.

First, is not the concept of the ineffable Real so featureless as to be redundant, incapable of doing any work? Reply: The concept of the Real does do vital work. For the Real is that which there must be if religious experience in its variety of forms is not purely imaginative projection but a response to a transcendent reality. The difference between affirming and not affirming the Real is the difference between a religious and a naturalistic interpretation of religion in its variety of forms.

But, second, how can we worship the noumenal Real? Surely an object of worship must have some definite characteristics, such as being good, loving and so on. Reply: We do not worship the Real in its infinite transcendent nature, beyond the scope of our human categories, but the Real as humanly thought and experienced within our own tradition. In religious practice we relate ourselves to a particular 'face' or appearance or manifestation of the ultimate divine reality.

But, third, do not the different traditions make many mutually contradictory truth claims – that the divine reality is personal, that it is nonpersonal; that it is unitary, that it is triune; and so on? Reply: These different and incompatible truth claims are claims about different manifestations of the Real to humanity. As such they do not contradict one another. That one group conceives and experiences the Real in one way is not incompatible with another group's conceiving and experiencing the Real in another way, each described in its own theology. There is contradiction only if we assume that there can be only one authentic manifestation of the Real to humanity.

Fourth, in seeing the various objects of worship and foci of religious contemplation as not being themselves ultimate, but appearances of the ultimate to human consciousness, does not this hypothesis contradict the self-understanding of each of the religions? And is this not gross presumption? The reply here is a counterquestion: Does not the traditional Christian view contradict the self-understanding of every religion except itself? And is it not a lesser presumption to apply the same principle to one's own religion also?

Fifth, on what basis can we judge that the figure of the Heavenly Father, for example, is indeed an authentic manifestation of the Real? Answer: On the basis of its capacity to promote the salvific transformation of human life.

But then, sixth, if we say that the figure of the Heavenly Father is a manifestation of the Real because it is salvific, and that it is salvific because it is a manifestation of the Real, are we not moving in a circle? Reply: Yes, the hypothesis is ultimately circular, as indeed every comprehensive hypothesis must be. The circle is entered, in this case, by the faith that human religious experience is not purely imaginative projection but is also a response to a transcendent reality. The hypothesis should be judged by its comprehensiveness, its internal consistency and its adequacy to the data – in this case, the data of the history of religions.

But, seventh, surely in denying that the Real in itself is personal, is one not asserting that it is nonpersonal, and thus arriving at a Hindu or Buddhist conclusion? Reply: The suggestion is more radical than that, namely, that these dualisms of human thought – personal/impersonal, good/bad, substance/process and so on – do not apply to the Real in itself. Its nature is beyond the scope of our human conceptual systems.

Eighth, so the Real is not properly thought of as being good or loving? Reply: No, these human concepts do not apply to the Real in itself. But we have found, within all the great world religions, that the Real is good, or benign, from our human point of view, as the ground of our highest good, which is the transformed state that we can speak of as eternal life, or nirvana, or moksha and so on.

Ninth, can we not, however, modify the ineffability of the Real in itself by saying that it has analogous attributes to those of its *personae* and *impersonae*? Thus, if the Heavenly Father of Christian belief is an authentic manifestation of the Real, must not the Real in itself be loving and fatherlike, at least in an analogous sense? The reply is again a counterquestion: What could it mean for the Real to be both analogically personal and analogically nonpersonal, both analogically conscious and analogically not conscious, both analogically purposive and analogically not purposive, both analogically a substance and analogically a nonsubstantial process? Would this not be a mass of contradictions? If, however, these mutually incompatible attributes are attributes of different manifestations of the Real to human consciousness, the contradictions disappear.

Tenth, why postulate *one* Real? The different religions report different realities, so why not affirm all of them? Reply: For two reasons. One is the difficulty of making sense of the relationship between a plurality of ultimates. Does the Holy Trinity preside over Christian countries, Allah over Muslim countries and so on? And what about those parts of the world where people of different religions live mixed together? And, more fundamentally, if there exists a God who is the creator *ex nihilo* of everything other than God, how can there also be the eternal uncreated process of *pratita samutpada*?

The other reason is that the moral and spiritual fruits produced by response to the different experienced ultimates are so essentially similar, within the cultural differences of their different traditions, that it seems more reasonable to postulate a common source of this salvific transformation.

There are many other issues, and a growing literature about them. But the task of this chapter has been the relatively modest one of introducing the newly perceived global context within which Christian theologians will increasingly feel obliged to think in the future.

10

JÜRGEN MOLTMANN: Dialogue or Mission? Christianity and the Religions in an Endangered World

Jürgen Moltmann (b.1926), one of the leading Protestant theologians of the post war period, was for many years Professor of Theology at the University of Tübingen. His many works of systematic theology began with Theology of Hope *(English trans. London, 1967) and concluded with* The Coming of God *(English trans. London, 1996). His strongly trinitarian, future-oriented, theology has constantly concerned itself with questions of social justice and ecology.*

Let me begin with a personal experience and an honest doubt.

1. When I was in India, I was fascinated by the glorious Hindu and Jain temples, with their crowd of praying and sacrificing people. For thousands of years the same figures, the same stories, the same rituals. What wisdom in suffering, what experience of life, love and death is preserved here, kept alive down to the present day! I think of the Vishnu temple in Srinagar, and the Jain sanctuary on Mount Abu. When I was there I often found myself asking: do I as a Christian really want these religious marvels to disappear and to be replaced everywhere by Christian churches? And yet, does this mean that I don't want all these people to hear the gospel of Christ, and experience the Spirit of life, and hope for the new creation and the fullness of life? I feel torn. On the one hand I am impressed by the wonderful world of the Indian religions. On the other, I am captive to faith in Christ, and to hope for his kingdom. What ought I to do? Should I relinquish Christ's command to go

out and preach the gospel, and do my utmost through interfaith dialogue for religious tolerance and understanding between the religions? Or should I reject the dialogue, and devote myself entirely to mission? 'Go and make disciples of all nations,' says the missionary charge according to Matthew, not 'Engage in conversations with all the religious groups!' Or are dialogue and mission not contradictory after all?

2. When a new appointment had to be made to the Chair for Missionary Studies in our theological faculty in Tübingen, objections were raised in the senate by members of other faculties: mission was no longer in keeping with the times, it was said; what was needed were programmes for dialogue. So ought we to rename the Chair for Missionary Studies, and call it a Chair for the Study of Christian Dialogue – or simply pass it over to the Faculty for Religious Studies, and make it a chair for the study of religions in general, the Christian religion included? If we do that, ought we not then logically to turn the denominational faculties into departments for religious studies? But if we really come down to it: what *is* Christian mission? Is it the extension of the Christian empire, Christian civilization, or what today goes under the high-sounding title of 'the community of Western values'? Or does it aim to spread the Christian churches, or to convert people to the Christian faith? Or is mission perhaps something quite different? Is it perhaps the invitation to the future of life?

In this chapter I shall try first to take stock of our experiences of interfaith dialogue up to now. (What *is* a dialogue of this kind with people of different faiths and different philosophies of life? What ought we to be discussing? When we enter into a dialogue of this kind, what are our premises and what are our expectations? And what is the outcome?) Second, I shall try to develop a new interpretation of mission which presupposes dialogue, is continually engaged in dialogue, never breaks it off or pushes it aside, which makes dialogue possible because it is necessary – but uses it for more than just an encounter.

I am starting from two simple facts.

1. Without the religious and cultural dialogue between religious communities, no one will be able to understand anything – no Christian, no Jew, no Muslim, and no Hindu or Buddhist. People who just stay in their own little circles and stew in their own juice become stupefied, because wherever they are they always hear only the same thing, the thing which endorses them. But sooner or later, what is no different will become for the people who are no

different a matter of indifference. It is only from the other that we become aware of what we ourselves are, and sure of our identity.

2. No one has ever become a Christian or a Jew or a Muslim or a Hindu or a Buddhist through interfaith dialogue. The dialogue between the religious communities has a tranquillizing effect on things as they actually are, and is in tendency completely conservative. We all remain just what we were, but in dialogue we 'converse', or are simply nice to each other; otherwise we leave each other in peace, religiously speaking. Without peace between the world religions there will be no peace in the world, says my friend Hans Küng. He is right. If we don't talk to each other today perhaps we shall be shooting at each other tomorrow. And yet in view of the many deadly perils in the world in which the religious communities live, we can surely expect rather more of these communities than a cease-fire and a 'leave us in peace'.

So I shall ask critically: dialogue yes – but to what end? Mission, yes – but in what direction?

I. THE PRESENT STATE OF INTERFAITH DIALOGUE

The history of the religions has seen abundant opportunities for encounter, and a rich variety of ways of living together. Dialogue is only one of them, and it is a specifically modern, originally Western possibility at that, for it presupposes the separation between religion and state power, as well as individual religious liberty.

1. The original and most widespread form was and is a unity of religion and state. In antiquity, the states were religious states, and great religions were state religions. Worship was accounted the first civic duty, and the kings and emperors, Pharaohs and Caesars were the high priests of the territories over which they ruled. As the father of his country (*pater patriae*), the Roman Caesar was at the same time the *pontifex maximus* for Jupiter, the father of the gods. In the world of the Egyptian Pharaohs, the great Persian kings and the Chinese emperors, things were no different. The state religion legitimated the absolutism of the rulers. Their rule therefore became a 'holy rule' which promised their subjects salvation. Anyone who refused to conform to the public state cult counted as an enemy of the gods and the realm. That person evoked the wrath of the gods, which brought misfortune to country and people, and he therefore had to be sacrificed. Countries in which Buddhism or Islam have been made the state religion still exist today. Countries in which Marxism-Leninism was made the state ideology existed earlier in the

Eastern bloc, now a thing of the past. In the Holy Roman Empire, the Emperor Constantine and his successors Theodosius and Justinian made Christianity the imperial religion for their realm, with its many peoples.

In the Western world this unity of state and Christian religion existed right down to the present – in Germany until the Weimar Constitution of 1919, where Article 48 says for the first time: 'There is no state church.' The 'religious' state united under a single denomination was for long a political ideal: one king – one law – one religion. It was with this absolutist motto that the Protestant minorities were driven out of France, Austria, Italy and Hungary, and Catholics out of England.

If a religion becomes a political religion in this sense, then religious wars are more likely to result than religious dialogue. The other denomination of one's own religion will be persecuted as apostasy. The other state religion will be eradicated as idolatry and devil worship, and its adherents forcibly converted. The encounter between state religions usually led to the annihilation of the weaker one, and to the defection of its adherents, who ranged themselves on the side of the gods of the bigger battalions. Wars of religion, or wars in which the religions became the driving powers of aggression – as in Bosnia – always have to do with political religions.

But the political religions of the ancient world were not as totalitarian as the modern ones. The state cult was binding on everyone; but beneath that threshold the Roman empire, with its myriad peoples, was tolerant. Families could worship their private gods, the *penates,* in their own homes. The private associations could keep their Mithras cult, and the diverse military units their national gods. Things were no different in the Chinese empire and in Buddhist countries. On these levels – the levels below the state cult – religions spread, new ones sprang up, and there was dialogue and an easy-going co-existence among the different religious communities, which were made up of families, kinships, clans and castes.

If religious communities affirmed the right to elevation as the religion of the state – if, that is, they came forward with an absolute and universal claim – a public trial of power was, from time immemorial, open to the contestants, like the contest between Moses and Pharaoh's 'magicians' in Egypt, or – a rather more modern example – the public disputations between the priests and the missionaries, the representatives of the religious communities which were battling for cultic power in the state. The forum was the seat of central power – the king's court, or the city council. After the arguments for 'the true' religion and against the false one had been exchanged, the king or the city council decided which religion was to hold sway in the country, as the 'true' and 'beneficial' one, and which religion had to be banished, because it was 'false' and 'would bring misfortune'. The religious disputation was a dialogue leading to a public political decision, a kind of court proceeding, with indictment, defence and verdict. This was also the way the Reformation was introduced into the Holy Roman Empire in the sixteenth century. After the Leipzig disputation between Luther and Eck, the Reformation faith was established in Saxony by the Electoral Prince. After the Zürich disputation, for which Zwingli formulated the theses, the Reformation was introduced into the city by the city council.

What does this brief glance at the widespread unity of religion and state suggest to us about interfaith dialogue?

(a) In Asia and Africa (except for Ethiopia), a non-political – i.e., a non-Constantinian – Christianity has existed ever since the first century as a religious minority living tolerantly with other religious groups. Strong family ties ensure the survival of these Christian communities in India and Egypt. The only mission these churches know is non-violent mission, mission through conviction, simply through the process of co-existence. Of course there were and are dialogues with representatives of other religious groups, but they have no great importance. The Protestant church in China did not grow out of religious or ideological dialogue; it emerged out of martyrdom during Mao's brutal, anti-religious cultural revolution. It survived in house churches and in steadfast Christians, and today has between sixty and eighty million members. The Orthodox Church in the former Soviet Union never entered into dialogue with state representatives of the ruling Marxist-Leninist ideology, and even in 1967 refused to participate in our last Christian-Marxist dialogue in Marienbad; and yet it has outlived the Marxist state religion.

(b) In the Western world, religious pluralism, and with it interfaith dialogue, developed very differently, for here the foundation was the ancient *corpus christianum*. Until the Reformation, Christianity in its Roman Catholic form was the imperial religion. After the Reformation, denominationally unified 'religious' states were established according to the motto *cuius regio eius religio*. The denominational divisions of Christianity and the existence of Jewish communities promoted the modern type of the secular state, which is neutral towards religion. This developed in Holland first of all, then in

Prussia, later in France, and so on. Initially, the secularization of the state means only that governmental power has no competence in religious questions and must let the religious groups settle their internal affairs by themselves, 'although within the limits of the law to which all are subject' – that law being the human and civil right to religious liberty. The separation of church and state, and the right to religious liberty, have made of the denominationally unified 'religious' states of the Christian world modern *multifaith societies*. What do we mean by that?

(i)   In a state constituted in this way, all religious communities must be treated alike.

(ii) The state ensures the individual's religious liberty: everyone is free to enter a religious group or to leave it, and is also free while he or she belongs to it. The state cannot allow any religion to dispute the right to religious liberty.

(iii) All religious communities are free within the limits of the rule of law which is valid for all. No secular state can permit groups in the name of their religion to torture witches, burn heretics, mutilate girls, burn widows, sacrifice children, torment animals, train suicide squads, or terrorize and execute members who have defected. It is only if this frame of reference is clear to the different religious communities in the secular society that they can enter into dialogue with each other. The state must reject as attacks on its free constitutional structure any attempt to abolish the separation between religion and state, and to set up a theocracy, as well as efforts to subjugate adherents of a religious group psychologically; for the state is responsible for the multifaith society's frame of reference. The religions are subordinate to religious freedom, not religious freedom to a religion.

But this frame of reference modifies quite considerably the life of the religious communities that accept it. They automatically lose their total claim, and become relative to the personal religious liberty of the people. If religion is no longer 'a matter for the state', it becomes 'a private affair'. We respect the liberty of other people in religious matters, and require them to respect ours. Personal decisions of faith are not really open to discussion, because they are not open to dispute. Everyone can believe what he or she likes, and no institution has the right to lay down rules for them; only, they must not make an absolute claim for what they believe, and take this to radical lengths. Because decision in religious questions is shifted from the state to the individual, religions change their character. They are no longer a civic duty; they are a spiritual offer in the service sector of the market society's supermarket economy. They offer 'spiritual resources' for 'the mastery of contingencies', to use the language of secular sociologists – meaning by that the mastery of such critical situations as disablement, sickness, loss, or death. The religions which are processed for the religious market of the Western, multifaith society are therefore no longer what they once were, or what they are elsewhere. What emerges is a Christianity without expectation of the kingdom of God, a Judaism without the land of Israel, and an Islam without a geographical 'house of Islam'.

The earlier absolute, in our case the Christian claim in a Christian world, has been replaced by the secular world's claim to religious pluralism, which is maintained just as exclusively. It is impermissible to make anything absolute – except pluralism. In 1968, in his criticism of the bourgeois world, Herbert Marcuse called this 'repressive tolerance'. If we add the modern marketing of religions in the modern world, it is then the repressive tolerance of the consumer society. Modern interfaith dialogue is evidently meant to minister to the establishment of religious peace in religious pluralism. This is something new in the history of religion. Up to now this modern religious peace has not had a particularly enlivening effect on the faith communities: rather, it has put them out of commission socially and politically, turning them into a personal 'do as you please'.

In the three biblical religions, Judaism, Christianity and Islam, the general opinion would seem to be that one must have a monogamous relationship to one's religion – one person, one religion. But in Asia, the pluralism of the religions can be lived polygamously too. In Japan there is the Three Religions Movement, in Taiwan the Five Religions Movement. In India one can also live the religions successively, according to the stage in life one has reached. In Japan one can be married in a Christian ceremony, celebrate the New Year in a Shinto temple, and meditate among the Buddhists. So there is no need to take such a narrow view of religion as we are accustomed to do. Of course one can also dispense with all religious offers, on the ground that they make no difference to life as it is actually lived.

2. The programme of modern interfaith dialogue is really a conservative programme. It completely leaves out all the criticism of religion made by Feuerbach, Marx and Freud. Through conversations, the religious communities

are supposed to dismantle their prejudices, get rid of their bogey-man images and their aggressions, and arrive at peaceful co-existence in mutual respect. This is vitally important. Multifaith societies can be incomparably fruitful and lively, but they can also explode and be deadly, as history shows. But if peaceful co-existence is the goal of dialogue, then in contrast to the religious disputations we mentioned earlier, dialogue has no higher goal than itself: dialogue is the goal of dialogue. Dialogue doesn't lead beyond dialogue, but only to a deepening of dialogue. In interfaith dialogue the common path is also the goal. It is under-standable that in the countries of the Western world interest in these dialogues is considerable, for here multifaith societies are supposed to develop, and yet social peace has to be maintained. But it is equally understandable that in Islamic countries and among Hindus in India and Buddhists in Burma interest in the Western offer of dialogue is relatively slight.

If interfaith dialogue is directed towards the ethical goals of tolerance and freedom, what the communities have in common is generally speaking put in the foreground; and all the hitherto absolutist religions therefore now vie with each other to be accounted the most tolerant. If the religious concern is in the foreground, the unbridgeable differences surface. In Iran the mullahs didn't want to talk with Christian 'pluralists', but only with convinced Christian theologians, who take their own religion seriously to the point of making an absolute claim for it. We would do the same thing with Muslims and Buddhists and Marxists.

Experiences of dialogue on an international level up to now show a number of imbalances. I am mentioning them, not in order to hinder the dialogue, but so as to make it more serious. We all know the dialogues which run according to the following pattern: a Christian theologian puts questions – a rabbi, a mullah or a swami readily replies. But they ask nothing on their own account, because they aren't interested in Christianity. At most they may make critical remarks about the decadence of the Western world, which they take to be the Christian world. Many mullahs reject interfaith dialogue, because self-criticism is foreign to them, and they are therefore not prepared to allow any criticism of Islam; instead they simply give propaganda speeches everywhere on behalf of the Qur'an. They prefer to talk about a 'cultural dialogue' such as was held at the Islam conference in Cairo in 1996. A well-known pioneer of Christian-Jewish dialogue in Germany noticed the one-sidedness after twenty years, and said to me rather sadly: 'The Jews never asked me anything.' The result is that some dialogues turn into discussions between Christian theologians in the presence of astonished and silent rabbis, swamis or Buddhist monks. 'Of course you can ask us anything at all,' they say – and see that as their contribution to the dialogue.

Another imbalance is that minorities are always very interested in public dialogue, but majorities are not. Representatives of Islam have no interest in dialogues with Coptic Christians in Egypt, or with Christian minorities in Iran or Turkey, Iraq or Syria; but in the Christian countries of Europe they gladly finance Muslim-Christian dialogues as a way of presenting themselves. I experienced this myself in Turin and Naples. When I suggested that the next Christian-Muslim dialogue should be held just as publicly in Cairo or Riad, the Muslims quite coolly waved the proposal aside. In Christian countries which are now multifaith, they demand tolerance for Islam, a tolerance which they notoriously deny to Christians, Jews and Hindus in their own 'house of Islam'. Religious freedom is fine when it permits Christians to become Muslims, but it would be a bad thing if it allowed Muslims to become Christians. At the centre of Catholic Christendom in Rome, a costly and lavish mosque was built with Saudi-Arabian money. In Riad, not even Christian crosses can be worn round the necks or on the clothing of Christian clergy. The Archbishop of Canterbury told me that he had to change on the plane. But the minimum requirement for dialogue is reciprocal hospitality and mutual respect.

3. There are two different forms of interfaith dialogue: direct dialogue about the different religious ideas of the participants, and indirect dialogue, about ethical, social and ecological topics of common concern.

The *direct dialogue* is the religious dialogue between different so-called world religions – religions, that is, which are not confined to a single people and a single culture, but appeal to each and every human being, and are therefore to be found everywhere in the world. Among these, of the Abrahamic religions Christianity and Islam may be mentioned especially; of the Asian religions, Hinduism, Buddhism and Confucianism. Over against the allegedly primitive animist religions, these used once to be called the 'advanced' religions.

In spite of all the political impediments imposed by anti-semitism, the Christian-Jewish dialogue is the most fruitful, for we share 'a single book and a single hope', as Martin Buber put it. The dialogue is a dialogue over an open book, so to speak – the Tenach/Old Testament – and a dispute about interpretation in the spirit of the Torah or the spirit of the gospel.

The Christian-Muslim dialogue is burdened not only by a painful political history on both sides, but also by the fundamentalism which elevates the Qur'an or the Bible into the infallible divine Word, and forbids all historical criticism or self-criticism as Western or modern decadence. As the publications show, it is difficult to get beyond mutual missionizing or propaganda speechifying. But for this dialogue too there is a shared pre-history in the Tenach/Old Testament, and in Abraham a shared father in faith.

Christian-Buddhist dialogue is exceedingly difficult, once one gets beyond the initial exchange of superficial courtesies. An American-Japanese dialogue group has therefore drawn up a long-term programme which indicates possible approaches. The Buddhist interpretations of Christian texts by Masao Abe and Christian interpretations of Buddhist texts by David Tracy are extremely helpful.

Chinese Confucianism seems at first quite convincing as a family ethic, but if it is used for the purposes of Asian educative dictatorships opposed to allegedly Western human rights (as was earlier the case in Korea and is still so in Singapore), Confucianism ceases to be available as dialogue partner.

Taoism is much more exciting. Ever since Leibniz in the seventeenth century, Laotse ('Tao te King') has been famed as a 'natural theology', while today it is extolled as an ecological cosmology. The parallels to Jewish Wisdom literature and to Christian cosmos mysticism are certainly astounding. But there are very few Taoist scholars in the world today.

The ideal of interfaith dialogue is that the world religions should arrive at peace with each other, and should be brought to co-operate in efforts for world peace. But this is of course a Western idea, for 'book' religions are better equipped for spoken dialogue and logical argumentation than meditative or ritual ones. This is already evident from the fact that in all the different dialogue programmes, the animist religions of Africa, America and Australia do not crop up at all.

Indirect dialogue takes place today on Earth Day, for example, at global forum conferences, and at conferences on the environment held under the aegis of the UN and UNESCO. The purpose here is not the exchange of religious ideas, or a theological dispute about 'the truth'. The underlying concern is a shared perception of the perils in which the world stands today, and the common search for ways out of those perils. How, up to now, have the major religions of the world helped to justify the spoilations of the world – and what can they do to save it? Where do the religions harbour a resignation hostile to life, or forces – apocalyptic forces, for example – which are destructive of the world and prepared for violence? And what changes are necessary if the religions are to become forces which affirm humanity's life and preserve the world?

This dialogue is indirect because we are all talking, not about ourselves or each other, but about a third factor. Hans Küng's programme for 'a global ethic' is really also a call to a general, indirect dialogue of the religions about an ethic which will preserve the world from devastation and ruin. This at least, was the message of the Parliament of the World's Religions held in Chicago in 1993.

The ecological crisis or catastrophe from which the Third World particularly is suffering requires the 'advanced' religions to return to the earth. Up to now these religions have had little to say at the environmental conferences I have mentioned except for generalities, whereas representatives of the despised 'primitive', animist religions disseminate profound wisdom about the cycles and rhythms of the earth. At a conference of this kind in Moscow in 1990 we heard the 'indigenous' children of the earth – the Mayas of Central America, Africans from the Cameroons, and Aborigines from Australia – talk about 'mother earth' and our 'grandmother the moon', and their harmony with the spirit (Tao) of the cosmos; and we were moved. The ancient wisdom of these peoples in their dealings with the organism of the earth is certainly pre-industrial; but in a post-industrial age it is going to become highly relevant. We only have to translate this past into our future. Today it is not just a question of peace between the world religions which dominate the world of men and women. It is also a question of rediscovering 'the religion of the earth', which the human religions must approach in sympathetic understanding, if the organism of the earth is to survive, and we with it.

II. MISSION IS THE INVITATION TO LIFE

Having thus summed up the present position of dialogue between the religions today, we may pass on to the second part of our discussion, and look at ideas for a new concept of mission. Here a fresh approach would seem to be called for.

1. Earlier, Christian mission meant the spread of the Christian *imperium*. The salvation of the nations was supposed to lie in their subjugation to the

'holy rule' of the Christian emperor, for his rule was nothing less than the Thousand Years' Empire of Christ on earth, the empire at the end of history, in which Christ will reign with his own, and they will judge the nations. Under these auspices, Charlemagne 'missionized' the Saxons, Otto the Great the Slavs, Columbus the Caribbean, Hernando Cortés the Aztecs, and Pizzaro the Incas. Baptism or death was the apocalyptic motto. In the nineteenth century, the violent Christian *imperium* was replaced by 'Christian civilization' and by the cultural mission of Christianity in Africa and Asia. This found the support of European economic imperialism. In our own century 'the community of Western values' bears only faint traces of that earlier political and cultural Christian messianism.

2. Later came Christian mission as the spread of Christian churches from Rome *urbi et orbi,* from Wittenberg, Geneva and Canterbury. The salvation of men and women is to be found in their subjection to 'the holy rule' of the Christian church, for its rule is nothing other than the Thousand Years' Empire of Christ, in which Christ will reign with those who are his, and will judge the nations. The church is 'the mother and preceptress of the nations', as a papal encyclical asserts. Mission and the spread of the church have led to the world-wide dissemination of Roman Catholic, Anglican, Methodist and Lutheran churches, and of all Europe's other Christian denominations. We may safely say that to the degree to which self-styled 'Christendom' disintegrated in Europe, the churches as churches – not as European state religions – became present all over the world. The European secularization of state and culture made the churches, through their mission, 'secular' in the original sense of the word, that is to say world-wide.

3. Finally, ever since the nineteenth century we have been familiar with mission as the evangelization of humanity. That means awakening personal experiences of faith in God's Spirit, and bringing people to make their own personal decisions of faith. Salvation lies in the acknowledgement of Christ's 'holy rule'. 'Accept Christ as your personal Lord and Saviour, and you will be saved.' This kind of mission too is deeply influenced by the expected future of God and his presence in the Spirit.

Common to these three forms of Christian mission is the fact that they are messianically and apocalyptically motivated. They all start from something which in the present exists only in particularist form, and try to globalize it, whether it be the Christian *imperium* or the Christian church or the Christian experience of conversion.

I would suggest proceeding in the reverse direction. If we understand mission, not as an aggressive appropriation of the whole, but as an invitation to God's future, then we begin with that universal future of the nations and the earth, and give it present force in the gospel of hope and in the service of love. We invite people of other religions and ideologies to work together for that future which we try to imagine in the symbols of the kingdom of God, eternal life, and the new creation of heaven and earth. The religions and cultures of other people will not thereby be destroyed; they will be interpenetrated by the Spirit of hope, and opened for the future of the world. This corresponds very well to the invitation to that indirect dialogue about the present dangers to the world, and ways of surmounting them. Why, one must finally ask, should we alone worry about life and survival in this self-destructive world? But how is that to be theologically interpreted?

Mission in the original theological sense of the word is *missio Dei* – God's sending. But what does God send? According to biblical understanding (both Jewish and Christian) he sends nothing less than his *Spirit* into this world, through the Christ, the Messiah. This is the Spirit who is the life-giver and who is therefore called *the Spirit of life,* or *the source of life.* According to the Gospel of John, what God brings into the world through Christ can be summed up in a single word, *life.* 'I live and you shall live also' (John 14:19). What is meant is the fulfiled life – the wholly and entirely living life – the shared life – the eternal life – the fullness of life. It is experienced in the new livingness of love. Nor is it just human life that is meant, for according to the prophetic message this living power of God will be poured out 'on all flesh', which in the language of the Old Testament means everything living. God's sending is biocentrically oriented, not anthropocentrically. It is not concerned with the political or religious rule of human beings over the world, and not merely with the salvation of human souls, but with the liberation, salvation and final redemption of the life shared.

Its goal is therefore 'the new creation of all things'. The eternal life which is the gift of the Spirit who is the life-giver is not a life other than this life here and now; it is the power through which this life here will be different. This mortal, temporal life gains a share in the divine life, and through that becomes life that is eternal: *'This* perishable nature must put on the imperishable, and *this* mortal nature must put on immortality', stresses Paul (I Cor. 15:53). So Nietzsche was right: 'Eternal life is eternal livingness.' If God's sending embraces the whole of life, the shared life of all the living, it must not be reduced to religion and inwardness and 'the salvation of our souls', important though our 'souls' are.

Jesus didn't bring a new religion into the world. He brought new life. He didn't found 'Christianity', nor did he set up an ecclesial rule over the nations. He brought life into this violent and dying world, the life 'that was from the beginning, which we have looked upon and touched ... and the life was made manifest, and we saw it, and testify to it, and we proclaim to you the life that is eternal ...' (1 John 1:1–2). Christ is the divine Yes to life. That Yes leads to the healing of the sick, to the acceptance of the marginalized, to the forgiveness of sins, and to the saving of impaired life from the powers of destruction. This is the way the Gospels tell about Jesus' mission. And according to the Gospels this is also the character of the mission of the women and men who live in his Spirit (Matt. 10:7–8).

If we apply this sending – this mission – to the situation of life as it is today, then we come to at least three points of intersection.

1. It is not only our human life that is in deadly danger. Ever since Hiroshima in 1945 this has been true for life itself. Tens of thousands of nuclear weapons are lying ready for 'the final solution' of the question of the human race. In the nuclear winter that will follow their deployment, all higher life on earth will die. The nuclear end of life is possible at any time, even if at present it is not probable; so in this sense we are living in an 'end-time'. Through political efforts for peace we can extend our time limit – but no time is conceivable in which human beings will no longer be capable of doing what they can do today. The formulae for the weapons of mass annihilation can never again be forgotten once they have been discovered. The mission for life requires unconditional service for peace, and work for the abolition of war as a means of settling conflicts. Humanity is intended for life, for God is a 'God of life'. In this context, or at this point of intersection, mission is the invitation to life.

2. Ever since Chernobyl in 1986, all life has been in deadly danger, not just human life. A whole region was contaminated by radioactivity, and made uninhabitable for centuries. Two hundred times more radioactivity was released in Chernobyl than in Hiroshima and Nagasaki. Up to now about 150,000 people in the area have died from radiation-related illnesses. And children are still dying, for example from leukaemia.

For the invitation to life, the conclusion from this has to be a new 'reverence for life', as Albert Schweitzer put it. At this point of intersection, mission is the invitation to joint resistance against technologies hostile to life, and the development of a way of dealing with energy which will be nature-friendly.

3. Over-population means more and more 'surplus people' whom nobody wants and nobody needs. Violence against life is on the increase, even in the name of religion. The abandonment of the street children, child prostitution, the unemployment of both women and men, the squeezing out of the old from the health services: these are only some aspects of the cynical way our society deals with young, old, and sick or impaired life. The production of 'surplus life' and the acts of violence perpetrated against this 'surplus life' are also among the deadly dangers of the modern world, just as are the weapons of mass destruction and the ecological crimes against nature. Here mission is the invitation to responsible dealings with life itself.

In distinction from the religious pluralism of our society, these threats to life permit no pluralism – at least no alternatives to life. The seriousness of the situation forbids the post-modernist free-for-all. 'Anything goes' has long since given way to 'nothing goes at all any more'.

In this context, the question is not whether other religions can also be 'paths to salvation': whether in religions other than Christianity people are also searching for God, and can perhaps find God; whether, that is , there are 'anonymous Christians' among members of other religious communities too, as Karl Rahner conjectured – or however the questions about the theological significance of other religions may be formulated. In this context the question is rather the question about *life* in other religions, and also, of course, the question about life in the non-religious, secular world. The mission to which God sends men and women means inviting *all* human beings, the religious and the non-religious, to life, to the affirmation of life, to the protection of life, to shared life, and to eternal life. Everything which ministers to life in other religions and cultures is good, and must be absorbed into the coming 'culture of life'. Everything which among us and other people is a hindrance to life, destroys it, or sacrifices it is bad, and must be overcome as a 'barbarism of death'.

Earlier, the significance for Christianity of the plurality of the religions was treated theologically under the heading of original sin, and the myth of the Tower of Babel. Today some theologians think that religious truth itself is pluriform, and must therefore manifest itself in a plurality of religions. For me, the theological 'site' at which people of other religions come into view is pneumatology and, within the doctrine of the Holy Spirit of life, the teaching about the protean variety of life's potentialities and life's powers – the potentialities and powers we call charismata. Which forms and concepts in the world of the religions minister to life? Can a religion or a culture become a charisma of God's Spirit for people once they become Christians and begin to love life with the love of God?

Earlier, when the religions fell under the doctrine of original sin, people who became Christians had to cut themselves off radically from the 'superstition' of their forefathers and the 'idolatry' of their people. According to the new pluralistic theology of religions, people don't have to become Christians at all if they have found the divine truth in their own religion. In my own view, everything a person is, and everything that has moulded that person culturally and religiously, can become a charisma, if he or she is called by Christ, and loves life, and helps to work for the kingdom of God. 'Everyone as the Lord has called them' (1 Cor. 7:17). So there are Jewish Christians and Gentile Christians, each with their own dignity. There are many different gifts, but one Spirit (1 Cor. 12:4). There are many, many forms of life, but it is one life.

Lastly, conditions won't change *unless people change.* How else can they change? People must be different if the world is to be different. If we want peace on earth, we must become peaceable men and women. If we want a future for our children and our children's children we ourselves must overcome our lethargy and our egoism and be born again to a living hope for the future. If life is to survive, and if its deadly dangers are to be surmounted, faith must be awakened in us and other people, a 'faith that moves mountains'. The unconditional love for life must awaken in us. There is no future without hope. There is no life without love. There is no new assurance without faith. It is the task of evangelization and of the witness of Christian life to proclaim the living Christ and to awaken in us the Spirit of life.

11

POPE JOHN PAUL II: Address of the Holy Father to the Congregation for the Doctrine of the Faith

John Paul II (b. 1920) became Pope in 1978. A philosopher and theologian in his own right, he has taken an increasingly conservative line, not least over the question of Christianity and the other world religions. Without repudiating the stance of Vatican II (see chapter 3 above), he has reaffirmed the uniqueness and finality of Christ very strongly, a position reinforced and extended by Cardinal Ratzinger in the Congregation for the Doctrine of the Faith's declaration, "'Dominus Jesus": On the Unicity and Salvific Universality of Jesus Christ and the Church', extracts from which are appended here to the Pope's Address.

YOUR EMINENCES, VENERABLE BROTHERS IN THE EPISCOPATE AND THE PRIESTHOOD, DEAR FAITHFUL COLLABORATORS

1. It is a great joy for me to meet you at the end of your plenary assembly. I want to express my gratitude and appreciation for the work that your dicastery accomplishes each day in the service of the Church for the good of souls, in harmony with the Successor of Peter, the first guardian and defender of the sacred deposit of faith.

I thank Cardinal Joseph Ratzinger for the sentiments he has expressed on everyone's behalf in his address to me, and for explaining the topics that you have carefully considered during your assembly, which was especially dedicated to studying the problem of the uniqueness of Christ and to revising the norms of the so-called 'graviora delicta' ['more serious transgressions']

2. I would now like to dwell briefly on the principal topics discussed at your meeting. Your dicastery has considered it timely and necessary to begin studying the themes of the uniqueness and salvific universality of Christ and the Church. The reaffirmation of the Church's doctrine on these themes is being proposed in order to show 'the light of the Gospel of the glory of Christ' (2 Cor. 4:4) to the world and to refute errors and serious ambiguities that have taken shape and are spreading in various circles.

In recent years a mentality has arisen in theological and ecclesial circles that tends to relativize Christ's revelation and his unique and universal mediation of salvation, as well as to diminish the need for Christ's Church as the universal sacrament of salvation.

To remedy this relativistic mentality, the definitive and complete character of Christ's revelation must first of all be emphasized. Faithful to the word of God, the Second Vatican Council teaches: 'The most intimate truth which this revelation gives us about God and the salvation of man shines forth in Christ, who is himself both the mediator and the fullness of all revelation' (Dogm. Const. *Dei Verbum*, n. 2).

For this reason, in the Encyclical Letter *Redemptoris missio* I reminded the Church of her duty to proclaim the Gospel as the fullness of truth: 'In this definitive Word of his revelation, God has made himself known in the fullest possible way. He has revealed to mankind who he is. This definitive self-revelation of God is the fundamental reason why the Church is missionary by her very nature. She cannot do other than proclaim the Gospel, that is, the fullness of the truth which God has enabled us to know about himself' (n. 5).

3. The theory on the limited nature of Christ's revelation, which would find its complement in other religions, is thus contrary to the faith of the Church. The underlying reason for this assertion claims to be based on the fact that the truth about God could not be grasped and manifested in its totality and completeness by any historical religion, and so not even by Christianity or by Jesus Christ. This position, however, contradicts the affirmations of faith that the full and complete revelation of God's saving mystery is given in Jesus Christ, while the understanding of this infinite mystery is to be explored and deepened in the light of the Spirit of truth, who guides us in the era of the Church 'into all the truth' (John 16:13).

The words, works and entire historical event of Jesus, while being limited as human realities, still have the divine Person of the incarnate Word as their source and therefore contain in themselves the definitive and complete revelation of his saving ways and of the divine mystery itself. The truth about God is not abolished or diminished because it is expressed in human language. On the contrary, it remains one, full and complete, because the one who speaks and acts is the incarnate Son of God.

4. Connected with the uniqueness of Christ's salvific mediation is the uniqueness of the Church he founded. The Lord Jesus, in fact, established his Church as a saving reality: as his Body, through which he himself accomplishes salvation in history. Just as there is only one Christ, so his Body is one alone: 'one, holy, catholic and apostolic Church' (cf. *Symbolum fidei*, DS 48). The Second Vatican Council says in this regard: 'Basing itself on Scripture and Tradition, this holy Council teaches that the Church, a pilgrim on earth, is necessary for salvation' (Dogm. Const. *Lumen gentium*, n. 14).

It is a mistake, then, to regard the Church as a way of salvation along with those constituted by other religions, which would be complementary to the Church, even if converging with her on the eschatological kingdom of God. Therefore we must reject a certain indifferentist mentality 'characterized by a religious relativism which leads to the belief that one religion is as good as another' (cf. Encyc. Let. *Redemptoris missio*, n. 36).

It is true that non-Christians – as the Second Vatican Council recalled – can 'gain' eternal life 'under the influence of grace', if 'they seek God with a sincere heart' (*Lumen gentium*, n. 16). But in their sincere search for the truth of God, they are in fact 'related' to Christ and to his Body, the Church (cf. ibid.). They nevertheless find themselves in an unsatisfactory situation compared to that of those in the Church who have the fullness of the means of salvation. Understandably, then, in accordance with the Lord's command (cf. Matt. 28:19–20) and as a requirement of her love for all people, the Church 'proclaims, and is in duty bound to proclaim without fail, Christ who is "the Way, the Truth and the Life" (John 14:6). In him, in whom God reconciled all things to himself, men find the fullness of their religious life' (Decl. *Nostra aetate*, n. 2).

5. In the Encyclical Letter *Ut unum sint*, I solemnly confirmed the Catholic Church's commitment to the 'restoration of unity', in continuity with the great cause of ecumenism which the Second Vatican Council had so much at heart. Together with the Pontifical Council for Promoting Christian Unity,

you helped to reach the agreement on fundamental truths of the doctrine of justification that was signed on 31 October last year in Augsburg. Trusting in the help of divine grace, let us go forward on this journey, even if there are difficulties. Our ardent desire to reach the day of full communion with the other Churches and Ecclesial Communities cannot obscure the truth that the Church of Christ is not a utopia to be reconstructed by our human powers from the fragments we find today. The Decree *Unitatis redintegratio* spoke explicitly of the unity which 'we believe subsists in the Catholic Church as something she can never lose, and we hope that it will continue to increase until the end of time' (n. 4).

Dear Brothers, in the service that your Congregation offers to the Successor of Peter and to the Church's Magisterium you help to ensure that Christ's revelation continues to be in history 'the true lodestar' of all humanity (cf. Encyc. Let. *Fides et ratio*, n. 15).

In congratulating you on your important and valuable ministry, I encourage you to continue with new enthusiasm in your service to the saving truth: *Christus heri, hodie et semper!*

With these sentiments I cordially give you all a special Apostolic Blessing as a pledge of my affection and gratitude.

EXTRACTS FROM THE DECLARATION 'DOMINUS IESUS' ON THE UNICITY AND SALVIFIC UNIVERSALITY OF JESUS CHRIST AND THE CHURCH

In the course of the centuries, the Church has proclaimed and witnessed with fidelity to the Gospel of Jesus. At the close of the second millennium, however, this mission is still far from complete. For that reason, Saint Paul's words are now more relevant than ever: 'Preaching the Gospel is not a reason for me to boast; it is a necessity laid on me: woe to me if I do not preach the Gospel!' (1 Cor. 9:16). This explains the Magisterium's particular attention to giving reasons for and supporting the evangelizing mission of the Church, above all in connection with the religious traditions of the world.

In considering the values which these religions witness to and offer humanity, with an open and positive approach, the Second Vatican Council's Declaration on the relation of the Church to non-Christian religions states: 'The Catholic Church rejects nothing of what is true and holy in these religions. She has a high regard for the manner of life and conduct, the precepts and teachings, which, although differing in many ways from her own teaching, nonetheless often reflect a ray of that truth which enlightens all men.' Continuing in this line of thought, the Church's proclamation of Jesus Christ, 'the way, the truth, and the life' (John 14:6), today also makes use of the practice of inter-religious dialogue. Such dialogue certainly does not replace, but rather accompanies the *missio ad gentes*, directed toward that 'mystery of unity', from which 'it follows that all men and women who are saved share, though differently, in the same mystery of salvation in Jesus Christ through his Spirit'. Inter-religious dialogue, which is part of the Church's evangelizing mission, requires an attitude of understanding and a relationship of mutual knowledge and reciprocal enrichment, in obedience to the truth and with respect for freedom. ...

The Church's constant missionary proclamation is endangered today by relativistic theories which seek to justify religious pluralism, not only *de facto* but also *de iure* (or *in principle*). As a consequence, it is held that certain truths have been superseded; for example, the definitive and complete character of the revelation of Jesus Christ, the nature of Christian faith as compared with that of belief in other religions, the inspired nature of the books of Sacred Scripture, the personal unity between the Eternal Word and Jesus of Nazareth, the unity of the economy of the Incarnate Word and the Holy Spirit, the unicity and salvific universality of the mystery of Jesus Christ, the universal salvific mediation of the Church, the inseparability – while recognizing the distinction – of the kingdom of God, the kingdom of Christ, and the Church, and the subsistence of the one Church of Christ in the Catholic Church.

   The roots of these problems are to be found in certain presuppositions of both a philosophical and theological nature, which hinder the understanding and acceptance of the revealed truth. Some of these can be mentioned: the conviction of the elusiveness and inexpressibility of divine truth, even by Christian revelation; relativistic attitudes toward truth itself, according to which what is true for some would not be true for others; the radical opposition posited between the logical mentality of the West and the symbolic mentality of the East; the subjectivism which, by regarding reason as the only source of knowledge, becomes incapable of raising its 'gaze to the heights, not daring to rise to the truth of being', the difficulty in understanding and accepting the presence of definitive and eschatological events in history; the metaphysical emptying of the historical incarnation of the Eternal Logos, reduced to a mere appearing of God in history; the eclecticism of those who, in theological research, uncritically absorb ideas from a variety of philosophical and theological contexts without regard for consistency, systematic connection, or compatibility with Christian truth; finally, the tendency to read and to interpret Sacred Scripture outside the Tradition and Magisterium of the Church.

On the basis of such presuppositions, which may evince different nuances, certain theological proposals are developed – at times presented as assertions, and at times as hypotheses – in which Christian revelation and the mystery of Jesus Christ and the Church lose their character of absolute truth and salvific universality, or at least shadows of doubt and uncertainty are cast upon them.

As a remedy for this relativistic mentality, which is becoming ever more common, it is necessary above all to reassert the definitive and complete character of the revelation of Jesus Christ. In fact, it must be *firmly believed* that, in the mystery of Jesus Christ, the Incarnate Son of God, who is 'the way, the truth, and the life' (John 14:6), the full revelation of divine truth is given: 'No one knows the Son except the Father, and no one knows the Father except the Son and anyone to whom the Son wishes to reveal him' (Matt. 11:27); 'No one has ever seen God; God the only Son, who is in the bosom of the Father has revealed him' (John 1:18), 'For in Christ the whole fullness of divinity dwells in bodily form' (Col. 2:9–10). ...

Only the revelation of Jesus Christ, therefore, 'introduces into our history a universal and ultimate truth which stirs the human mind to ceaseless effort'.

Therefore, the theory of the limited, incomplete, or imperfect character of the revelation of Jesus Christ, which would be complementary to that found in other religions, is contrary to the Church's faith. Such a position would claim to be based on the notion that the truth about God cannot be grasped and manifested in its globality and completeness by any historical religion, neither by Christianity nor by Jesus Christ.

Such a position is in radical contradiction with the foregoing statements of Catholic faith according to which the full and complete revelation of the salvific mystery of God is given in Jesus Christ. Therefore, the words, deeds, and entire historical event of Jesus, though limited as human realities, have nevertheless the divine Person of the Incarnate Word, 'true God and true man' as their subject. For this reason, they possess in themselves the definitiveness and completeness of the revelation of God's salvific ways, even if the depth of the divine mystery in itself remains transcendent and inexhaustible. The truth about God is not abolished or reduced because it is spoken in human language; rather, it is unique, full, and complete, because he who speaks and acts is the Incarnate Son of God. Thus, faith requires us to profess that the Word made flesh, in his entire mystery, who moves from incarnation to glorification, is the source, participated but real, as well as the fulfilment of every salvific revelation of God to humanity, and that the Holy Spirit, who is Christ's Spirit, will teach this 'entire truth' (John 16:13) to the Apostles and, through them, to the whole Church. ...

It must therefore be *firmly believed* as a truth of Catholic faith that the universal salvific will of the One and Triune God is offered and accomplished once for all in the mystery of the incarnation, death and resurrection of the Son of God.

Bearing in mind this article of faith, theology today, in its reflection on the existence of other religious experiences and on their meaning in God's salvific plan, is invited to explore if and in what way the historical figures and positive elements of these religions may fall within the divine plan of salvation. In this undertaking, theological research has a vast field of work under the guidance of the Church's Magisterium. The Second Vatican Council, in fact, has stated that: 'the unique mediation of the Redeemer does not exclude, but rather gives rise to a manifold cooperation which is but a participation in this one source'. The content of this participated mediation should be explored more deeply, but must remain always consistent with the principle of Christ's unique mediation: 'Although participated forms of mediation of different kinds and degrees are not excluded, they acquire meaning and value *only* from Christ's own mediation, and they cannot be understood as parallel or complementary to his.' Hence, those solutions that propose a salvific action of God beyond the unique mediation of Christ would be contrary to Christian and Catholic faith. ...

From what has been stated above, some points follow that are necessary for theological reflection as it explores the relationship of the Church and the other religions to salvation.

Above all else, it must be *firmly believed* that 'the Church, a pilgrim now on earth, is necessary for salvation: the one Christ is the mediator and the way of salvation; he is present to us in his body which is the Church. He himself explicitly asserted the necessity of faith and baptism (cf. Mark 16:16; John 3:5), and thereby affirmed at the same time the necessity of the Church which men enter through baptism as through a door.' This doctrine must not be set against the universal salvific will of God (cf. 1 Tim. 2:4); 'it is necessary to keep these two truths together, namely, the real possibility of salvation in Christ for all mankind and the necessity of the Church for this salvation'.

The Church is the 'universal sacrament of salvation', since, united always in a mysterious way to the Saviour Jesus Christ, her Head, and subordinated to him, she has, in God's plan, an indispensable relationship with the salvation of every human being. For those who are not formally and visibly members of the Church, 'salvation in Christ is accessible by virtue of a grace which, while having a mysterious relationship to the Church, does not make them formally part of the Church, but enlightens them in a way which is accommodated to their spiritual and material situation. This grace comes from Christ; it is the result of his sacrifice and is communicated by the Holy Spirit', it has a relationship with the Church, which 'according to the plan of the Father, has her origin in the mission of the Son and the Holy Spirit'.

With respect to the *way* in which the salvific grace of God – which is always given by means of Christ in the Spirit and has a mysterious relationship to the Church – comes to individual non-Christians, the Second Vatican Council limited itself to the statement that God bestows it 'in ways known to himself'. Theologians are seeking to understand this question more fully. Their work is to be encouraged, since it is certainly useful for understanding better God's salvific plan and the ways in which it is accomplished. However, from what has been stated above about the mediation of Jesus Christ and the 'unique and special relationship' which the Church has with the kingdom of God among men – which in substance is the universal kingdom of Christ the Saviour – it is clear that it would be contrary to the faith to consider the Church as *one way* of salvation alongside those constituted by the other religions, seen as complementary to the Church or substantially equivalent to her, even if these are said to be converging with the Church toward the eschatological kingdom of God.

Certainly, the various religious traditions contain and offer religious elements which come from God, and which are part of what 'the Spirit brings about in human hearts and in the history of peoples, in cultures, and religions'. Indeed, some prayers and rituals of the other religions may assume a role of preparation for the Gospel, in that they are occasions or pedagogical helps in which the human heart is prompted to be open to the action of God.

One cannot attribute to these, however, a divine origin or an *ex opere operato* salvific efficacy, which is proper to the Christian sacraments. Furthermore, it cannot be overlooked that other rituals, insofar as they depend on superstitions or other errors (cf. 1 Cor. 10:20–21), constitute an obstacle to salvation.

With the coming of the Saviour Jesus Christ, God has willed that the Church founded by him be the instrument for the salvation of *all* humanity (cf. Acts 17:30–31). This truth of faith does not lessen the sincere respect which the Church has for the religions of the world, but at the same time, it rules out, in a radical way, that mentality of indifferentism 'characterized by a religious relativism which leads to the belief that "one religion is as good as another".' If it is true that the followers of other religions can receive divine grace, it is also certain that *objectively speaking* they are in a gravely deficient situation in comparison with those who, in the Church, have the fullness of the means of salvation. However, 'all the children of the Church should nevertheless remember that their exalted condition results, not from their own merits, but from the grace of Christ. If they fail to respond in thought, word, and deed to that grace, not only shall they not be saved, but they shall be more severely judged.' One understands then that, following the Lord's command (cf. Matt. 28:19–20) and as a requirement of her love for all people, the Church 'proclaims and is in duty bound to proclaim without fail, Christ who is the way, the truth, and the life (John 14:6). In him, in whom God reconciled all things to himself (cf. 2 Cor. 5:18–19), men find the fullness of their religious life.'

In inter-religious dialogue as well, the mission *ad gentes* 'today as always retains its full force and necessity'. 'Indeed, God "desires all men to be saved and come to the knowledge of the truth" (1 Tim. 2:4); that is, God wills the salvation of everyone through the knowledge of the truth. Salvation is found in the truth. Those who obey the promptings of the Spirit of truth are already on the way of salvation. But the Church, to whom this truth has been entrusted, must go out to meet their desire, so as to bring them the truth. Because she believes in God's universal plan of salvation, the Church must be missionary.' Inter-religious dialogue, therefore, as part of her evangelizing mission, is just one of the actions of the Church in her mission *ad gentes*. *Equality*, which is a presupposition of inter-religious dialogue, refers to the equal personal dignity of the parties in dialogue, not to doctrinal content, nor even less to the position of Jesus Christ – who is God himself made man – in relation to the founders of the other religions. Indeed, the Church, guided by charity and respect for freedom, must be primarily committed to proclaiming to all people the truth definitively revealed by the Lord, and to announcing the necessity of conversion to Jesus Christ and of adherence to the Church through Baptism and the other sacraments, in order to participate fully in communion with God, the Father, Son and Holy Spirit. Thus, the certainty of the universal salvific will of God does not diminish, but rather increases the duty and urgency of the proclamation of salvation and of conversion to the Lord Jesus Christ.

Acknowledgements

'The Revelation of God as the Abolition of Religion' consists of extracts from Karl Barth's *Church Dogmatics*, Vol. I, part 2 (English trans., 1956), section 17, and is reprinted by kind permission of the publishers, T. & T. Clark Ltd, of Edinburgh. The selection given here was first made by O. C. Thomas for his *Attitudes Towards Other Religions* (SCM Press, London, 1969) and is reused with gratitude.

'Christianity and the Non-Christian Religions' is taken from Karl Rahner's *Theological Investigations*, Vol. V. (1966), and is reprinted by kind permission of the publishers, Darton, Longman and Todd Ltd, London and The Crossroad Publishing Company, New York.

The extracts from the Second Vatican Council's *Declaration on the Relation of the Church to Non-Christian Religions* (English trans., Thomas Athill) are reprinted by kind permission of the Catholic Truth Society, London.

'The Christian in a Religiously Plural World' is taken from *Religious Diversity: Essays by Wilfred Cantwell Smith*, edited by Willard G. Oxtoby (Harper & Row, New York, 1976), and is reprinted by kind permission of the publisher.

'The Place of Non-Christian Religions and Cultures in the Evolution of Third World Theology' is taken from Aloysius Pieris' *Theology of Liberation in Asia* (Orbis, Maryknoll, 1986) and is reprinted by kind permission of the author.

'The Christian Faith and the World Religions' is taken from *Keeping the Faith. Essays to Mark the Centenary of Lux Mundi*, ed. G. Wainwright (Fortress Press, Philadelphia and T.&T. Clark, Edinburgh, 1988) and is reprinted by kind permission of the author's literary executor.

'Is There One True Religion? An Essay in Establishing Ecumenical Criteria' is taken from Hans Küng's Theology for the Third Millennium (English trans., Harper Collins, Glasgow, 1988) and is reprinted by kind permission of the author.

'Christian Theology of Liberation and Interfaith Dialogue' consists in extracts from Paul Knitter's article of that title which appeared in the Anarardi Journal of Theological Reflection, Vol. VI, 1 (Jan.–June 1993) and is reprinted by kind permission of the author.

'The Theological Challenge of Religious Pluralism' was first published in *Introduction to Christian Theology*, edited by Roger A. Badham (Westminster/John Knox Press, Louisville, KY, 1998) and is reprinted by permission of the author.

'"Dialogue of Mission?" Christianity and the Religions in an Endangered World' is taken from Jürgen Moltmann's *God for a Secular Society. The Public Relevance of Theology* (English trans., SCM Press, London, 1999) and is reprinted by kind permission of the author.

Pope John Paul II's Address (28 January 2000) and the Congregation for the Doctrine of the Faith's Declaration (6 August 2000) are made available on the Vatican web site (www.vatican.va).

Bibliography

I. CHRISTIAN ATTITUDES TO OTHER RELIGIONS

K. P. Aleaz, *Theology of Religions*. Moumita, Calcutta, 1998

Gerald Anderson and Thomas Stransky, eds, *Christ's Lordship and Religious Pluralism*. Orbis, Maryknoll, NY, 1981

J. N. D. Anderson, *Christianity and Comparative Religion*. Tyndale Press, Wheaton, Illinois, 1970/Inter-Varsity Press, London, 1971

—, *Christianity and the World Religions*. Inter-Varsity Press, Leicester, 1984

Hasan Askari, *Spiritual Quest: An Inter-Religious Dimension*. Severn Mirrors Publishing House, Pudsey, 1991

Michael Barnes, *Religions in Conversation: Christian Identity and Religious Pluralism*. SPCK, London, 1989

Karl Barth, *Church Dogmatics*, Vol. 1/2, section 17 (1939). T. & T. Clark, Edinburgh, 1956

Reinhold Bernhardt, *Christianity Without Absolutes*. SCM Press, London, 1994

Walbert Buhlmann, *All Have the Same God*. St Paul Publications, Slough, 1979

William Burrows, ed., *Redemption and Dialogue*. Orbis, Maryknoll, NY, 1993

Naomi Burton, ed., *The Asian Journal of Thomas Merton*. New Directions, New York, 1973/Sheldon Press, London, 1974

Arnulf Camps, *Partners in Dialogue: Christianity and Other World Religions*. Orbis, Maryknoll, NY, 1983

John B. Cobb, *Christ in a Pluralistic Age*. Westminster Press, Philadelphia, 1975

Harvey Cox, *Many Mansions: A Christian's Encounter with Other Faiths*. Collins, London, 1988

Harold Coward, *Pluralism in the World Religions: A Short Introduction*. Oneworld, Oxford, 2000

Kenneth Cracknell, *Towards a New Relationship: Christians and People of Other Faiths*. Epworth Press, London, 1986

Kenneth Cragg, *Christianity in World Perspective*. Lutterworth Press, London, 1968
— *The Christian and Other Religion*. Mowbray, London, 1977
— *The Christ and the Faiths*. SPCK, London, 1986

Charles Davis, *Christ and the World Religions*. Hodder & Stoughton, London, 1970

Donald Dawe and John Carman, eds, *Christian Faith in a Religiously Plural World*. Orbis, Maryknoll, NY, 1978

Gavin D'Costa, ed., *John Hick's Theology of Religions*. University Press of America, New York/London, 1987
— *Christian Uniqueness Reconsidered*. Orbis, Maryknoll, NY, 1990
— *The Meeting of Religions and the Trinity*. Orbis, Maryknoll, NY/T. & T. Clark, Edinburgh, 2000

E. C. Dewick, *The Christian Attitude to Other Religions*. Cambridge University Press, 1953

John S. Dunne, *The Way of All the Earth*. Macmillan, New York/Collier Macmillan, London, 1972

Jacques Dupuis, *Jesus Christ at the Encounter of World Religions*. Orbis, Maryknoll, NY, 1991
— *Towards a Christian Theology of Religious Pluralism*. Orbis, Maryknoll, NY, 1997

James Dupuis, *Jesus Christ and His Spirit*. Theological Publications of India, Bangalore, 1977

H. H. Farmer, *Revelation and Religion*. Nisbet, London, 1954
— *Reconciliation and Religion: Some Aspects of the Uniqueness of Christianity as a Reconciling Faith*. Ed. Christopher Partridge, Edwin Mellon Press, Lampeter, 1998

Antony Fernando, *Christianity Made Intelligible, as One of the World's Religions*. Inter-Cultural Book Promotions, Kadawata, Sri Lanka, 1990

Martin Forward, ed., *God of All Faith*. Methodist Home Church Mission Division, London, 1989
— *Ultimate Visions*. Oneworld, Oxford, 1995

Walter Freytag, *The Gospel and the Religions*. SCM Press, London, 1957

Chester Gillis, *Pluralism: A New Paradigm for Theology*. Louvain, Peters Press, 1993

George Gispert-Sauch, ed., *God's Word among Men*, Vidyajoti, Delhi, 1973
— *Dialogue and Community*, World Council of Churches, Geneva, 1977

Robert Grant, *Gods and the One God*. Westminster Press, Philadelphia, 1986

Bede Griffiths, *The Marriage of East and West*. Collins, London, 1982

David Hart, *Non-Realism and the World Faiths*. Mowbray, London, 1995

S. Mark Heim, *Salvations: Truth and Difference in Religion*. Orbis, Maryknoll, NY, 1995

— ed., *Grounds for Understanding*. Eerdmans, Grand Rapids, Michigan, 1998
— *The Depth of the Riches: A Trinitarian Theology of Religious Ends*. Eerdmans, Grand Rapids, Michigan, 2000
John Hick, *God and the Universe of Faiths*. Oneworld, Oxford, 1993
— ed., *Truth and Dialogue*. Sheldon Press, London/Westminster Press, Philadelphia, 1974
— *God has Many Names*. Macmillan, London, 1980
— *Problems of Religious Pluralism*. Macmillan, London/St Martin's Press, NY, 1985
— *The Rainbow of Faiths*. SCM Press, London, 1995, published in the United States as *A Christian Theology of Religions*, Westminster/John Knox Press, Louisville, 1995
John Hick and Paul Knitter, eds, *The Myth of Christian Uniqueness*. Orbis, Maryknoll, NY/SCM Press, London, 1987
Eugene Hillman, *The Wider Ecumenism: Anonymous Christianity and the Church*. Burns & Oates, London/Herder & Herder, New York, 1968
— *Many Paths: A Catholic Approach to Religious Pluralism*. Orbis, Maryknoll, NY/SCM Press, London, 1989
W. E. Hocking, *Living Religions and a World Faith*. Allen & Unwin, London/Macmillan, New York, 1940
H. Jai Singh, ed., *Inter-Religious Dialogue*. Institute for the Study of Religion and Society, Bangalore, 1967
E. O. James, *Christianity and Other Religions*. Hodder & Stoughton, London, 1968
George Knight, *I Am: The God of the Bible and the Religions of Man*. Eerdmans, Grand Rapids, MI, 1983
Paul Knitter, *No Other Name?* Orbis, Maryknoll, NY, 1995
— *One Earth Many Religions: Multifaith Dialogue and Global Responsibility*. Orbis, Maryknoll, NY, 1995
Paul Knitter, John Cobb, Leonard Swidler and Monika Hellwig, *Death or Dialogue*. SCM Press, London, 1990
Hendrik Kraemer, *The Christian Message in a Non-Christian World*. Harper & Row, New York/Edinburgh House Press, London, 1938
— *Religion and the Christian Faith*. Lutterworth Press, London, 1956
— *World Cultures and World Religions: The Coming Dialogue*. Lutterworth Press, London, 1960
— *Why Christianity of all Religions?* Lutterworth Press, London/Westminster Press, Philadelphia, 1962
Hans Küng, 'The World Religions in God's Plan of Salvation' in *Christian Revelation and World Religions*, ed. Joseph Neuner, Burns & Oates, London, 1967
— *On Being a Christian*, Part A, III. Doubleday, New York/Collins, London, 1976
Hans Küng and Jürgen Moltmann, eds, *Christianity among World Religions*. T. & T. Clark, Edinburgh (Concilium), 1986
— *Jesus and the Other Names*. Orbis, Maryknoll, NY, 1995

A. T. van Leeuwen, *Christianity in World History*. Edinburgh House Press, London, 1964/Scribner's, New York, 1968

David Lochead, *The Dialogical Imperative: A Christian Reflection on Interfaith Encounter.* Oribs, Maryknoll, NY/SCM Press, London, 1988

John Macquarrie, *The Mediators*. SCM Press, London, 1995

Stephen Neill, *Christian Faith and Other Faiths*. Oxford University Press, 1961

Harold Netland, *Dissonant Voices: Religious Pluralism and the Question of Truth*. Eerdmans, Grand Rapids, MI/Apollos, Leicester, 1991

Joseph Neuner, ed., *Christian Revelation and World Religions*. Burns & Oates, London, 1967

Lesslie Newbigin, *The Finality of Christ*. SCM Press, London/John Knox Press, Atlanta, 1969

— *The Gospel in a Pluralist Society*. Eerdmans, Grand Rapids, MI, 1989

Bruce Nicholls, ed., *The Unique Christ in Our Pluralist World*. World Evangelical Fellowship, Baker, Grand Rapids, MI, 1994

Dennis Ockholm and Timothy Phillips, eds, *More Than One Way? Four Views on Salvation in a Pluralistic World*. Zondervan, Grand Rapids, MI, 1989

Schubert Ogden, *Is There Only One True Religion or Are There Many?* Southern Methodist University Press, Dallas, 1992

Raymond Panikkar, *The Trinity and the Religious Experience of Man*. Darton, Longman & Todd, London, 1973

Christopher Partridge, *H. H. Farmer's Theological Interpretation of Religion: Towards a Personalist Theology of Religions*. Edwin Mellon Press, Lampeter, 1998

J. Pathrapankal, *Service and Salvation*. Theological Publications of India, Bangalore, 1973

E. Perry, *The Gospel in Dispute: the Relation of Christian Faith to Other Missionary Religions*. Doubleday, New York, 1958

Alan Race, *Christians and Religious Pluralism*, 2nd edn. SCM Press, London, 1994

Karl Rahner, 'Christianity and the Non-Christian Religions' in *Theological Investigations*, Vol. 5. Darton, Longman & Todd, London/Seabury Press, New York, 1966

— 'Reflections on Dialogue within a Pluralistic Society' in *Theological Investigations*, Vol. 6, 1969

— 'Anonymous Christianity and the Missionary Task of the Church' in *Theological Investigations*, Vol. 12, 1974

— 'Observations on the Problem of the "Anonymous Christian"' in *Theological Investigations*, Vol. 14, 1976

— 'Christ in Non-Christian Religions' in *God's Word among Men*, ed., G. Gispert-Sauch. Vidyajoti, Delhi, 1973

— 'Anonymous and Explicit Faith' and 'The One Christ and the Universality of Salvation' in *Theological Investigations*, Vol. 16, 1979

Lucien Richard, *What Are They Saying about Christ and World Religions?* Paulist Press, New York, 1981

Glyn Richards, *Towards a Theology of Religions*, Routledge, London and New York, 1989

J. A. T. Robinson, *Truth is Two-Eyed*. SCM Press, London, 1979

Stanley Samartha, ed., *Faith in the Midst of Faiths*. World Council of Churches, Geneva, 1977

— *One Christ – Many Religions*. Orbis, Maryknoll, NY, 1991

— *Between Two Cultures*. World Council of Churches, Geneva, 1996

John Sanders, *No Other Name: An Investigation into the Destiny of the Unevangelized*. Eerdmans, Grand Rapids, MI, 1992

H. R. Schlette, *Towards a Theology of Religions*. Burns & Oates, London, 1966

Albert Schweitzer, *Christianity and the Religions of the World*. Allen & Unwin, London, 1922/Holt, New York, 1939/Macmillan, London, 1951

Byron Sherwin and Harold Kasimov, eds, *John Paul II and Interreligious Dialogue*. Orbis, Maryknoll, NY, 1999

H. van Straelen, *The Catholic Encounter with World Religions*. Burns & Oates, London/Newman Press, New York, 1966

Donald Swearer, *Dialogue: The Key to Understanding Other Religions*. Westminster Press, Philadelphia, 1977

Leonard Swidler, *Towards a Universal Theology of Religion*. Orbis, Maryknoll, NY. 1987

— *After the Absolute*. Fortress Press, Minneapolis, 1990

M. M. Thomas, *Man and the Universe of Faiths*. Christian Literature Society, Madras, 1975

Terry Thomas, *Inter-Religious Encounter*. Open University, Milton Keynes, 1978

Paul Tillich, *Christianity and the Encounter of the World Religions*. Columbia University Press, New York, 1963

— *The Future of Religions*. Harper & Row, New York/Greenwood Press, London, 1966

Arnold Toynbee, *Christianity Among the Religions of the World*. Scribner, New York, 1957

David Tracy, *Dialogue with the Other*. Peters Press, Louvain, 1990

Ernst Troeltsch, *The Absoluteness of Christianity* (1901). John Knox Press, Atlanta, 1971/SCM Press, London, 1973

— 'The Place of Christianity among the World Religions' (1923) in *Christian Thought*. Meridian, New York/University of London Press, 1957

Kevin Vanhoozer, ed., *The Trinity in a Pluralistic Age*. Eerdmans, Grand Rapids, MI, 1997

Ishanand Vempeny, *Inspiration in the Non-Biblical Scriptures*. Theological Publications of India, Bangalore, 1973

Max Warren, *I Believe in the Great Commission*, Hodder & Stoughton, London, 1976

Maurice Wiles, *Christian Theology and Inter-religious Dialogue.* SCM Press, London/Trinity Press International, Philadelphia, 1992
R. C. Zaehner, *At Sundry Times.* Faber & Faber, London, 1958
— *The Convergent Spirit.* Routledge & Kegan Paul, 1963, published in the United States as *Matter & Spirit.* Harper & Row, New York, 1963
— *The Catholic Church and World Religions.* Burns & Oates, London, 1964
— *Concordant Discord.* Oxford University Press, 1970

II. HISTORY OF CHRISTIAN ATTITUDES TO OTHER RELIGIONS

Carl F. Hallencreutz, *New Approaches to Men of Other Faiths.* World Council of Churches, Geneva, 1977
Stephen Neill, *A History of Christianity in India* (2 vols.), Cambridge University Press, 1984
Eric J. Sharpe, *Not to Destroy but to Fulfil.* Gleerups, Lund, 1965
— *Comparative Religion: a History.* Duckworth, London, 1975
Francis Sullivan, *Salvation Outside the Church?* Geoffrey Chapman, London, 1992

III. THE MISSIONARY AND ECUMENICAL MOVEMENTS

World Missionary Conference, 1910, 10 vols. Oliphant, Anderson and Ferrier, London, 1910
International Missionary Council, Jerusalem Conference 1928. Oxford University Press, 1928
International Missionary Council, Tambaram (Madras) Conference, 1938, 7 vols. Oxford University Press, 1939
Guidelines on Dialogue with People of Living Faiths and Ideologies. World Council of Churches, Geneva, 1979
Marcus Braybooke, *Pilgrimage of Hope: One Hundred Years of Global Interfaith Dialogue.* SCM Press, London, 1992
— *Inter-faith Worship.* Galliard, London, 1974
Kenneth Cracknell, *Justice, Courtesy and Love.* Epworth Press, London, 1995
John Hick and Hasan Askari, eds, *The Experience of Religious Diversity.* Gower, Aldershot, 1985
W. E. Hocking, *Re-thinking Missions.* Harper & Row, New York, 1932
Norman Goodall, ed., *Missions Under the Cross (IMC, Willingen, 1952).* International Missionary Council, London, 1953
Karl-Josef Kuschel, *Abraham: A Symbol of Hope for Jews, Christians and Muslims.* SCM Press, London, 1995
Harold Lindsell, ed., *The Church's Worldwide Mission.* World Books, Waco, Texas, 1966

Paul Mojzes and Leonard Swidler, *Christian Mission and Interreligious Dialogue.* Edwin Mellon Press, New York, 1991

Ronald Orchard, ed., *International Missionary Council Ghana, 1958.* Edinburgh House Press, London, 1958

— *Witness in Six Continents (WCC Commission on World Mission & Evangelism, Mexico City, 1963).* Edinburgh House Press, London, 1964

Vinoth Ramachandra, *The Recovery of Mission.* Paternoster Press, Carlisle, 1996

Stanley Samartha, ed., *Dialogue Between Men of Living Faiths (Ajaltoun, 1970).* World Council of Churches, Geneva, 1971

— *Living Faiths and the Ecumenical Movement.* World Council of Churches, Geneva, 1971

— *Towards World Community (Colombo, 1974).* World Council of Churches, Geneva, 1975

Pauline Webb, *Salvation Today* (Bangkok, 1973). SCM Press, London, 1974

IV. PHILOSOPHICAL DISCUSSIONS

Peter Byrne, *Prolegomena to Religious Pluralism.* Macmillan, London/St Martin's Press, New York, 1995

William A. Christian, *Meaning and Truth in Religion.* Princeton University Press, 1964

— *Oppositions of Religious Doctrines.* Macmillan, London/Herder & Herder, New York, 1972

— *Doctrines of Religious Communities.* Yale University Press, 1987

John B. Cobb, *The Structure of Christian Existence.* Westminster Press, Philadelphia, 1967/Lutterworth Press, London, 1968

— *Christ in a Pluralistic Age.* Westminster Press, Philadelphia, 1975

Frederick Copleston, *Religion and the One.* Crossroads, New York, 1982

Jerald Gort, Hendrik Vroom, Rein Fernhout and Anton Wessels, eds, *Dialogue and Syncretism.* Eerdmans, Grand Rapids, MI/Rodopi, Amsterdam, 1989

— *On Sharing Religious Experience.* Eerdmans, Grand Rapids, MI/Rodopi, Amsterdam, 1992

Paul Griffiths, *An Apology for Apologetics.* Orbis, Maryknoll, NY, 1991

Ian Hamnett, ed., *Religious Pluralism and Unbelief,* Routledge, London and New York, 1990

John Hick, *An Interpretation of Religion.* Macmillan, London/Yale University Press, 1989

James Kellenberger, ed., *Inter-religious Models and Criteria.* Macmillan, London, 1993

Charles Lewis, ed., *Relativism and Religion.* Macmillan, London, 1995

Robert Neville, *Behind the Masks of God.* State University of New York Press, Albany, 1991

Ninian Smart, *Beyond Ideology*. Harper & Row, San Francisco, 1981
Linda Tessier, ed., *Concepts of the Ultimate*. Macmillan, London, 1989
Keith Ward, *Images of Eternity. Concepts of God in Five Religious Traditions*. Oneworld, Oxford, 1998
Hendrik Vroom, *Religions and Truth*. Eerdmans, Grand Rapids, MI/Rodopi, Amsterdam, 1989

V. CHRISTIANITY AND BUDDHISM

A Zen Buddhist Pilgrimage. The Zen–Christian Colloquium, Hong Kong, 1981
Towards the Meeting with Buddhism. Secretariat for Non-Christians, Rome 1970
Masao Abe, *Buddhism and Interfaith Dialogue*. Macmillan, London, 1995
George Appleton, *On the Eightfold Path*. SCM Press, London, 1961
Hermann Beckh, *From Buddha to Christ*. Floris, Edinburgh, 1977
Naomi Burton, Patrick Hart and James Laughlin, eds, *The Asian Journal of Thomas Merton*. Sheldon Press, London, 1974
Roger Corless and Paul Knitter, eds, *Buddhist Emptiness and Christian Trinity*. Paulist Press, New York, 1990
Heinrich Dumoulin, *Christianity Meets Buddhism*. Open Court, LaSalle, Illinois, 1974
Antony Fernando, *Buddhism and Christianity*. Ecumenical Institute, Colombo, 1981
H. von Glasenapp, *Buddhism and Christianity*. Buddhist Publication Society, Kandy, 1963
Aelred Graham, *Conversations Christian and Buddhist*. Harcourt Brace, New York, 1971
G. W. Houston, ed., *Dharma and Gospel*. Sri Satguru Publications, Delhi, 1984
Christopher Ives, *Zen Awakening and Society*. Macmillan, London, 1992
William Johnston, *Silent Music*. Harper & Row, New York/Collins, London, 1978
— *The Inner Eye of Love*. Harper & Row, New York/Collins, London, 1978
Winston L. King, *Buddhism and Christianity*. Westminster Press, Philadelphia, 1962
Chwen Lee and Thomas Hand, *A Taste of Water: Christianity Through Taoist–Buddhist Eyes*. Paulist Press, New York, 1990
Raimundo Panikkar, *The Silence of God: The Answer of the Buddha*. Orbis, Maryknoll, NY, 1989
William Peiris, *Edwin Arnold: His Life and Contribution to Buddhism*. Buddhist Publication Society, Kandy, 1970
Lynn, A. da Silva, *The Problem of the Self in Buddhism and Christianity*. Macmillan, London/Barnes & Noble, New York, 1979
Ninian Smart, *Buddhism and Christianity: Rivals or Allies?* Macmillan, London, 1993
B. H. Streeter, *The Buddha and the Christ*. Macmillan, New York, 1932

VI. CHRISTIANITY AND HINDUISM

Abhishiktananda (H. le Saux) *Prayer.* Indian SPCK, Delhi, 1967
— *Hindu–Christian Meeting Point*. Christian Institute for the Study of Religion and Society, Bangalore, 1969

— *Guru and Disciple.* SPCK, London, 1974

— *Saccidananda: A Christian Approach to Advaitic Experience.* Indian SPCK, Delhi, 1974

— *The Further Shore.* Indian SPCK, Delhi, 1975

Daniel Bassuk, *Incarnation in Hinduism and Christianity.* Macmillan, London, 1987

Marcus Braybrooke, *Together to the Truth: Developments in Hindu and Christian Thought since 1800.* Indian SPCK, Delhi, 1971

John B. Chethimattam, *Patterns of Indian Thought.* Geoffrey Chapman, London/ Orbis, Maryknoll, NY, 1971

Harold Coward, ed., *Hindu–Christian Dialogue.* Orbis, Maryknoll, NY, 1989

R. De Smet and J. Neuner, eds, *Religious Hinduism: A Presentation and Appraisal.* St Paul's Press, Allahabad, 1964

J. N. Farquhar, *The Crown of Hinduism (1913).* Oxford University Press, 1930

M. K. Gandhi, *In Search of the Supreme,* ed. V. B. Kher, Vol. III, Section 7. Navajivan, Ahmedabad, 1962

S. K. George, *Gandhi's Challenge to Christianity.* Navajivan, Ahmedabad, 1947

Bede Griffiths, *Christian Ashram.* Darton, Longman & Todd, London, 1966

— *Christ in India.* Scribner, New York, 1967

— *Vedanta and Christian Faith.* Dawn Horse Press, 1973

— *Return to the Centre.* Collins, London/Templegate, New York, 1976

A. G. Hogg, *The Christian Message to the Hindu.* SCM Press, London/Macmillan, New York, 1974

— *Karma and Redemption (1909).* Christian Literature Society, Madras, 1970

Roger Hooker, *Journey into Varanasi.* Church Missionary Society, London, 1978

Klaus Klostermaier, *Hindu and Christian in Vrindaban.* SCM Press, London, 1969

S. Kulandran, *Grace in Christianity and Hinduism.* Lutterworth Press, London, 1964

J. Mattam, *Land of the Trinity: Modern Christian Approaches to Hinduism.* Theological Publications of India, Bangalore, 1975

Nirmal Minz, *Mahatma Gandhi and Hindu–Christian Dialogue.* Christian Literature Society, Madras, 1970

John Moffitt, *Journey to Gorakhpur.* Sheldon Press, London, 1973

Raymond Panikkar, *The Unknown Christ of Hinduism.* Darton, Longman & Todd, London, 1964

Geoffrey Parrinder, *Avatar and Incarnation.* Oneworld, Oxford, 1997

Sarvapelli Radhakrishnan, *East and West in Religion.* George Allen & Unwin, London, 1933

— *Eastern Religions and Western Thought.* Oxford University Press, 1939

K. L. Seshagiri Rao, *Mahatma Gandhi and C. F. Andrews: A Study in Hindu–Christian Dialogue.* Punjabi University, 1969

Stanley Samartha, *The Hindu Response to the Unbound Christ.* Christian Literature Society, Madras, 1974

Arvind Sharma, *The Concept of Universal Religion in Modern Hindu Thought.* Macmillan, London, 1998

Eric Sharpe, *Faith Meets Faith; Some Christian Attitudes to Hinduism in the Nineteenth and Twentieth Centuries.* SCM Press, London, 1977

Ninian Smart, *The Yogi and the Devotee: The Interplay between the Upanishads and Catholic Theology.* George Allen & Unwin, London, 1968

T. Thangaraj, *The Crucified Guru.* Abingdon Press, Nashville, 1994

M. M. Thomas, *The Acknowledged Christ of the Indian Renaissance.* SCM Press, London, 1969

VII. CHRISTIANITY AND ISLAM

Islam and Christian–Muslim Relations (Journal). Centre for the study of Islam and Christian–Muslim Relations, University of Birmingham, 1990–

Guidelines for a Dialogue between Muslims and Christians. Secretariat for Non-Christians, Rome, 1969

Christians Meeting Muslims; Ten Years of Christian–Muslim Dialogue. World Council of Churches, Geneva, 1977

J. T. Addison, *The Christian Approach to the Moslem.* Columbia University Press, New York, 1942

T. Andrae, *Mohammed: the Man and his Faith.* Harper & Row, New York, 1955

Munawar Ahmed Anees, Syed Z. Abedin and Ziauddin Sardar, *Christian–Muslim Relations; yesterday, today and tomorrow.* Grey Seal, London, 1991

Hasan Askari, *Inter-Religion.* Printwell Publications, Aligarh, 1977

J. L. Barton, *The Christian approach to Islam.* Pilgrim Press, Boston, 1918

G. Bassetti-Sani, *Louis Massignon – Christian Ecumenist.* Franciscan Herald Press, Chicago, 1974

E. W. Bethmann, *Bridge to Islam.* George Allen & Unwin, London, 1953

D. Brown, *Christianity and Islam* (5 vols). Sheldon Press, London, 1967–70: *Jesus and God; The Christian Scriptures; The Cross of the Messiah; The Divine Trinity; The Church and the Churches A New Threshold: Guidelines for the Churches in their Relations with Muslim Communities.* British Council of Churches, London, 1962

— *The Way of the Prophet.* Highway Press, London, 1962

L. E. Browne, *The Eclipse of Christianity in Asia.* Cambridge University Press, 1933

— *The Prospects of Islam.* SCM Press, London, 1944

W. W. Cash, *Christendom and Islam: their contacts and cultures down the centuries.* SCM Press, London, 1977

Kenneth Cragg, *The Call of the Minaret.* Oneworld, Oxford, 2000

— ed., *Alive to God: Muslim and Christian Prayer.* Oxford University Press, 1970

— *The Dome and the Rock.* SPCK, London, 1964

— *The Event of the Qur'an.* Oneworld, Oxford, 1994

— *The House of Islam.* Dickenson, Belmont, California, 1969

— *The Mind of the Qur'an*. George Allen & Unwin, London, 1973
— *The Privilege of Man*. Athlone Press, London, 1968
— *Sandals at the Mosque*. SCM Press, London, 1959
— *The Wisdom of the Sufis*. Sheldon Press, London, 1976
— trans. and Introduction, *The Hallowed Valley – a Muslim Philosophy of Religion*, by M. K. Hussain. American University in Cairo Press, 1977
— trans. and Introduction, *Theology of Unity*, by Mohammed Abdul. George Allen & Unwin, London, 1966
N. Daniel, *The Arabs and Medieval Europe*. Longman, London, 1979
— *Islam and the West: the Making of an Image*. Oneworld, Oxford, 2000
R. Frieling, *Christianity and Islam: a battle for the true image of man*. Floris Books, Edinburgh, 1978
T. Gairdner, *The Rebuke of Islam*. SPG, London, 1910
A. Guillaume, *Islam*. Penguin, London, 1954
E. Hahn, *Jesus in Islam: a Christian View*. Christian Centre, Krishnagiri, 1975
— *Muhammed, the Prophet of Islam*. Henry Martyn Institute, Hyderabad, n.d.
John Hick and Edmund Meltzer, eds, *Three Faiths – One God: A Jewish, Christian, Muslim Encounter.* State University of New York Press, Albany, 1989
Albert Hourani, *Western Attitudes Towards Islam*. Montefiore Memorial Lecture, Southampton University, 1974
J. Jomier, *The Bible and the Koran*. Desclée, New York, 1964
J. Kritzeck, *Peter the Venerable and Islam*. Princeton University Press, 1964
L. Levonian, *Studies in the Relationship between Islam and Christianity*. George Allen & Unwin, London, 1940
D. B. Macdonald, *Aspects of Islam*. Macmillan, London, 1911
G. E. Marrison, *The Christian Approach to the Muslim*. Lutterworth Press, London, 1968
C. R. Marsh, *Share Your Faith with a Muslim*. Moody, Chicago, 1975
I. Maybaum, *Trialogue between Jew, Christian and Muslim*. Routledge & Kegan Paul, London, 1973
W. M. Miller, *A Christian Response to Islam*. Presbyterian & Reformed Publishing Co., USA, 1976
J. R. Mott, ed., *The Moslem World Today*. Hodder & Stoughton, London, 1925
W. Muir, trans., *The Apology of al-Kindi (Christian–Muslim Dialogue)*. SPCK, London, 1911
B. Padwick, *Muslim Devotions*. SPCK, London, 1961
— *Temple Gairdner of Cairo*. SPCK, London, 1930
G. Parrinder, *Jesus in the Qur'an*. Oneworld, Oxford, 1995
Moshe Perlmann, trans., *Ibn Kammuna's Examination of the Three Faiths*. University of California Press, Los Angeles and London, 1971
C. Rahbar, *The God of Justice*. E. J. Brill, Leiden, 1960
D. J. Sahas, *John of Damascus on Islam*. E. J. Brill, Leiden 1972

Stanley Samartha and John B. Taylor, eds, *Christian–Muslim Dialogue* (Broumana Consultation, 1972). World Council of Churches, Geneva, 1973

Annemarie Schimmel and Abdoldjavad Falaturi, eds, *We Believe in One God: The Experience of God in Christianity and Islam.* Burns & Oates, London, 1979

F. Schuon, *Understanding Islam.* George Allen & Unwin, London, 1965

P. Seale, *Qur'an and Bible.* Croom Helm, London, 1978

W. Cantwell Smith, *Islam in Modern History.* Mentor Books, New York, 1959/ London, 1965

R. W. Southern, *Western Views of Islam in the Middle Ages.* Harvard University Press, 1962

H. Spencer, *Islam and the Gospel of God: a comparison of the central doctrines of Christianity and Islam.* SPCK, London, 1956

J. W. Sweetman, *Islam and Christian Theology* (4 vols.). Lutterworth Press, London, 1945–67

W. Montgomery Watt, *Muhammad: Prophet and Statesman.* Oxford University Press, 1961

— *Islamic Revelation.* Edinburgh University Press, 1969

— *Truth in the Religions.* Edinburgh University Press, 1963

— *Muslim–Christian Encounters: Perceptions and Misperceptions.* Routledge, London, 1991

C. V. Werff, *Christian Mission to Muslims – the Record.* William Carey Library, Pasadena, 1977

Andrew Wingate, *Encounter in the Spirit: Muslim–Christian Meetings in Birmingham.* World Council of Churches, Geneva, 1988

S. M. Zwemmer, *Islam – a Challenge to Faith.* New York, 1907

— *The Moslem Christ.* London, 1915

— *Raymund Lull: first Missionary to the Moslems.* New York, 1902

VIII. CHRISTIANITY AND JUDAISM

Jewish–Christian Dialogue. World Council of Churches, Geneva, 1975

Leo Baeck, *Judaism and Christianity.* Jewish Publication Society of America, 1958/ Harper Torchbooks, New York, 1966

Paul Borchsenius, *Two Ways to God.* Valentine, Mitchell, NY, 1968

James Charlesworth, ed., *Jesus' Jewishness.* Crossroad, New York, 1991

Dan Cohn-Sherbok, *On Earth as it is in Heaven: Jews, Christians, and Liberation Theology.* Orbis, Maryknoll, NY, 1987

A. Roy Eckhardt, *Elder and Younger Brothers: the Encounter of Jews and Christians.* Scribner, New York, 1967

Charles Glock and Rodney Stark, *Christian Beliefs and Anti-Semitism.* Harper & Row, New York, 1966

Walter Jacob, *Christianity Through Jewish Eyes.* Hebrew Union College Press, New York, 1974

Jacob Katz, *Exclusivism and Tolerance.* Schocken, New York, 1975

Charlotte Klein, *Anti-Judaism in Christian Theology.* Fortress Press, Philadelphia/SPCK, London, 1978

Hans Küng and Pinchas Lapide, *Brother or Lord?* Collins, Fount, London/Doubleday, New York, 1977

I. Maybaum, *Trialogue between Jew, Christian and Muslim.* Routledge and Kegan Paul, London, 1973

Gabriel Moran, *Uniqueness: The Problem in Jewish and Christian Traditions.* Orbis, Maryknoll, NY, 1992

James Parkes, *Prelude to Dialogue.* Valentine, Mitchell, New York, 1969

— *The Conflict of the Church and the Synagogue.* Atheneum, New York, 1969

John Pawlikowski, *What Are They Saying about Christian–Jewish Relations?* Paulist Press, New York, 1980

— *Christ in the Light of Christian–Jewish Dialogue.* Paulist Press, New York, 1982

John D. Rayner, *Towards Mutual Understanding.* James Clarke, London, 1960

Rosemary Reuther, *Faith and Fratricide: The Theological Roots of Anti-Semitism.* Seabury Press, New York, 1979

F. Rosenzweig, *The Star of Redemption.* Routledge & Kegan Paul, London, 1971

E. P. Sanders, *Jesus and Judaism.* SCM Press, London, 1985

Samuel Sandmel, *We Jews and You Christians.* Lippincott, New York, 1967

— *The Genius of Paul.* Fortress Press, Philadelphia, 1970

— *A Jewish Understanding of the New Testament.* SPCK, London, 1977

— *Judaism and Christian Beginnings.* Oxford University Press, 1978

— *Anti-Semitism in the New Testament?* Fortress Press, Philadelphia, 1978

Peter Schneider, *Sweeter than Honey.* SCM Press, London, 1966

— *The Dialogue of Christians and Jews.* Seabury Press, New York, 1967

Norman Solomon, *Judaism and World Religion.* Macmillan, London, 1991

Leonard Swidler, *Yeshua: A Model for Moderns.* Sheed & Ward, London, 1988

Paul Van Buren, *A Theology of Jewish–Christian Reality.* Harper & Row, San Francisco, 1997

Geza Vermes, *The Religion of Jesus the Jew.* SCM Press, London, 1993

Trude Weiss-Rosmarin, *Judaism and Christianity: the Differences.* Jonathan David, New York, 1972

IX. CHRISTIANITY AND THE PRIMAL RELIGIONS

Kwesi Dickson and Paul Ellingworth, eds, *Biblical Revelation and African Beliefs.* Lutterworth Press, London, 1969

Bengt Sundkler, *The Christianity in Africa.* SCM Press, London, 1960

John V. Taylor, *The Primal Vision: Christian Presence and African Religion.* SCM Press, London/Fortress Press, Philadelphia, 1963

— ed., *Primal World Views: Christian Dialogue with Traditional Thought*. Daystar Press, Ibadan, 1976

Keith Ward, *Religion and Revelation (Part 2)*. Clarendon Press, Oxford, 1994

E. Westermann, *Africa and Christianity*. Oxford University Press, 1937

X. CHRISTIANITY AND CHINESE RELIGIONS

Hans Küng and Jula Ching, *Christianity and Chinese Religions*. Doubleday, New York and London, 1989

Index